977.01 Joh
Johnson Donald S.
La Salle : a perilous
   odyssey from Canada to
   the Gulf of Mexico /

$26.95
ocm49494992

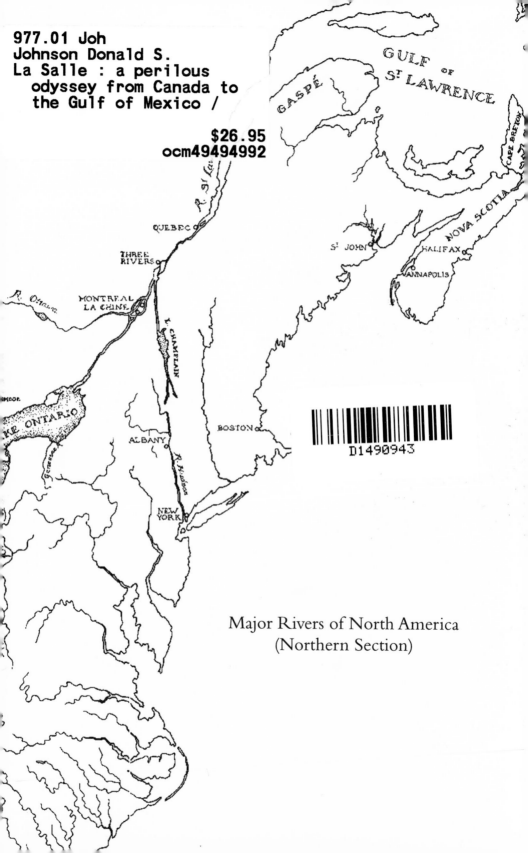

Major Rivers of North America
(Northern Section)

D1490943

LA SALLE

LA SALLE

*A Perilous Odyssey from Canada
to the Gulf of Mexico*

DONALD S. JOHNSON

Cooper Square Press

First Cooper Square Press edition 2002

This Cooper Square Press hardcover edition of *La Salle: A Perilous Odyssey from Canada to the Gulf of Mexico* is an original publication. It is published by arrangement with the author.

Copyright © 2002 by Donald S. Johnson

All rights reserved.
No part of this book may be reproduced in any form or by any electronic or mechanical means, including information storage and retrieval systems, without written permission from the publisher, except by a reviewer who may quote passages in a review.

Published by Cooper Square Press
A Member of the Rowman & Littlefield Publishing Group
200 Park Avenue South, Suite 1109
New York, New York 10003-1503
www.coopersquarepress.com

Distributed by National Book Network

Library of Congress Cataloging-in-Publication Data

Johnson, Donald, 1932–
    La Salle : a perilous odyssey from Canada to the Gulf of Mexico / Donald Johnson.— 1st Cooper Square Press ed.
        p.   cm.
    Includes bibliographical references and index.
    ISBN 0-8154-1240-1 (cloth : alk. paper)
    1. La Salle, Robert Cavelier, sieur de, 1643–1687.   2. Mississippi River Valley Discovery and exploration—French.   3. Canada—History—to 1763 (New France) 4. Explorers—America—Biography.   5. Explorers—France—Biography.   I. Title.
F1030.5 .J85 2002
    77'.01—dc21   2002004683

♾ ™ The paper used in this publication meets the minimum requirements of American National Standard for Information Sciences—Permanence of Paper for Printed Library Materials, ANSI/NISO Z39.48–1992.
Manufactured in the United States of America.

Man shapes his own destinies when the fortitude of the soul corresponds with the vigorous organization of the mind.

CHARLES GAYARRÂE

Engraving of La Salle as a young man.

For Ewan and Sonoko

CONTENTS

LIST OF ILLUSTRATIONS

ACKNOWLEDGMENTS

With particular thanks to Ed Jordan who tirelessly translated so many of the original documents from French into English; to the Osher Map Library in Portland, Maine, for making available maps that aided in the cartographic history of La Salle's exploration; and finally, to my agent, Ed Knappman, and editor, Michael Dorr, who turned my manuscript into the finely wrought book presented here.

PREFACE

One question an author can always count on to be asked, is "How did you happen to write a book on this subject?" In response, I had heard about the discovery of the remains of the vessel *Belle* by the Texas Historical Commission. A gift from the Sun King, Louis XIV of France, to Sieur de la Salle, the *Belle* lay covered in the mud and sand of Matagorda Bay, Texas, victim of shipwreck for over three hundred years. In 1995 the ship was brought to light. If only a few rotting timbers, a scattering of musket and cannonballs, with perhaps the addition of a random personal artifact, such as pewter plate or pottery, was revealed, the project of excavation would still be very worthwhile. The Texas Historical Commission found a great deal more— a vessel in remarkable state of preservation, filled with all the items intended to create a new colony. So complete were the remains, that it seemed time was held in abeyance, waiting to start anew for these adventurers.

I visited the site in Texas and in witnessing the revitalization of this important part of American history, became engrossed. There was another element that helped influence my decision to take up this subject. As a child growing up in Minnesota I was surrounded by place-names of people— Hennepin, Marquette, Jolliet, and Nicollet—who accompanied La Salle on his ventures, or were part of his era. Finally, as an adult, I would get to really learn about them, and attach deeds to their names.

As I gathered background on La Salle, I was delighted to find the wealth of material available, particularly the number of first-hand accounts. Though La Salle kept journals and made maps, unfortunately they have not survived. Most of them were lost in the shipwreck of the *Belle* in 1684. Those, however, who were a part of his three great expeditions, particularly his last voyage to the mouth of the Mississippi, all wrote their version of what happened. At the time, Europe eagerly awaited the latest reports from this mysterious land and the peoples who inhabited it, and publishers rushed to supply the demand. There were numerous French editions of Father Hennepin's works: *Description de la Louisiane* (1683), *Nouvelle Découverte* (1697), and *Nouveau Voyage* (1689), which were almost immediately translated into Italian, Dutch, German, and English. To have access to these writings was far superior than having to rely on the later reconstruction of events by historians.

The lack of journals or memoirs by La Salle was an impediment, but fortunately, numerous other writings and letters to and from La Salle exist. Pierre Margry, Assistant Director of the Archives of Marine and Colonies at Paris, collected all that he could about New France. These were published in Paris in 1876–1888 under the title of *Découvertes et Etablissements des Français dans l'Ouest et dans le Sud de l'Amérique Septentrionale (1614–1754), Mémoires et Documents Originaux*. The first three volumes contain all the original documents and letters relating to La Salle that Magry could obtain from various public archives of France, Canada, and other private sources.

Besides the primary sources of information there were histories published almost immediately following the exploration of New France and discovery of the Mississippi River. These early works provide much descriptive material, and benefit greatly in their accuracy by not being corrupted with changes of interpretation through time. Of all the books written on the history of Cavalier de La Salle, undoubtedly the one best known is Francis *Parkman's La Salle and the Discovery of the Great West*. First published in 1878 as part of a much larger five volumes work, *France and England in North America*, it remains the most complete and authoritative account of La Salle. Parkman drew upon the papers collected by Pierre Margry for much of his material on La Salle.

It seemed that with the overwhelming amount of first-hand material and original documents, it would be an easy task to recapitulate the adventures of La Salle and bring them up to date with the recent excavation of his vessel, *Belle*. After reading this material, my initial delight soon turned to dismay. The accounts by those who accompanied La Salle, the histories, and the *Récites* (Relations) were a morass of confusion and contradictions, not just in details, but major events as well. My task became much like the classic Japanese tale of *Rashoman*, wherein which is the "true" account, and whose "truth" does one choose to believe. Furthermore, scholarly and critical treatises provide ample evidence of willful misstatements by some authors, outright plagiarism by others, and at times, total fabrications of fantasy in the writing. When the author was not to blame, the publisher was guilty of these deeds. Editors often tampered with the reports of the writer, and inserted fallacious material into the writings if they felt it would increase interest in the book and create more sales.

Even Pierre Margry's monumental work is not above reproach. Critics point out that to support his unshakable belief that La Salle was the first person to discover the Mississippi River, Margry was subjective in his judgment of what to include in his catalogue of documents. He omitted portions of documents, or falsified them to suit his purpose.

There is uncertainty as to exactly how La Salle filled the years between the time he first arrived in Canada to begin a settlement at La Chine on the St. Lawrence River, until his descent of the Mississippi River to its mouth. Some historians doubt that during this time La Salle explored the Ohio River and met with the Seneca Iroquois, as claimed. Affirmative evidence is found in the lengthy journal written by Abbé Eusèbe Renaudot, titled "Récit d'un ami de l'abbe Galinée" ("The account of a friend, the Abbé Galinée"). La Salle, under the urgings of the Sulpician Seminary in Montreal, combined his proposed expedition with that of the Abbé René de Brehart de Galinée. La Salle was in search of a passage to the Pacific Ocean, and Galinée was looking to convert to the Roman faith the Indians he would find in the valleys of the Ohio and Mississippi. Pierre Magry and Francis Parkman accepted the account of Galinée without question. In contrast, the historian Jean Delanglez presents strong arguments that the entire idea of La Salle's descent of the Ohio River was an "elaborate hoax— pure fiction, resting on worthless evidence."

Such is one of the many dilemmas in which I found myself; whether to give support to the story of La Salle's discovering and exploring the Ohio River. If the Galinée account was a manufactured document, with the sole purpose to deceive, and disparage the Jesuit accomplishments in America, it was done with much care and effort. Even with its errors and contradictions, it still has a ring of truthfulness about it. If La Salle was not thus occupied during these years (1669–1670), what *was* he doing then? Even if his exploration of the Ohio cannot be fully documented, it still has the right to be told. Sometimes myth and legend form a surer degree of truth and reality than the mere collection of facts. Thus, the reader is advised in advance, of my prejudice in this particular segment of La Salle's life.

There is also the matter of the use of words like "Savage" and "Indian," which today is not politically correct. Since they were perceived in those terms, and in common usage during La Salle's time, I have retained them as a matter of historical perspective. When Europeans first came to these shores, their view of the native peoples they met with were far different than now. The Reverend Samuel Purchas, a noted early seventeenth-century historian, considered the Indians "bad people, having little of humanity but shape, ignorant of civilities, of arts, of religion, more brutish than the beasts they hunt." Almost 150 years later, when Francis Parkman wrote his history on La Salle, there was little to change this opinion. La Salle, himself, had witnessed the cruelty that the Indians could inflict, not only upon the white man, but captives of other tribes during the frequent wars.

Throughout the book, I have changed all place-names to present-day names, to make the geography more understandable. An appendix at the back of the book gives all the names and variations of spellings as they were originally used in the journals and on maps. Footnotes are not indicated with numbers in the text, but reference to the source of quotations is found in the endnotes. I feel this method produces a better flow to the narrative, yet still allows identification of the source material.

All maps throughout the book have been redrawn from reproductions in various atlases of cartography. Frequently, these images are of poor quality; second-, or even third-generation reproductions. By converting the maps to line art, I have considerably enhanced their clarity. And by stripping away all unnecessary detail, attention is focused on the relevant information. Unfortunately, these acts also eliminate the great beauty and wealth of historical information contained in these maps. For further enjoyment and enlightenment, I urge the reader to seek out the original of these maps and charts. If a cartographic library is not accessible, there is always the aforementioned atlases. Most of these maps are also available for viewing on the Internet.

There is good reason for the great *number* of maps contained herein. Cartography reveals more succinctly than the written word, and is grasped more quickly by the mind, mankind's search for, and knowledge about the surface of our globe. Inherent in maps is the intricate relationship of space and time, wherein history and geography are simultaneously presented. So entwined are history and geography that the study of one is scarcely possible without the other. Captain John Smith, of the famed Virginia Colony, said: "As geography without history seems like a carcass without motion, so history without geography wanders as a vagrant without habitation." Fortunately, in cartography the two are combined. Although the passage of time, so essential to history, is absent when any *single* map is absent, it is readily observed in a sequential *group* of maps.

The reader will find a variety of spellings in other books for Henri de Tonti, La Salle's trusted friend and companion throughout much of his travels. Born in Italy with the name of Henri de Tonti, he retired to France, where he changed it to the Gallic version of Henry de Tonty. Since he was in the service of France while accompanying La Salle, and signed his name with the new spelling during this period of his life, I have chosen to use it rather than the more customary Italian version.

At this point it is customary for the author to absolve those who have worked with him from any responsibility for the errors and problems that may be found in the book, and to claim them solely as his own. I do not know when this practice started, but in 1627, Captain John Smith did it in the preface to his *Sea Grammar*. Since I have not seen it expressed better elsewhere, I will let Captain Smith speak for me.

Honest Readers,
If my desire to doe good hath transported mee beyond myselfe, I intreat you ex-
cuse me, and take for requitall this rude bundle of many ages observations; al-
though they be not so punctually compiled as I could wish, and it may bee you

expect. At this present I cannot much amend them; if any will bestow that paines, I shall thinke him my friend, and honour his endevuors. In the interim accept them as they are, and ponder errours in the balance of good will.

Your friend,
John Smith

IMPORTANT INDIVIDUALS

Father Jolliet

Jesuit missionary, explorer and cartographer. Descended the Mississippi River in 1673 as far as confluence with the Arkansas River.

Father Marquette

Récollet Franciscan missionary. Accompanied Jolliet on 1673 expedition.

Father Louis Hennepin

Flemish Récollet Friar. Accompanied La Salle as Chaplain and historian on La Salle's first expedition. Explored mouth of Mississippi from confluence of Illinois River, northward to Minnesota.

Father Chrestien Le Clercq

Récollet missionary. Accompanied La Salle on voyage to Gulf of Mexico.

Father Luke Buisset

Hennepin, Le Clercq, and Buisset were confreres of Zénobe Membré. All four were sent to New France as missionaries in 1675.

Father Anastase Douay

Accompanied La Salle on his third and last expedition from Fort St. Louis, Texas.

Sieur de Lhuh (Daniel Greysolon du Lhut)

A celebrated Coureur de bois. Born at Lyons, France, and cousin of Henri Tonti. His enterprises were independent of those of La Salle, but like La Salle, carried out under authorization of Count Frontenac. Rescued Hennepin at the end of his journey in Minnesota.

Sieur La Forest

A lieutenant under La Salle, left in charge of Fort Frontenac. La Forest remained there until 1685, when he joined Tonti in Illinois. Five years later,

La Forest and Henri de Tonti obtained a grant of Fort St. Louis, and a limited trading permit; favors which were afterwards revoked.

Jean–Baptiste Colbert (1619–1683)

Controller General (Minister) to King Louis XIV. La Salle named the Mississippi R. as the Colbert River.

Jean Talon

Appointed by King Louis XIV as Intendant of New France. Successor to Courcelle. Commissioned on March 23, 1665, and served until 1668. After a one year leave of absence he again served from 1670 to 1672.

Daumont de Saint-Lusson

Subdelagate of Intendant Talon.

Jacques Duchesneau

Talon's successor as Intendant of New France.

Jacques de Menles

Replaces Deuchesneau in 1682 as Intendant of Canada.

Marquis de Tracy

Lieutenant-General of Canada, 1663 to 1665.

Daniel de Rémy, Sieur de Courcelle

Governor of Canada. Commissioned March 23, 1665, and served until April 7, 1672.

Louis de Baude, Count of Palluau and Frontenac (Count Frontenac)

Appointed Governor, and Lieutenant General of Canada in 1672. Recalled to France in 1682. Served a second administration in New France from 1689 to 1698.

Chevalier Montmagny

Second Governor (after Champlain) of New France.

Toussaint Rose

Secretary to King Louis XIV.

Prince de Conti

A prominent courtier who married a daughter of King Louis XIV. A patron of La Salle.

Louis de Baude, Count of Pallusu and Frontenac (Count Frontenac)

Appointed Governor, and Lieutenant-General of Canada in 1672. Recalled to France in 1682. Served a second administration in New France from 1689 to 1698.

Joseph-Antoine Le Febvre de La Barre

Governor of Canada in 1682, following Frontenac.

Chevalier Montmagny

Second Governor (after Champlain) of New France.

Toussaint Rose

Secretary to King Louis XIV.

Prince de Conti

A prominent courtier who married a daughter of King Louis XIV. A patron of La Salle.

Marquis de Seignelay

Son of Jean-Baptiste Colbert. Secretary and Minister of State under King Louis XIV. Intendant General of Commerce and Navigation of France.

Le Mouyne d'Iberville

First Royal Governor of Louisiana.

Le Monyne de Bienville

Second Royal Governor of Louisiana.

Antoine de la Mothe Cadillac

Third Royal Governor of Louisiana.

Pierre Margry

Director of Archives of the Marme and Colonies at Paris. Author of six volume book on collected papers relating to La Salle.

Henri de Tonti

Italian by birth, French by necessity. La Salle's Lieutenant and trusted friend. Tonti built Fort St. Louis on the Illinois River, where he remained until 1700. He then joined d'Iberville on the Mississippi. In 1704 he died of yellow fever at Mobile.

Henri Joutel

Official historian for La Salle's last voyage, and personal friend of La Salle.

LA SALLE AND HIS RELATIVES

René-Robert Cavelier, Sieur de la Salle

A pupil of the Jesuits in Rouen, France, until his fifteenth year. Became a novice in that order at Paris, October 5, 1658. Two years later he took the vows of Jesuit, and assumed the name of Ignatius. Was known in the order as Frère Robert Ignace.

Abbé Jean Cavelier

Brother of La Salle.

Sieur Cavelier

Nephew of La Salle.

Sieur de Morangé

Another nephew of La Salle.

Nicolas de La Salle (Otherwise known as the little M. de la Salle)

Was *not* related to Robert de la Salle. A companion of La Salle during the 1682 expedition. Held title of Commissary in Louisiana from 1701 to 1709. Believed to be the son of the Chief Clerk of the Marine Department. Published *Relation de la descouverte que M. de La Salle a faite de la rivière de Mississippi en 1682, et de son retour jusqu'a Québec.* Known by the shorter title of *Récit de Nicolas de la Salle, 1682.*

CHRONOLOGY OF LA SALLE
IN NEW FRANCE

1643   Rène-Robert Cavelier, Sieur de la Salle is born in Rouen, France.

1666   La Salle arrives in Canada and spends next three years establishing settlement at La Chine on the St. Lawrence River, and making short, local explorations of surrounding territory.

Treaty of peace signed with Iroquois Nation.

1669   La Salle (with Galinée) visits land of Senecas to establish peace between Senecas and France.

First expedition to discover the Mississippi River, by way of the Ohio River.

1671   Second expedition to discover the Mississippi River, by way of the Illinois River.

1674   La Salle goes to France, gains funds for Fort Frontenac, and is given Seigniory of the fort, and a title of nobility.

1675   Building of Fort Frontenac and La Salle's commercial enterprise.

1677   (Nov.) La Salle returns to France, receives permission from King Louis XIV to explore western parts of New France.

(Nov.) Begins exploration, builds Fort Conti at Niagara, and constructs ship named *Griffin*.

1679   (Feb.) Returns to Fort Frontenac and financial ruin.

(Aug.) Back to Fort Conti. Sails the *Griffin* on Lake Erie, to Strait of Detroit, and into Lake Huron.

(Sept.) *Griffin* sailed from Green Bay to Michillimackinac and Niagara, but is shipwrecked before it reaches Michillimackinac.

(Nov.) Fort St. Joseph established at mouth of St. Joseph (Miamis) River.

Fort Crêvecoeur built.

(March) La Salle leaves Fort Crêvecoeur for Fort Frontenac.

(Aug.) Second journey to Illinois country.

(Sept.) Fort Crêvecoeur destroyed.

1681   Third expedition to explore the Mississippi River, and to descend to Gulf of Mexico.

1682   (Feb.) La Salle enters the Mississippi River, and descends to Gulf of Mexico.

(April) Mouth of Mississippi reached. Formal possession of Mississippi Valley taken for France and named "Louisiana."

(Dec.) Fort St. Louis of Illinois built.

1683   (Jan.–Aug.) La Salle and Tonty at Fort St. Louis.

(Nov.) La Salle sails for France to gain support for permanent settlement at mouth of Mississippi River.

1684   (April) Receives commission from king to settle lands in France's dominion in North America from Fort St. Louis on the Illinois River to New Biscay.

(Aug.) Fleet of four vessels—the *Joly, La Belle, L'Aimable,* and *Saint-François*—leaves Rochelle, France for mouth of Mississippi.

(Sept.) *Joly, Aimable,* and *Belle* arrive safely at Saint Dominique.

1685   (Jan.) Landfall made on Texas Gulf Coast.

(Feb.) *Belle* enters Matagorda Bay, but *Aimable* runs aground, and breaks up while attempting to enter.

(March) *Joly* returns to France.

(April) Construction begun on Fort St. Louis on the Garcitas River.

(June) Fort St. Louis completed.

(Oct.) La Salle, with fifty men, leave to search for the Mississippi River.

1686   (Jan.) *Belle* wrecked in Matagorda Bay.

(March) La Salle party returns to Fort St. Louis.

(April) La Salle, plus twenty others, leave for the Illinois, and on to Canada to obtain help for the Gulf colony.

1687   (Jan.) La Salle, with seventeen men, makes second attempt to reach the Illinois and Montréal.

(March) La Salle is murdered.

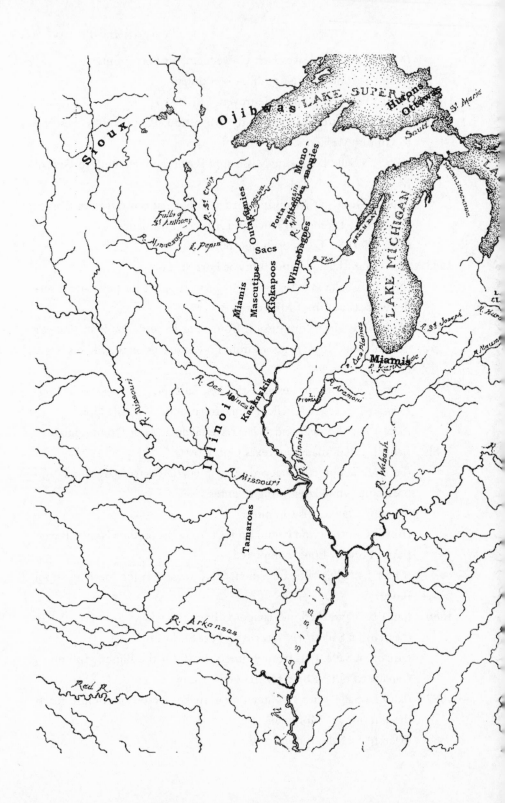

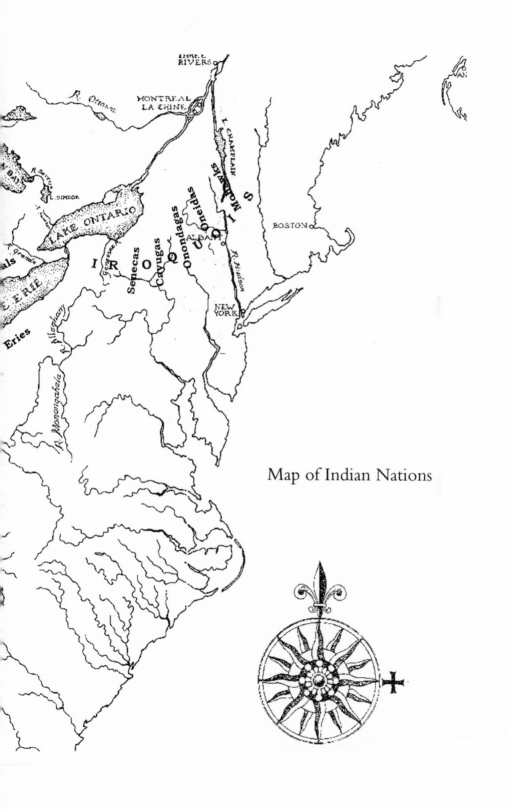

THREE
RIVERS

MONTREAL
LA CHINE

OTTAWA

L. SIMCOE

LAKE ONTARIO

L. CHAMPLAIN

I R O Q U O I S

Senecas   Cayugas   Onondagas   Oneidas

MOHAWKS

ALBANY

BOSTON

R. Hudson

E R I E

Eries

R. Allegheny

R. Monongahela

NEW
YORK

Map of Indian Nations

PART I

In Contest for the New World

U ntil the mid-sixteenth century, European mariners relied for navigation upon their intimate knowledge of coastal waters, keeping to familiar routes, never far from the sight of land. For instruments, no more than a lead line to determine depth, a compass for direction, and a sandglass to keep track of time, were needed to plot their course. Experience with the tides, currents, and type of bottom found within these boundaries, plus a careful dead-reckoning, sufficed to enable sailors to arrive at their desired ports. Gradually, tentative travels along the coasts expanded into longer passages farther offshore, and the great age of exploration of the Atlantic began.

The primary cause and the greatest driving force behind this outburst of oceanic activity was the search for a sea route to the Far East, to the territories of Cathay and Cipangu (Japan), to gain better access to the treasures sought by all of Europe—silks, spices, precious stones, and perfumes. For centuries these goods traveled overland by caravan to Mecca and Alexandria, there to be bartered for western goods and transported farther northward. In the Mediterranean, Venetian ships monopolized the spice trade, while Genoese ships handled the silk trade through their merchant colonies in Constantinople and Kaffa. But when the Turks conquered Constantinople in 1453 and Alexandria shortly thereafter, this major trade route was severely limited, if not altogether cut off, and the nations of Europe had to search for other routes to the riches of the Orient.

With overland travel eastward blocked by the Pyrenees Mountains, and Muslim centers of trade in the Mediterranean virtually monopolized by Venice and Genoa, Spain and Portugal had to turn toward the west, to the uncharted Atlantic. Portuguese mariners sailed the Atlantic coast of Africa, where they established colonies and trading stations. Each voyage advanced a little farther before turning homeward, and by 1434 Gil Eanes, a navigator from the Algarve, made an unprecedented journey as far south as Cape Bojador at the western bulge of Africa. Sailors pushed the limits of their voyages still farther, until they passed Dakar, Guinea, and reached Sierra Leone, only 10° above the equator. In 1487, two Portuguese mariners, Bartholomeu Dias and Pèro da Covilhã, were able to double the Cape of Good Hope and enter the Indian Ocean. Nine years later, Vasco da Gama not only rounded the Cape, but sailed all the way to Calicut, India. By the middle of the sixteenth century, Portugal had more than fifty forts and trading posts, ranging around Africa, to Goa at India, and all the way to Macao on Mainland China.

In the other direction, Spanish mariners crossed the Atlantic and revealed the existence of an entire New World. The voyages of Christopher Columbus gave for the Spanish monarchy a vast Caribbean empire, and in 1519 the Spanish conquistador Hernando Cortés captured Tenochitlán (Mexico City), the capital of the Aztec empire. Other Spanish explorers extended this dominion from Florida in the north to the Yucatan in the south, and onward to Peru in South America. Spanish ships also rounded Cape Horn and reached the Philippines and the Spice Islands, where they established ports of trade.

As these explorations revealed each new land and archipelago, Portugal and Spain claimed ownership. In 1479–1480, with the Treaty of Alcáçovas, Spain and Portugal arranged a comprehensive division of their possessions in the Atlantic Ocean. Portugal then petitioned Rome to sanction this treaty. And in the following year, 1481, Pope Sixtus IV issued the Bull of *Aeterni regis* which affirmed what had been agreed to by the two nations. Shortly thereafter, Columbus's epic voyage to the New World left Spain concerned over her sovereign rights to the newly discovered lands. In 1493, Ferdinand and Isabella persuaded Pope Alexander VI, a Spaniard, to issue another Bull granting Spain rights to the islands reached by Columbus. A vertical line was drawn at "one hundred leagues toward the west and south from any of the islands commonly known as the Azores and Cape Verde." The location of this line was ambiguous, but it undoubtedly gave more territory in the Atlantic to Spain than to Portugal.

Dissatisfied with the inequities continually produced by these Bulls, Spain and Portugal decided to resolve their differences independently of the papacy. They reached a compromise in the 1494 Treaty of Tordesillas, with each power agreeing that:

> . . . a boundary or straight line be determined and drawn north and south, from pole to pole, on the Ocean Sea, from the Arctic to the Antarctic Pole. This line shall be drawn straight . . . at a distance of 370 leagues west of the Cape Verde Islands. And all lands on the eastern side of the said bound . . . shall belong to the said King of Portugal and his successors. And all other lands shall belong to the said King and Queen of Castile.

For a while it seemed this would quiet the ownership disputes. After Magellan's expedition of 1519–1522, the Orient became accessible to Spain by sailing west. Spanish ports on the Pacific coast of Mexico provided a direct route to the Philippines, eliminating the need to make the long, perilous voyage around Cape Horn. Sugar produced in Hispaniola and other Caribbean islands, along with gold and other minerals plundered from Peru and Mexico brought great wealth to Spain.

Portugal had her trade routes around the Cape of Good Hope to Mozambique and Zanzibar on the east coast of Africa, and to Goa, India, Malacca, and Macao.✤ From her colonies along the African coast, Portugal extracted wealth from gold mines, the sale of ivory, and in the trade of black slaves. From Malacca, and the Spice Islands, she derived enormous profits from the

✤ Malacca, a Portuguese territory since 1509, is on the west coast of the Malay Peninsula, and is not to be confused with the Molucca Islands (commonly called the Spice Islands) in East Indonesia between the island of Celebes and New Guinea.

trade in spices. By the end of the first quarter of the sixteenth century, the two great maritime powers of Spain and Portugal had divided the world between them and shifted the economic and political balance in Europe. Spain had discovered the West Indies and Seas Occidental, while Portugal had discovered the East Indies and Seas Oriental; between the two, they encompassed the world in the southern oceans. Their maritime supremacy remained unchallenged until the very end of the sixteenth century.

If the countries of northern Europe were to wrest their share of profit from trade on the far side of the world, they would have to find a route unimpeded by the powers of Spain and Portugal in the southern seas. At the time, England had neither the ability nor the inclination to engage in battles on the sea or by diplomacy on land. King Henry VIII, married to Catherine of Aragon, was not interested in creating conflict with the Spanish monarchy. French Kings, as well, avoided direct challenge of the division of the world as defined by international law and backed by papal authority. The potential for wealth from Asian trade was so great, however, that England and France continued to try to reach the East Indies, despite the papal Bulls and treaties. Prohibited by Spain and Portugal from entering the southern seas, they turned to concentrate their efforts in northern latitudes.

The idea of a northern route to the Far East was never doubted to exist, but waited only to be validated by some adventurous mariner. In his *Discourse of a Discovery for a New Passage to Cataia* (1576), Sir Humphrey Gilbert felt that everything considered, and weighed together, the only reason the Northwest Passage had not yet been discovered is that the honor is being "reserved for some noble Prince, or worthy man thereby to make himself rich, and the world happy." Presumably, since the Portuguese and Spanish already had their trade routes to the Far East by the Southeast and Southwest, the best of all—the Northwest Passage—was being reserved by God for some Englishman. One hundred years later, after attempts by the English mariners, Martin Frobisher, John Davis, and Henry Hudson failed, Father Christian Le Clercq, a Récollet Missionary, concluded in his *First Establishment of the Faith in New France* that "we [the French] have every reason to believe that this enterprise [finding the Northwest Passage] was reserved for Monsieur de la Salle."

Political as well as physical constraints slowed the endeavors of England and France to pursue the Northwest Passage to Cathay. Under the rule of King Henry VII of England, John Cabot was given ships, men, and the power to "saile to all parts, countrys and seas of the East, of the West, and of the North, to seeke out, discover, and find whatsoever isles, countrys, regions or provinces . . . in what part of the world soever they be, which before this time had beene unknowen to all Christians." Cabot left Bristol, England, in 1497 to find a short route to the Indies. He arrived in Newfoundland, and took possession of this "newe founde ilande" for his sovereign. John Cabot did not achieve his goal of reaching China, but he did accomplish something perhaps more important: as a result of this voyage, England claimed possession of the entire North American continent.

OLD RIVALRIES

News of Cabot's voyage spread quickly. Spanish ambassadors in England relayed letters about Cabot's activities to their Catholic sovereigns, informing Ferdinand and Isabella that the land they (the English) found already belonged to Spain, for "it is at the end of that which belongs to your highness by the convention [Treaty of Tordesillas] with Portugal." King Henry ignored the complaints made to him that the islands and mainland found by John Cabot did not belong to England, since according to the treaty they already belonged to Spain.

In 1508 Sebastian Cabot, son of John Cabot, left England to search for a northwestern route to the Far East. He explored the coastline of North America from sixty miles north of the Arctic Circle, south to Cape Hatteras, or possibly even the Bahama Islands. He too failed to find the passage.

France, as well, sought the elusive passage to gain her share in wealth from the Asian trade. In the second quarter of the sixteenth century, Giovanni da Verrazano, a Florentine navigator, was convinced that the route to Cathay lay somewhere in the middle of the North American continent. Under the French flag, he set sail for America in 1524. Verrazano closed with the coast at about 34° N, near Cape Fear, southernmost of North Carolina's three capes. From there he headed south. Then, probably realizing he was as close to potentially hostile Spanish ships as he cared to come, he turned north. Verrazano continued to follow the coast until he reached the northern end of Newfoundland, and from there he headed back home. Upon his return, in a long letter to King Francis I, Verrazano described the voyage, and his observations that completely changed the current ideas of the cosmography of the world.

With this voyage, the last unexplored section of the coastline of North and South America was closed. Verrazano showed that the new continent, extending from the tip of Patagonia to within 1,200 miles of the North Pole, was unbroken by any strait or passage leading to the Pacific Ocean. This did not end the search for the Northwest Passage; it merely shifted it farther north. Spurred by the desire for immense wealth gained from the Far East trade, French and English mariners continued to make voyages in the western Atlantic, in spite of Spanish opposition. "Gallia Nova," or "Francesca," as Verrazano named his newly discovered lands, was the start of French and Spanish rivalries in North America.

Throughout these French and English explorations Spain remained firm in her claim that she owned all land beyond 370 leagues west of the Cape Verde Islands as demarcated in the Treaty of Tordesillas and backed by the Vatican. To substantiate her claim and promote new voyages, France took action to remove the Spanish impediment to her explorations. Fortunately for Francis I, Pope Clement VII was a Medici, and thus allied with France against Charles V of Spain. Also, the pope's niece, Catherine de' Medici, was betrothed to the duc d'Orleans, future King Henry II of France. When they met in Marseilles for the wedding celebration in 1533, King Francis persuaded the pope to change the *Inter caetera* bull issued in 1493 by Alexander VII. Pope Clement proclaimed that the edict of Alexander "applied only to lands already discovered, not to those found by other sovereigns." With this, a new concept of colonialism emerged; one in which ownership of newly discovered land and the exclusive right to trade there were valid only if those claiming sovereignty of the region permanently occupied it, and had fixed establishments there.

In the second quarter of the sixteenth century, Captain Jacques Cartier of France made three voyages to the New World. With royal support, and now, approval of the Vatican, he sailed in 1534 to "the kingdom of Terres Neufves [Newfoundland], to discover certain isles and countries where there is said to be found a vast quantity of gold and other rich things." ♣ Cartier's commission from Francis I was a direct challenge to Spanish rights in North America. Like his predecessors, Cartier's primary goal was to find the Northwest Passage. He entered the Gulf of St. Lawrence and made a complete circuit of its waters before the approaching winter forced his return to France. In the following year Cartier again voyaged to Canada to prove his theory that the "grand river of Hochleaga," as the St. Lawrence River was called, might provide a passage through North America to the Far East. To his dismay, the impassable series of rapids above the present-day city of Montréal repudiated the promise that the St. Lawrence River would provide a navigable passage to the Pacific Ocean.

♣ Cartier's landfall was at Cape Buona Vista, on the eastern shore of Newfoundland. This is the same landfall believed by most—but not all—to be that of John Cabot in 1497, and possibly the landfall of the Portuguese mariner, Corte-Real in 1501.

On October 17, 1540, Jacques Cartier received a grant from the king for a third voyage to Canada, this time to colonize the new lands he discovered. Shortly afterward, Jean-François de la Rocque, Sieur de Roberval, received a similar commission. Roberval was to sail with Cartier "for conquest of these lands and to make settlements in the said country." However, the combined effects of an insufficient supply of provisions, hostile Indians, and a severe winter of hardship and suffering caused both mariners to abandon their plans and return to France. No further attempt was made by France to establish a permanent colony in Canada for another sixty-four years.

Spain, however, never relinquished her claim of ownership of all of North America. Pope Clement's edict ending the *Inter caetera* by Alexander VI, which restricted any nation from sailing west of a vertical line 370 leagues west of the Cape Verde Islands, satisfied French interests, but was not accepted by Spain. According to Spain, her title to the entire continent was assured by papal Bull and the Treaty of Tordesillas.

These issues, which remained unresolved between the two nations, were addressed at the end of the war between Spain and France during the negotiations of the Treaty of Nice in 1538. The treaty included a phrase guaranteeing "free navigation to the subjects of both parties." The French took this to mean they had the right to voyage anywhere they pleased, east or west of the line, as long as it was to lands not already occupied by Spain; while Spain believed it restricted French vessels to free navigation *east* of the line of demarcation. Furthermore, according to Spain, she did not have to occupy all parts of the land to claim ownership of it. The two countries did agree, however, "not to attack each other's possessions."

But the law of diplomatic treaty and the law of the sea are two entirely different matters. Though peace was settled in Europe between the two nations, Spanish and French rivalry in the New World continued unabated. In the second half of the sixteenth century, piracy and privateering was rampant, and violence at sea, common in European waters, was carried to North American waters as well. Any ship, be it Dutch, English, French, Spanish, or Portuguese, regardless of allegiances or treaties, was fair game for any other—every vessel was a predator, and every vessel was prey. Privateering was simply considered a form of commercial enterprise.

French pirates ranged the West Indies, capturing Spanish treasury ships and destroying Spanish settlements in Puerto Rico and Hispaniola. And in 1555, a fleet of French pirates invaded, and demolished the Spanish stronghold of Havana, Cuba. Spanish ships, in turn, asserted their rights in North America by attacking French fishing settlements in far northern latitudes off the coast of Labrador and Newfoundland.

In addition to the pirate vessels, the French navy maintained a fleet of six ships in the Caribbean and Gulf of Mexico to protect French interests. Entreaties by Jean-Baptiste Colbert, minister of King Louis XIV, to the Spanish king for trading privileges in the Spanish colonies and free navigation for French ships in the Gulf of Mexico were denied. What could not be obtained by diplomacy would have to be taken by force. In the last quarter of the seventeenth century, the conquest of Spanish colonies on the Gulf coast and seizure of the gold and silver mines in Mexico became the ultimate ambition of King Louis XIV of France.

Subsequent treaties between Spain and France, such as the Treaty of

Vaucelles in 1556, and the Treaty of Cateau-Cambrésis in 1559, did little to settle the problem. France was not willing to give up her claim to North America, and insisted on total freedom of the seas for her ships. Those lands that she "discovered" and were not already claimed by Spain or Portugal were considered French territory—occupied or not. Spain, on the other hand, would not relinquish her monopoly of the American continent and ownership of all waters west of the papal line of demarcation.

As matters between the two nations stood at the end of 1559, the old line of Demarcation of Alexander VI, a line intended to establish peace between Spain and Portugal, became the boundary for war. Under the treaty of peace, as long as French ships remained east of that line they would have no fear of being attacked; west of that line, however, freedom to navigate the waters, and to colonize any lands there, would depend upon the victor in battle. Thus, Spain and France were in the strange position of being at peace in Europe, and at war in America.

Despite Spanish claims of sole territorial rights in the Caribbean; claims justified by occupation following the discoveries and explorations of Christopher Columbus; claims backed by the edict of Alexander VIII; there was no way Spain could keep marauding vessels of other nations out of these waters—the prize was too great. France and England were determined to gain their share of wealth from the region's natural products of tobacco, sugar, rum, and molasses. French pirates cruised among the Caribbean archipelagos and ranged the shores of the Gulf of Mexico from Florida to the Yucatan, looting and capturing what they could. By 1640, France conquered and possessed the West Indian islands of Tortuga, Guadeloupe, Martinique, and the northern coast of Santo Domingo. Important as these islands were unto themselves, they also served as bases at the gateway to the Mexican coast, with its even greater riches of gold and silver.

ENGLISH SETTLEMENTS

In the closing decades of the sixteenth century, England's Queen Elizabeth warned Spain that "the pope had no right to partition the world, and to give and take kingdoms to whomever he pleased." John Cabot's landfall at Newfoundland in 1497 had given England her claim of ownership of North America and the right to colonize those lands. Accordingly, in 1606, King James I granted land patents to two companies: the London Company, or as sometimes called, the Southern Virginia Colony, which included the territory of Virginia; and the Plymouth Company, or Northern Virginia Colony, whose property included Maine, Acadia, and adjacent regions. These two patents covered land from the 34th degree of latitude (about fifty miles north of Charleston, South Carolina) to the 45th degree of latitude at Eastport, Maine. Thereby, the Plymouth Company owned the entire coastline of Maine, as well as a major part of Nova Scotia.

Captain John Smith is well known as the founder of Jamestown, on the James River of Chesapeake Bay, for the London Company; his counterpart in founding a settlement for the Plymouth Company was George Popham. So little was known about this coast that when the Popham colony was formed at the mouth of the Kennebec River in Maine (then called the Sagadahoc River), Popham wrote to England claiming that a large sea existed only seven days journey to the west, by which China could be reached. Captain John Smith likewise believed that "a strait, sound, or river north of the Virginia colony, somewhere under 40° N latitude, might lead to a Western Sea." From there, he thought, perhaps by traveling through the Great Lakes, one would pass into the Pacific Ocean.

In giving these two patents, the fact that the southern border of the Plymouth Company overlapped the northern border of the London Company was apparently unnoticed. Not overlooked, however, was the presence of French settlements within the limits of King James's patents. In a fit of self-righteous wrath, the governor of Virginia, Sir Thomas Dale, decided the French intruders must be expelled. Commanded by Captain Samuel Argall, a fleet of three ships sailed to Mt. Desert Island, Maine, where the fledgling French settlement with Jesuit missionaries was demolished. In less than a day Argall and his men sailed across the Bay of Fundy (renamed now, Argall Bay) and attacked the settlement of Port Royal, burning it to the ground. Having accomplished what he had set out to do—eliminate the French settlements of Acadia—Argall returned to Virginia.

The setback to Acadia was only temporary, and within a few years Port Royal was rebuilt. The French were not removed from their foothold in North America, but the southern boundary of Acadia was shifted more than 240 miles farther north from its original limit to the eastern shore of Penobscot Bay, Maine (roughly 44° N latitude). Within a period of fifty years, control of Acadia shifted back and forth between British and French hands eleven times.

HOLLAND IN AMERICA

Holland also played a role in the development of this region. Although Henry Hudson was an Englishman, his voyage to North America in 1609 was under the auspices of the Dutch East India Company of Amsterdam. After a brief stay in Maine (at the mouth of the St. George River), he sailed south to Chesapeake Bay. Hudson had in mind to visit his friend Captain John Smith and discuss with him his ideas about the Northwest Passage, but contrary winds prevented Hudson's vessel from entering the Chesapeake, and he forsook this plan. Continuing northward along the coast, Hudson entered the river that now bears his name and sailed its length for 150 miles to where it no longer became navigable, then returned home. The Hudson River was disproved as one more potential route leading to the Pacific. By virtue of this voyage Holland also claimed a large portion of North America. Contemporary maps displayed the title "New Netherland" in the region from Delaware Bay, north to Nova Scotia, overlapping both the English and French claims.

Dutch dominance over this vast territory lasted well into the second half of the seventeenth century. Holland's interest in North America never lay in colonization; it was the commercial interest of trade that prompted her involvement. Gradually, through treaties with England, the domain of New Netherland contracted to the area now called Delaware, New Jersey, Pennsylvania, New York, and Connecticut, and finally dwindled to her most important settlements and trade-stations along the Hudson River.

A FRENCH START

French colonization in North America began from two centers: one, in the far northern latitudes around the Bay of Fundy (named *La Bai Française,* or French Bay); the other, south, in the Caribbean and Gulf of Mexico. The coast explored by Verrazano in 1524, and claimed for France, as well as the visits by Jacques Cartier, provided sufficient grounds for France to amplify her hold thereby establishing permanent settlements. The natural products of the land, its forests, fur-bearing animals, minerals, and other commodities, though not capable of yielding the kind of profits the Spanish wrested from their possessions to the south, began to have an appeal. Coupled with the desire for trade and profits was the resolve to convert the inhabitants there to the Christian faith.

This enterprise, for the glory of France, was entrusted to the leadership of Pierre du Guast, Sieur de Monts, a nobleman from the province of Xaintonage. On November 8th, of 1603, King Henry IV of France granted to de Monts a patent to the land of La Cadie (Acadia); prescribed from the 40th to the 46th degree of latitude, it extended roughly from the latitude of Philadelphia, along the coast north to Nova Scotia and Cape Breton Island. As lieutenant general, de Monts represented France "in the territories, coasts, and confines of La Cadie." He was to "establish, extend, and make to be known our [France's] name, might, and authority. And under the same to subject, submit, and bring to obedience all the people of the said land and the borders thereof."

The following year, de Monts and his pilot Samuel Champlain sailed for New France. The site selected for this first settlement, a small island in the middle of the St. Croix River of Passamaquoddy Bay on the western shore of the Bay of Fundy, was a disaster. Those who survived the disease of scurvy and the cruel winter quickly departed and sailed to the Nova Scotia side of the bay where they founded the first permanent French settlement of Port Royal, now called Annapolis Royal.

PART II

Canada, or the Nouvelle France

Champlain found the initial locations in Acadia unsuitable for any kind of permanent settlement and made another attempt in 1608—this time, on the St. Lawrence. The bitter cold winters he experienced there in an earlier exploration precluded this being his initial choice. But he realized now that for his colony to succeed it had to depend on a profit from the trade in furs; that meant being farther north where the beaver were more plentiful. Selecting the Indian village of Stadacona (first visited by Jacques Cartier in 1535) Champlain founded a new colony on the St. Lawrence River. The Indians called it *Kebec,* meaning "the narrowing of the waters." Champlain named it Québec. There, he built his residence and set about building a business with his monopoly in the fur trade.

Champlain's original desires for exploration and the ultimate goal of finding the Northwest Passage were not forgotten. In the following years he extended his travels beyond the rapids above Montréal, to the Iroquois River (now called Richelieu), which flows into Lake Ontario; he explored the Ottawa River, and managed to reach Georgian Bay of Lake Huron, thus providing a route to the upper Great Lakes which would be free from the threat of Iroquois attacks; and southward from Lake Ontario, into Iroquois country, to the lake in New York state, which now bears his name.

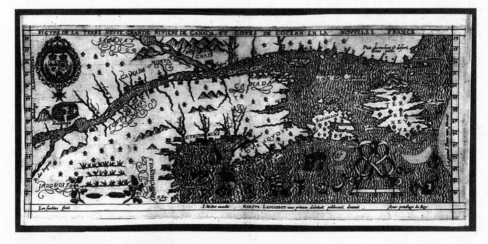

Drawn by March Lescarbot, and published in *Histoire de la Nouvelle-France* . . . Paris, Jean Milot, it represents the territories of Canada and the Atlantic coast of New France as explored at that time. Newfoundland (*Terre Nouve*), Cape Breton (*Bacaillos*), Nova Scotia (*Souriquois*), and Anticosti Island (*I. de l'Assomption*), with their offshore banks, are remarkably well delineated. Cape Cod is identified by the name of *Malebarre*, which was given to it by Samuel Champlain in his explorations in 1605 and 1606, on account of the dangerous bars and sandbanks he found there.

Hochleaga, shown in the enlarged detail, was the city visited by Jacques Cartier in 1535. At that time, over a thousand natives inhabited it. The large hill that dominated the stockaded city, Cartier named *Mont Royal*—*Hochleaga* became the future city of Montréal. *Map by Lescarbot, courtesy of the National Archives of Canada/NMC-97952.*

During his stay in Canada, Champlain befriended the Hurons and Algonquins in the wars against their traditional enemies, the Iroquois. The mingling in Indian politics that he initiated was a policy that continued throughout the history of New France. The French, by allying themselves with one tribe against another in the effort to maintain a balance of power in their own favor, created a hostility between themselves and the Iroquois—the effects of which were to return time and again in succeeding decades to drain their energies, reduce their profits, and thwart their progress of colonization.

Continually under threat of annihilation by the surrounding Indians, the newly commissioned Intendant of New France, Jean Talon, proceeded to carry out the orders given him by King Louis XIV. Protection against the Iroquois must be assured, he said:

> . . . *[they] are all perpetual and irreconcilable enemies of the Colony, having by the massacre of a number of French and the inhumanity which they exercise towards those who fall into their power, prevented the country being more peopled than it is at present and by their surprisals and unexpected forays always keeping the country in check; the King has resolved . . . to carry war even to their firesides in order totally to exterminate them, having no guarantee in their words, for they violate their faith as often as they find the inhabitants of the Colony at their mercy.*

The French colonists, under the leadership of Sieur de Tracy, moved against the Mohawks and destroyed their villages. The number of casualties was small, for the Indians fled to the woods. But the French had demonstrated to the other Iroquois Nations that they were not immune to the power of the French. Rather than risk losing a war to the French, and being destroyed, the Iroquois asked for, and received, a treaty of peace. The treaty was signed in Québec in 1666 and lasted for seventeen years.

Fearful of retaliation, and in spite of the treaty, Talon proposed this first attack be followed by a second offensive of even greater scope. He wanted to wage war, not only against the other Iroquois Nations, but the Dutch and English in North America, as well. But these plans gave way to others of reorganizing the commerce of New France and the expansion of its territory.

This treaty of peace prohibited attacks upon each other. However, the French considered the Indians as their vassals—subject to the rules of French subjects, controlled by force, if necessary, or subjugated by converting their religious beliefs into accepting Christianity. This was not the view held by the Indians. When the governor of Canada, de Courecelle, re-

Portrait of Jean Talon, appointed by King Louis XIV as Intendant of New France. Commissioned on March 23, 1665, he served until 1668. After a one-year leave of absence, he again served from 1670 to 1672. Painted by Frerè Luc, 1671. *Photo: courtesy of Musée des Augustines de l'Hôtel-Dieu de Québec.*

quested of the Senecas to not make war on other peaceful tribes, they challenged his right to interfere. They wanted to know "whether all the nations of this great continent became French subjects as soon as missionaries fixed themselves among them . . . were they no longer at liberty to demand satisfaction for insults [from other tribes] received?" They said they would "rather perish than diminish in the slightest degree their liberty and independence, and that it might be remembered that they had more than once made the French feel that they were not allies to be treated with hauteur or enemies to be despised." With such conflicting views as these, and where "theft from strangers was a virtue, and revenge a duty," any peace between the French and Iroquois was tenuous at best; quickly discarded at the least provocation.

The Franciscan (Récollets, and Sulpicians) and Jesuit missionaries did their best to instill the Christian Faith in the Indian. By developing their own settlements, and with constant religious teaching, they hoped to accomplish the saving of souls—and in some measure, reconcile the attitude of the Indians toward the French.

Decorated with the title of Bishop of Petraea, François Xavier de Laval-Montmorency (a Jesuit) was appointed first Bishop of Québec. He left France in the spring of 1659 to take charge of his new diocese. To the Jesuit priests, Claude Trouvé and François de Salignac, about to go on a mission to the Iroquois on the north coast of Lake Ontario, he gave extensive counsel. First, Laval reminded them that being sent "to work for the conversion of they heathen, they were engaged in the Church's most important work which obliges them to become worthy instruments of God." He advised them:

> . . . try to avoid the two extremities which are to be feared in those who devote themselves to the conversion of souls: hoping for too much, or despairing too much; those who are too optimistic are often the first to fall into despair at the sight of the great difficulties which are to be found in the task of converting the heathen, which is the work of God rather than of man. . . .
>
> . . . remember the text of the word of God, "fruit is brought forth in patience" [Luke 8:15]; those who do not have such patience are in danger, after having, at first, burned fiercely, of losing courage and abandoning the undertaking.

Excellent advice, which was heeded by these first missionaries. But for all their efforts, and under inconceivable hardships, at best they baptized a few babies, and the occasional adult near death who was willing to grasp at any chance for success from his impending doom. At worst, they suffered a martyrdom for their Faith.

As the first quarter of the seventeenth century ended, France's policy toward her fledgling colony in the New World changed. It was apparent that leaving the settlement of New France in the hands of a few individuals, with trade monopolies and the power to do as they wished, without some sort of planning and control, was not securing and expanding their empire. For nearly one hundred years the French had explored and partially inhabited the land of Acadia, stretching from Newfoundland to midcoast Maine and along the St. Lawrence River. For almost twenty-five years they were settled in Québec. For all that, the number of colonists scarcely numbered more than seventy-five—and these "were living in misery, exchanging yearly the hunger of winter for the starvation of spring."

In order for the fledgling communities to survive and prosper, they needed to grow. Men were needed to construct the forts for protection against Indian attacks, to build habitations for themselves and the farm animals, and to work the land to provide food. The villages needed more than the numbers of people arriving yearly from France; they needed families, and offspring—in short, they needed women. In the beginning, there was no set plan as to where they would come from. Some married women accompanied their husbands in the immigration to New France, and there was always a certain amount of cohabitation with the native women found here, but this was inadequate to provide the increased population.

A more definite, aggressive plan was needed. To this end, Jean-Baptiste Colbert, minister to King Louis XIV, initiated a recruitment program to procure young women for the colonization of New France. Called *Filles du roi* (Daughters of the king), funds for the project were provided by the royal treasury. In France, special agents made the selection. The women came from two social classes: one group destined for marriage to officers and gentlemen of noble birth were "young ladies" from good families and well educated; qual-

MARTYRE DU P. NICOLAS VIEL, RECOLLET ET DE SON
NEOPHYTE AHUNTSIC 1634.
D'APRES LE TABLEAU DE GEORGES DELFOSSE—ENREGISTRE

In 1625, Father Nicholas Viel became the first missionary in New France to suffer martyrdom for the faith. When Samuel Champlain heard that the Hurons were going to forsake
their alliance with the French, and instead side with the Iroquois, he dispatched missionaries—among them the Récollet Father Nicholas Viel—to the Huron country in an effort to
maintain the peace. When Father Viel and his young convert, Auhaitisque, returned to
Montréal, they were drowned purposely by their Huron guides in their hatred of the Christianizing thrust upon them. The scene of this martyrdom on the Ottawa River is now called
Sault-au-Récollet. *Photo: courtesy of the Bibliothèque Nationale du Québec, Québec, Canada.
Painted by George Delfosse, Montréal.*

Portrait of Jean-Baptiste Colbert, minister to King Louis XIV. Painted by Claude Levebvre, 1663. *Photo: courtesy of Réunion des Musées Nationaux / Art Resource, New York.*

ifications for those to more common settlers were that they be of good health and strong constitution to withstand the rigors facing them in New France— and of course, capable of bearing children. The selected women were all un- married and came mostly from farming families, thus were used to hard work.

The *Conseil de Québec* petitioned the king to select families "from the Isle de France, Normandy, Picardy, and the neighboring provinces, as the people there were, it was said, laborious, industrious, full of religious feeling, while the provinces near the seaports, where the shipments were made, contained many heretics, and a population less adapted to agriculture." They came from a wide variety of backgrounds, and all were considered "women of virtue."

Until such time as they could be transported to Québec, the women were housed by nuns, or widows and provided with food and clothing. Between the years of 1663 and 1673, around 600 *Filles du roi* emigrated to New France. But not all arrived safely. In 1664, passage across the Atlantic claimed the lives of sixty of the 300 who started out. Fifteen of the 300, left at the first point of land the ship reached in Newfoundland, and one woman was captured by the Iroquois.

The program had other problems as well. In the beginning, local priests were reluctant to perform these arranged marriages, and the duty was left to that of notaries. The *Conseil de Québec* had to pass laws officially forbidding anyone to prevent the marriage of the "girls who have come from France at the king's expense to marry, when they themselves wish to." The position the priests took was not unreasonable, since double and triple marriages were found to have been performed; to them, this was in contravention to the sacrament of marriage. To ease the situation, Colbert promised Talon that new convoys of girls would have certificates showing where they came from, that they were free and of marriageable state.

There were some who never did find marriage in the new land and became a burden to the communities who had to feed, clothe, and lodge them. Additionally, expenses were much higher than anticipated. And finally, there were a certain number of girls who complained about being ill-treated during the crossing. If this happened too often, and the information spread back to France, the number who chose to immigrate would dwindle substantially. Not wishing the king's project jeopardized, Talon said he would do "all he could to charm them out of their sadness."

The colony was in a wretched state: they were under constant threat of extermination from the Iroquois; few buildings were suitable for shelter or protection; and land was untilled. In contrast, within twenty-five years, the

English in the Virginia colonies grew and flourished. Already they had 4,000 inhabitants and a strong economic base in the tobacco and other natural resources sent back home.

To provide new stimulus to French growth in Canada, Cardinal de Richelieu, minister of the crown, created a vigorous plan to promote colonization—a plan based on strong trading companies such as those of the Dutch and English. He founded the "Company of One Hundred Associates," or "Company of New France." Drawn from wealthy merchants and nobles of Paris and other commercial cities, each of the members contributed a sum of money into the company and agreed: to send to New France in the ensuing year (1628) two or three hundred people skilled in various trades; by 1643 to increase the number of inhabitants to 4,000—these to be native-born Frenchmen and Catholics; and provide three priests for each settlement. In return, the king assigned to the Company of One Hundred Associates, the fort and village of Québec, all of New France (including that part of Florida inhabited by his predecessors), and the course of the Great River [St. Lawrence], along with islands, ports and harbors, et cetera.❖

All previous concessions given by the king were revoked, and the company received a full monopoly of trade—by land, or by sea—in leather, furs, and skins, commencing January 1, 1628, and ending December 31, 1643. The cod and whale fishing was withheld from the company in order that it may be for the benefit of all Frenchmen. Many other terms of rights and concessions were included in the king's commission, including special rewards to those who stayed in New France for six years before returning to their homeland.

❖ Fort Caroline (near present-day Jacksonville, Florida), founded by French Huguenots in 1564, was the first European settlement in the North America mainland. When Spain learned of the colony's existence in territory they considered their own, they attacked and killed all 140 of its inhabitants, except for sixty women and children taken as prisoner. Other Frenchmen, numbering 350, were found nearby and hacked to death with swords. The colony had lasted scarcely more than one year.

It was a well thought-out plan; one that if carried through with adherence to its provisions, would have succeeded. Replacing the earlier Huguenot settlers with Catholics did little to relieve religious strife; it merely shifted it to conflicts between the Jesuit and the Franciscan missionaries who took their place. And France simply did not have a surplus population to provide the sufficient number of settlers.

Less than a year passed, when the entire project received a severe blow. A small fleet of English privateers, commanded by David Kirke, attacked and captured nineteen of twenty French ships filled with colonists and supplies bound for New France. They took Québec as well.

At first, reaction at the French court was one of shock, for they had a treaty of peace with England, which was now so flagrantly disregarded. This changed to an attitude of acceptance and even of relief that Québec and Canada were no longer their responsibility or concern. The climate was harsh and unrelenting; they weren't able to provide the number of colonists to settle so vast a country; and even if they did settle it, of what use would it be, they asked? Profits they gained from the furs were not enough to warrant the expense. Opinion voice at the court was:

> . . . in the fifty years that we have known Canada, what have we derived from it? This country can, then, be of no use to us, or we must admit that the French are not suited for founding colonies. . . . Let us [instead] improve France, keep the men, profit by her advantages for trade; turn to account the industry of her inhabitants, and we shall see all the wealth of Asia, Africa, and the New World enter our ports.

Others, including Champlain, felt it was still worthwhile to retain France's hold in Canada. Though it yielded no gold or silver, such as the Spanish wrested from Peru and Mexico in their conquests, forests covered the country and would be of great value in shipbuilding, and the allure of fur trade always remained. The cod fishing alone was "enough to enrich a kingdom, required but little outlay, and was an excellent school to train sailors." As early as 1629, a cautionary warning was made about taking care "not to exhaust the source of supply [of beaver] by endeavoring to enrich themselves at once"—sound, but unheeded advice.

Upon these considerations, as well as maintaining his honor, King Louis XIV decided in favor of retaining Canada. France entered into negotiations with England to regain Quebec and was prepared to back it up with force if necessary. But England had no desire for their newly acquired territory; willingly, and quickly, they gave it back to France.✦ In addition to Québec, they returned all of New France, which included Acadia and Ile Royale (Cape Breton).

The transfer of ownership, and its return, did nothing to change conditions in New France. Its settlements lacked the forts to protect its inhabitants, the population was too few, and even the sole blessing—profit from the fur trade—was markedly diminished due to constant warfare with the Iroquois. With the exception of a few missionaries, who fearlessly, if injudiciously, traveled farther afield in order to bring the True Faith to the Indians, exploration of the wilderness west of Montréal had virtually ceased.

When the term of the Company of One Hundred Associates ended in 1644, its owners were all too happy to turn over all the property they owned, as well as their monopolies in trade, to the settlers. Now in ownership of New France, the settlers organized themselves into a corporation called *Compagnie des Habitants.* In recompense, they agreed to pay the old company 1,000 beaver pelts a year, assume all its debts, and pay the salaries of the government officials and the priests.

The *Compagnie des Habitants* fared little better than its predecessor. To aid in the operation of the company, the king created a council, called Conseil du Québec. Composed of the governors of Québec and Montreal plus the Jesuit superior (until there was a bishop), it was responsible for order and justice. Conditions in Canada continued to deteriorate. The Iroquois had seized the best beaver grounds in Ontario, selling the furs to the Dutch and English instead of the French. And the threat of annihilation by the Iroquois of the few remaining settlers was a constant threat.

In 1663, King Louis reorganized France's holdings in the New World. Canada was now considered, as any other French province, to be regulated by a governor, bishop, and Intendant. It was a political framework "without elective or responsible government." The next year, its commercial framework was also changed; it became part of a much larger trading territory—the French West India Company. By 1664, Canada consisted of

Portrait of King Louis XIV by Hyacinthe Rigaud, 1701. Painted when the Sun King was sixty-three years old, it shows him in full royal costume with all the symbols of his honors. *Photo: courtesy of Réunion des Musées Nationaux/Art Resource, New York.*

three settlements: Québec, Montréal, and Three Rivers; with the combined population of twenty-five hundred.

Such were the conditions in New France when La Salle arrived on the scene two years later in 1666. Canada was a wilderness, virtually unchanged—except for the relationship with the Iroquois—from the time of Jacques Cartier in 1534. It had a new form of government, still trying to define its role, and rife with conflicts between political and religious powers.

LA SALLE IN MONTRÉAL

Of most famous explorers, little is known about their early years. Not until they embark on some noble enterprise of discovery, and their names and deeds thrust into prominence, do their lives literally "begin." At a later time, biographers are then left to search about for some meager information with which to create a portrait of the character and abilities of their subject, hoping thereby to gain some prescient clues to their future behavior. Such is the case with René-Robert Cavelier, Sieur de la Salle, referred to simply as La Salle.

Assessing La Salle's character from all the contradictory material is as difficult as judging his true accomplishments. According to his Jesuit teachers in France, La Salle was a man of "excellent acquirements and unimpeachable morals." Many of La Salle's companions during his travels in New France were extravagant in their praise. Chevalier Tonty, who spent many years with La Salle, knew him to be "a man of undaunted courage." Henri Joutel, who accompanied La Salle and published an account of the last voyage to the Gulf of Mexico, wrote: "He was a man of regular Behavior, of a large Soul, well enough learned, and understanding in the Mathematicks, designing, bold, undaunted, dexterous, insinuating, not to be discourag'd at any Thing, ready at extricating himself out of any Difficulties, no way apprehensive of the greatest Fatigues, and wonder steady in Adversity." Joutel also commended La Salle for his truthfulness. He spoke only of what he knew about, says Joutel, and if there was apprehension about the veracity of the subject, or if he simply did not know, La Salle would not hesitate to say so. La Salle was firm in his belief that truth should not be frayed at the edges by doubt. Even Father Hennepin, who in his later volumes on the history of Louisiana usurped the credit from La Salle for his discoveries, paid homage to La Salle for his twenty years of unremitting efforts to bring Christianity to the "barbarous savages." To Hennepin, Réné-Robert Cavelier de la Salle was "a man of considerable merit, constant in adversities, fearless, generous, courteous, learned, and capable of everything."

Historians, as well, were unlimited in their praise of La Salle's character; his deeds exalted to being second only to those of Christopher Columbus. Jared Sparks, president of Harvard University in 1839 said: "No man surpassed the Sieur de la Salle in some of the higher attributes of character, such as personal courage and endurance, undaunted resolution, patience under trials, and perseverance in contending with obstacles."

For all those who saw in La Salle only the finest and noblest traits, there were others who mercilessly attacked his character, calling him unfit and an incompetent failure. These opponents claim that La Salle is vastly overrated, both in his personal qualities and his deeds; the elevation of La Salle to a hero figure, the result of highly romanticized ideals. He was said to be a "proud, domineering, and self-centered individual."

Some recent historians describe La Salle and his actions in clinical or psychiatric terms. La Salle is characterized, and the events of his life interpreted, from the perspective of a man who was paranoid and suffered from a manic-depressive disorder. Perhaps this approach to reevaluating our past heroes is but another phase of revisionist history.

This battle of contradictory evaluation about La Salle's character appears as early as 1744. A near contemporary historian, Pierre François-Xavier de Charlevoix, wrote in his *History of New France*:

Such is the lot of those men whom a mixture of great defects and great virtues draws from the common sphere. Their passions hurry them into faults; and if they do what others could not, their enterprises are not to the taste of all men. Their success excites the jealousy of those who remain in obscurity. They bene-

fit some and injure others; the latter take their revenge by decrying them with-
out moderation; the former exaggerate their merit. Hence the different portraits
drawn of them, none of which are really true; but as hatred and the itching for
slander always go further than gratitude and friendship, and calumny finds more
easy credence with the public than praise and eulogy, the enemies of the Sieur
de la Sale disfigured his portrait more than his friends embellished it.

In the following straight forward account of the exploits of La Salle the
reader may interpolate their own opinion about the judgment and reasoning power of La Salle and the psychological motives for his acts.

BORN IN 1643 into a moderately wealthy family of wholesale merchants
in Rouen, France, La Salle quickly exhibited a marked intellect, particularly in the sciences and mathematics. Accordingly, he received all the advantages of a liberal education as a pupil of the Jesuits. At the age of nine he
began his studies their local grammar school. Before his fifteenth birthday,
La Salle moved to Paris where he entered the novitiate. Two years later
(1660) he took the vows of the Jesuit order, choosing as his religious name,
Ignatious, the founder of the Society.

La Salle continued his education at the Collège of Henry IV, at La Flèche,
a Jesuit school famed as the best in France in the fields of mathematics and
physical sciences. Here he studied logic, physics, and mathematics, as well as
mastering the science of navigation. Self-discipline and scholarly excellence
were demanded of its pupils, and La Salle maintained these aims. But he also
began to exhibit other traits. His superiors noted that he was "stubborn,
domineering, and hot tempered," leading them to conclude that in La Salle
there was much that was contradictory to the life of a Jesuit.

La Salle grew restless and his studies suffered, until finally his teachers
considered him "a poor student, self-opinionated, and of very middling
judgement and prudence." In an attempt to maintain his place within the
Order, yet find some outlet of vigorous action, La Salle petitioned the general of the Society in Rome to send him to China to teach. He was turned
down in this, as well as in a later request to be sent to Portugal, since Por-

tugal would be a stepping-stone to the Chinese Mission. Unable to restrain his restless energies any longer, and the need to be his own master—traits that endured throughout La Salle's life—prompted him to withdraw from the Jesuit Order.

Unfortunately, under French law, his taking of the vows (even though later renounced) also left La Salle unable to inherit the estates and business of his recently deceased father. Thus, there was an imperative need to change his financial condition. Though La Salle had renounced his vows in the Jesuit Order, he always maintained deep religious convictions and kept as his companions Sulpician and Récollet friars.✤ These convictions created circumstances that help favor La Salle's decision to move to Canada. His older brother, Abbé Jean Cavelier, was already a priest of St. Sulpice in Montréal, and most likely it was upon his urgings that La Salle sailed for Canada in the spring of 1666.

✤ Both groups were of the Franciscan order. The Sulpicians, founded in Paris in 1641, maintained a parish church in Montréal and missions at various sites along the Great Lakes. Récollets were a reformed branch of the order founded by St. Francis of Assisi early in the thirteenth century. They arrived in New France in 1615 and preceded the Jesuits in establishing missions along the St. Lawrence River.

HERE, IN NEW FRANCE, economic opportunities were available for an adventurous, hardworking young man. His uncle, Henry Cavelier, was already established in Québec, selling woolens, guns, and brandy to the Indians in exchange for furs; and his cousin, Jacques Le Ber, was a successful merchant in Montréal. The region was rich in natural resources, and the demand in Europe for furs, particularly the beaver pelt, created fortunes for those involved in the trade.

As founders of Montréal, the priests of St. Sulpice became its sole proprietors and feudal lords, with the right to grant out lands to settlers. At the time, there were only three major settlements in Canada: Québec, Montréal, and Three Rivers, all located along the St. Lawrence River. Of the three, Montréal was the most dangerous for the French to occupy, being continually threatened by attack from tribes of the Five Nations, or Iroquois. These nations were the Seneca (westernmost, strongest, and most numerous),

Cayuga, Onondaga (central and most influential of the tribes), Oneida, and the Mohawk (fiercest, most implacable, and most treacherous of the five tribes).♣ Although some form of peace treaty had been negotiated before La Salle's arrival, it was tenuous and could likely be broken upon the slightest provocation. Generally, the Iroquois tribes favored alliance with the French, rather than the English, but this was no guarantee of peace in the ever shifting plays for power.

♣ After the Tuscarora tribe joined the Iroquois, it was called the Six Nations.

With the constant threat of violence, the best protection Montréal could have was a line of outpost settlements that could quickly convey warning of attack. Under their seigniorial power, the priests of St. Sulpice had the right to grant out lands in order to create a line of defense for their property. To encourage settlers, they gave the land at "very reasonable terms." Almost immediately, and without any fee, La Salle received from Abbé de Queylus (Superior of the Sulpician Seminary) a large tract of land above the great rapids on the St. Lawrence River, about eight or nine miles from Montréal.

These were the rapids that so dismayed Jacques Cartier when he first saw them on his second voyage to Canada in 1535. He called the rapids "a *sault* of water, the most impetuous one could possibly see." The water was far too shallow and much too swift for any vessel, other than a canoe, to pass; obviously the St. Lawrence River could not be the elusive Northwest Passage Cartier sought.

La Salle named his fledgling settlement on the St. Lawrence *Transport de la Seigneurie de St. Sulpice* and promptly started to clear the land and build a palisaded village.♣ Within the enclosure, he portioned off 280 acres of land for himself, about 133 acres for a common to be shared by all, and the rest to be sold to other settlers who would join him. For a yearly fee of three capons, a small sum of money, and a perpetual rent, the other settlers would receive one-third of an acre within the enclosure, plus forty acres outside for farming. In return for the grant of this land, La Salle had to pay a small fee to the seminary, but only if and when the property changed hands. No

♣ Later, the great rapids at this site were renamed La Chine, in mockery of the idea that the St. Lawrence River would lead to China.

matter how many settlers paid to join him, being ruler of his estate was not about to make a fortune for the young La Salle. He would have to depend upon the lucrative beaver and moose fur-trade, and for this the property on the St. Lawrence River—gateway to the interior—was ideally situated.

It quickly became apparent to the early French explorers that they were not going to become wealthy from gold and silver, such as the Spanish gained from their colonies to the south; but there was another source for riches in the New World—furs from the beaver and moose. When Pierre du Gaust, Sieur de Monts, had received permission from King Henry IV to colonize the New France called La Cadie, or Acadie, and was made lieutenant governor of that region, he counted on a monopoly of the fur-trade as the basis for his enterprise. After exploring the St. Lawrence River in 1608 Samuel de Champlain had perceived the advantage of constructing a fortified post on the river at the site of present-day Montréal. Here, he felt, one could control all traffic that passed through the lakes and rivers which drained into the St. Lawrence. The location here would prevent English and Dutch intrusion from the other direction and prevent their access to the supply of furs.

The life-blood of Canada—its sustenance—was the beaver trade, supplying the colony with 200,000 to 300,000 francs in profit yearly. France gained as well, retaining for itself as a form of taxation one-quarter of the beaver pelts and one-tenth of moose hides. In the absence of coin, beaver pelts long served as currency. To control and regulate the traffic in pelts, and to ensure its share of profits, the government set up a resident corporation of merchants. In 1647 this corporation, in conjunction with delegates representing Montréal, Québec, and Three Rivers, was managed by a council consisting of the governor of Montréal, superior of the Jesuits, and three important inhabitants. Annual fairs were set up at these three major settlements, and every summer the Indians would arrive with their canoes filled with pelts. In exchange for the furs, Indians received kettles, hatchets, knives, cloth, and other domestic items. Though the sale of alcohol was prohibited at these events, the ban could not be enforced, and the market fair usually ended in a drunken frenzy and debauchery.

Attempts to control the fur-trade were further thwarted by the practice of many Canadian inhabitants to establish temporary settlements outside the limits of the fair. With brandy as their ally, they bought the pelts at a low rate before they even reached the town fairs. Some individuals took to the woods completely, ranging across the wilderness, totally independent, buying pelts when and where they could. They were totally free of all local constraints and government restrictions, including the need for a license. Called *coureurs de bois* (bush-rangers), they were a law unto themselves. Edicts, threats, and punishments failed to prevent their siphoning off profits from Canada and the king. Not even the prospect of jail for life, or the threat of death, could stop these men. Marquis de Denonville, governor of Canada, called the *coureurs de bois* "a great evil . . . [and] deprives the country of its effective men, makes them indocile, debauched, and incapable of discipline." Their self-interest precluded working with any others to create a cohesive colony in New France. In their familiarity with the ways of the woods, roaming the rivers and lakes, these men were as savage as the natives they dealt with.

The fur-trade was not limited to a few adventurous renegades who had the courage and fortitude to make their way in the forest. It was the custom through all levels of the social structure in New France. Upon order of the king, the Jesuits and other religious orders in Canada were forbidden to trade in furs. Here too, as with *the coureurs de bois,* the rules were ignored. The Jesuit's role in the fur-trade extended far beyond merely allowing their buildings to be used as store-houses for safe-keeping of the pelts. Repeated admonishments from the civil authorities did not prevent them from engaging in the fur-trade for profit.

From the very beginning of the colony, the Jesuits supported themselves and their missions by the purchase and selling of furs. It is not clear, however, just how much profit they gained from the trade beyond what was necessary for their survival. According to La Salle, they made enormous profits. Confirmation of the extent of financial benefits is found in a letter written in 1649 by Paul Ragueneau, Father Superior, to the general of the Jesuits in Rome. There was always need, he said, for more priests of the order, as well as laborers and soldiers to help support and protect the missions, but it was "not necessary to increase the pecuniary aid given us." The Jesuits never denied they carried on a trade in pelts, but claimed their gain was not as much as commonly assumed. To those who challenged their involvement in the fur-trade, the Jesuits declared: "The said Reverend Father Jesuits have never been in the profession of sales and have never sold anything, but only that the wares they *give* to particular people are only so that they can have the necessities."

Count Frontenac, in a letter to Jean-Baptiste Colbert, Minister of Finance to King Louis XIV, said: "Speaking frankly to you, the Jesuits dream as much about the conversion of Castor [Beaver] as about that of souls." His accusations against the Jesuits were made again the following year (1673), when he said: "The Jesuits ought to content themselves with instructing the Indians in their old missions, instead of neglecting them to make new ones in countries where there are more beaver-skins to gain than souls to save."

Frontenac's qualities of an active mind, firm resolve, and the ability to conceive ambitious plans for New France that would encompass half of the North American continent, were, unfortunately, countered by less endearing attributes. Those who opposed his plans found an arrogant, angry, and vindictive man—one not to be crossed. When the attorney-general and two councilors fell into disfavor with Frontenac, he found pretext for exiling them. If he had been able to, he would also have confined the Intendant in prison for two years until his term of office was completed. His regard for missionaries, particularly the Jesuits, was of a low order, believing that "the state should be dominant, not the handmaiden of the Church and of the Jesuits who represented it."

Though Frontenac desired only the best for his monarch, and the good of New France, his own goals for personal glory often got in the way. He went so far as to usurp authority from the Council of Québec and assumed the title and functions of president. Word of his misconduct eventually made its way to court in France. Although he had influential alliances at court, King Louis found it necessary to reprimand his governor-general in New France, the Count de Frontenac. Reproaching him for disturbing the tranquility of New France, his said:

> You wish in the registers of the Sovereign Council to be styled chief and president of that council, which is entirely contrary to my ordinance concerning that body. . . .

Count Frontenac, governor and lieutenant-general of Canada from 1672 to 1682, and again from 1689 to 1698. This sculpture, executed in 1890, stands today at the National Assembly in Québec, Canada. Artist: Hébert, Louis Philippe (1850–1917). *Photo: courtesy of the National Archives of Canada/C-007183.*

I desire you to abandon that pretension, and rest contented with the title of governor and lieutenant-general for me. . . . You have no authority to keep the registers of the council in your hands, as you have assumed to do, and required; still less to take up the votes and pronounce the decisions; all these functions belong to the office of the president.

Frontenac brought further problems upon himself when he allied with the Sulpicians and Récollets in their disputes with the Jesuits. This created an animosity in the Jesuits toward Frontenac and his programs for expansion. In their missionary zeal, as well in their ambition to be being absolute rulers of the territories they inhabited, the Jesuits could not countenance competition by the Récollet or Sulpician priests, let alone the power of the Crown. Indeed, when King Louis XIV made Frontenac the governor of Canada, he expressly stated that Frontenac's function was "to transform a mission country into a Crown colony, with proper balance between the civil and ecclesiastical powers." Since the arrival of the Jesuit Fathers in Acadia in 1611, Quebec was their capital and stronghold. Frontenac was instructed to see that their authority did not push beyond the bounds of tolerance of the king. If this should occur, he was to "diplomatically oppose their designs," and inform his Majesty "so that he may be in a position to apply the proper remedy."

Those who favored the Jesuits, and their efforts as envoys of God, did not criticize their lack of success to civilize the barbarians and convert them to the "True Faith." If they failed, it was because "the seed of their word fell on a barren and fruitless soil." Others, however, censured the Jesuits not only for failing to convert the Indians to Christianity, but also for not making any real discoveries or explorations that would extend the temporal power of France—a goal considered equal to that of bringing the spirit of Faith to the savages. It did not go unnoticed that wherever the Jesuits maintained their missions throughout the immense territory from Cape Breton in the Gulf of St. Lawrence, all the way to the land of the Hurons, that as soon as the French no longer went there to trade because the furs were no longer plentiful, then, the reverend Fathers soon departed. For these critics, "the surest function of the missionaries was to minister to the French who go to trade."

The ecclesiastics were not the only ones prohibited by the king from trading in furs. French colonial officers were also restricted. Regardless of the regulations, civil servants did not hesitate to join in the trade for personal gain. Even as high an official as Count Frontenac was thus accused by Perrot, the governor of Montréal, of trafficking in furs. Perrot, in turn, received the same recrimination.

As for La Salle and the fur-trade, there are no documents that directly show the full extent of his participation. One of the inducements offered to any individual who would come to Canada and work in the missions was the right to trade with the Indians and sell the furs to the Company of New France at a fixed price.✤ During the first years of La Salle's stay on the St. Lawrence River he undoubtedly was actively engaged in buying and selling pelts, since building a sound financial basis for himself was one of the primary reasons he came to Canada. Later, when he needed money to finance his expedition, La Salle was able to offer furs as guarantee for loans.

✤ The Company of New France, formed by the king and headed by Richelieu, consisted of one hundred associates. It was granted a perpetual monopoly of the fur-trade and other commerce in New France.

EARLY EXPLORATIONS

La Salle's spent his sojourn on the St. Lawrence River by building up his seigniory. He constructed houses, prepared fortifications, cleared land, and started cultivation to provide food. When he could take time from these tasks, La Salle traveled among the neighboring Iroquois tribes, buying and selling beaver pelts to provide the funds for his enterprise. He even made several journeys into the forests north of the St. Lawrence, but concluded that efforts in this direction were unrewarding.

During these explorations he learned the language of the various Indian tribes he met. By 1669, La Salle could speak Iroquois, with its various dialects, as well as several other Indian languages. Similarities of language among the various tribes, particularly the Iroquois, though not identical, were close enough that by knowing one or more, La Salle could make himself understood in all. Those most alike were the Mohawk with the Oneida, and the Cayuga with the Seneca. His ability to converse with the Indians enabled him trade in furs more effectively, thereby increasing his profits. With this knowledge he could safely extend his range of travel and, combined with his powers of persuasion, acquire information unobtainable by other white men.

The fragile peace effected earlier between the French and Iroquois still held. In 1668 La Salle was visited by a band of Seneca Iroquois who came to Montreal for hunting and trading and stayed with him for the winter. Throughout the long, dark months, as the bitter cold wind howled and snow piled deep around the houses, everyone kept close to the fireplace for its bit of warmth. Like the snowflakes falling outside, the Seneca's thoughts drifted-back to their homes and lands beyond. They talked freely with La Salle and told him about a great river that began north in their country and flowed into the sea. They called it the Ohio, the Beautiful River, and said that its length was so great it took eight or nine months to reach its mouth. The river began, they said, at a three-day journey from the land of the Seneca. Following this river would eventually bring one to a country abundantly inhabited with deer and wild cattle (buffalo), and peopled by tribes whose number was beyond counting. La Salle's restless energies again took hold, and he began to contemplate what lay beyond the forests, rivers, and lakes already familiar to him. The dream of so many other explorers—French, English, and Dutch— to find a passage connecting the two oceans was rekindled and strengthened. Whether the Senecas meant the Ohio River or the Mississippi River is immaterial; what really mattered was that here was a potential navigable route by which the Pacific could be reached from the Atlantic.

TO THE VERMILION SEA

Little was known about the geography of the continent of North America. Only its fringes, the seaboard coasts, were explored and settled. The Jesuits had explored to the north as far as Hudson Bay and west to Lake Superior. This left the vast interior of the continent west of the Appalachian Mountains, and south to the Gulf of Mexico coast, almost totally unknown. As for the inland waterways, the St. Lawrence River and the Great Lakes, they were just beginning to appear with some semblance of accuracy on maps of the day, their actual extent still to be determined. If this river the Senecas called the Ohio did indeed reach the sea, La Salle conjectured its mouth would be at the Vermilion Sea (now called the Gulf of California).

Here was an idea to excite La Salle even more than wresting a habitable settlement from the wilderness on the banks of the St. Lawrence River, and more than adventurous short forays in quest of pelts. It provided the opportunity to partake in one of the greatest adventures known to seventeenth-century man—the search for the famed Northwest Passage. If this navigable route to the Pacific, hence to the Orient, could be found, the riches gained from spices, rare woods, precious stones, and silks would exceed beyond the wildest dreams any profit made by the sale of fish, timber, or beaver pelts from this region.

Should this prove to be another chimera, there was still the compensation of profit from trade with the many Indian tribes inhabiting the banks of the river. A new goal emerged for the youthful, adventurous La Salle; one that was to occupy every fiber of his body and thought of his mind for the next twenty years. He would explore this great river and follow it to its termination.

Eager to start, the following spring La Salle traveled to Québec to gain approval for his venture from Sieur de Courcelles, governor of Canada, and the Intendant, Jean Baptiste Talon.♣ Both were enthusiastic and gave their official approval. They wrote to Jean-Baptiste Colbert, Minister of King Louis XIV, and indicated their patronage. This did not include financial aid; that, La Salle would have to find for himself. He returned to Montréal and met

♣ The role of the Intendant in New France was to assist the governor. Commissioned by the king, it assured the Crown's power over local rule.

with Father Queylus, Superior of the Sulpician Seminary, who had granted La Salle his property in 1666. To support this venture, La Salle sold back to the Seminary of St. Sulpice all the property they had freely given him, which by now had increased in value because of the buildings and cleared acreage.

This, besides the small portion he sold independently, gave him sufficient funds to buy four canoes, all the provisions necessary, and to hire fourteen men to accompany him.

Friction and antagonism between the Franciscans and Jesuits, never far beneath the surface, arose and intruded itself in this venture. The Sulpicians, not wanting to be outdone by the Jesuits in the number of souls they saved—for the glory of God, and the honor to France—were already planning an expedition of their own. Beyond these sublime motives was the more practical goal of owning additional new land. Queylus reasoned that this would be an excellent opportunity to combine forces. La Salle could accomplish his discoveries, while the missionaries could convert to the Roman faith the populous tribes inhabiting those lands. Thus, two Sulpician missionaries, François Dollier de Casson and René de Brehart de Galinée, were added to La Salle's expedition. Swelling the numbers were ten more men from the Seminary, and three additional canoes to carry them, as well as the group of Senecas who stayed the winter with La Salle.

The canoes acquired for the expedition were the "North Canoe," a type based on Algonquin and Objibway styles. They were twenty-four feet long and capable of carrying up to 1,500 pounds of goods, plus the paddlers and passengers. An even larger canoe, called the "Montreal Canoe," was used by fur traders at the time. Thirty-three feet long, and six feet wide at the greatest beam, these canoes were capable of carrying up to 6,000 pounds of goods, and as many as eight or nine men. The following list, provided by the Fur Trade Museum in Lachine, Québec, emphasizes more than mere numbers can the prodigious quantity of goods the Montreal Canoe could hold and gives an idea of the kind of wares considered necessary for such an expedition.

19 bales of Merchandise. These were furs, pressed into bundles of 90 to 100 pounds each and covered with a protective wrapping.

1 bale each of General Items:

Black tobacco, plug tobacco, chewing tobacco, NorthWest twist, bell mouthed pails, copper pails, tin pails, jewelry, grease, iron (2 crates), steel, gunpowder (2 packages), shot, and bullets.

1 container each of Food Supplies:

ham, salt (1 keg), lard (200 pounds), beef, tongue, sausage, barley, rice, cheese, raisins, figs, prunes, and corn.

2 containers each of Food Supplies:

white sugar, brown sugar, butter, peas, ship's biscuits (8 bags)

3 crates each of other Merchandise:

hats, knifes, guns, traps, and soap

20 casks each of Spirits:

"high wine," rum, and other spirits

1 cask each of Spirits:

Port, Madeira, red wine, and French brandy

1 bundle each of Ship's Gear:

ax, tin plate, stove, pail, a roll of birch bark (used for repairs), pail, 12 to 18 pounds of pine gum (to seal leaking seams), trammel hook (made of iron, and adjustable in length to allow a cooking pot to hang closer or farther away from the fire), 5 tarpaulins, 5 fishing lines, and 6 bales of wattap (for lacing or sewing).

In addition to the general supplies listed above, each man was allowed to carry his own, personal bag of belongings, weighing up to forty pounds.

These canoes were a perfect marriage of locally available building materials and suitability to the terrain in which they were used. The ribs were made of cedar, light in weight, and impervious to rot. For strength, ash was used for the gunwales and thwarts. Birch bark, easily peeled in sheets from the paper birch tree (*Betula papyrifera*), covered the entire skeletal structure. Slender, flexible roots (called wattap) of the young spruce tree were used to sew or lace together the Indian canoes acquired for the expedition, which were constructed of birch-bark, reinforced with cedar ribs, and capable of carrying up to 1,500 pounds. The larger ones held as many as seven or eight men. Though usually propelled by paddles, if the wind was favorable, sails made of the same bark were set up. As much as 100 miles a day could be made going down river, and even more on the lakes with a good wind.

Delays were frequent, however, on account of the need to portage the canoes and all their belongings around the rapids. Carrying massive loads,

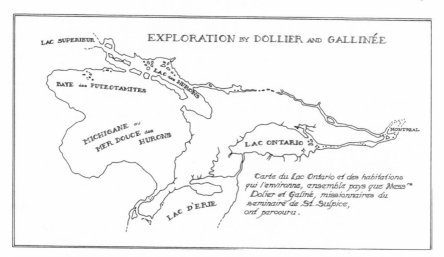

Exploration by Dollier and Gallinée in 1669–1670. Galinée was an accomplished navigator and cartographer. In this exploration he carried with him the cross-staff to measure altitude of a celestial body, and tables of declination of the sun to determine latitude. Galinée also had the mathematical ability to construct his map using the Mercator projection plan. In his journal, he says, "I have made it [the map] as a marine chart; that is to say, the meridians do not converge near the poles because I am more familiar with these maps than with the geographical ones, and, moreover, the former are commonly more exact than the others."

they stumbled over the rough, broken ground and fallen trees, often made treacherously slippery with a covering of pine needles. If they paid attention to where their feet were going, they were caught unawares by tree branches striking their bodies and snagging their clothing, all the while un-remittingly pestered by black-flies and mosquitoes.

Dollier de Casson was put in charge of the missionary faction, and the Senecas were to act as guides until they reached their homes. Galinée brought to the expedition his skills as a surveyor and mapmaker. His ability in astronomy also provided them the means to correctly determine the latitude of their findings, a necessary step to making a proper map. The group slowly worked their way up the St. Lawrence River, until finally they reached the eastern end of Lake Ontario, which opened up to them "like a great sea with no land beyond it." They had yet to reach the land of the Seneca, let alone the great river they were to explore, and already the hardship of travel took its toll. There was scarcely a man among them, Galinée said, who did not suffer from some illness or other.

The band of travelers made much better progress while paddling their canoes on the unruffled water of the lake, closely following the shore. In ten days they reached Irondequoit Bay, a broad, shallow bight on the southern shore of Lake Ontario. By Galinée's reckoning, they were about three hundred miles southwest of Montréal.

After thirty-five days of travel they at last reached the land of the Seneca, only a few miles from where the city of Rochester, New York, now stands. Only thirteen years before, no white man had ever visited this area, and not until the last two years did the Jesuits establish their missions in the four eastern divisions of the Iroquois nation. Here in the Seneca village, their mission was founded only the year before La Salle's arrival. The superior of this mission, Father Fremin, was not present to greet the newcomers, being at a general council of the Jesuits at Onondaga to help consider ways to promote their missionary goals among the Iroquois. In his stead were a number of Seneca Indians who invited everyone to their villages only a short distance away. Since La Salle hoped to find men here with the necessary knowledge to guide them to the Ohio, he agreed to accompany them. As a precaution, though, he kept most of his men back at the landing to guard the canoes.

At first, all went well. They exchanged presents, the Indians received knives, awls, glass beads, needles, and other utilitarian items in return for fruit, corn, and pumpkins. As was the custom, La Salle and his men were entertained and treated to feasting. Fresh meat from game was seldom available in this village; in its stead the guests were served the usual fare of the Senecas—boiled dog. It wasn't so much the dog meat that disgusted the men, but the incredibly filthy wooden bowls in which the three- or four-pound chunk was served. Covered in a layer of grease the bowls had apparently been accumulating from the day they were first made, Galinée remarked that "he was more desirous of rendering up what was in my stomach, than of taking into it anything new." The dishes of Indian meal, or corn, cooked in water and flavored with a bit of sunflower oil, or bear's fat, they found more palatable.

La Salle and the rest of his small party retired to the village, where a cabin was prepared for them, to wait for representatives of the other villages to arrive. A council was to be held to hear from the Frenchmen the object of their expedition. At length, when all the chiefs of the other villages were present, and there were about fifty or sixty of the principal men of the Seneca, the Council began. Again, they gave presents, this time of a more substantive nature, and the French expressed their desires to the Seneca. They said they considered the Senecas their brothers and had come to establish peace. They were here as representatives of the governor of Canada to see the people living along the Ohio River. To guide them there they needed a captive of that country, which they hoped the Seneca could provide.

The following day, La Salle and Galinée received the reply. They were assured they were welcome as brothers, and were told that "their Nation had never made war with the French, and did not desire to begin it in a time of peace." They also agreed to provide a captive youth to act as a guide, but that would have to wait until some of their party returned from trading with the Dutch.♣ The period of waiting—eight to ten days—began to worry La Salle, and agitate him. It was not in his nature to idly sit by and let circumstances direct his course. He was a man of action who

♣ From their center in Albany, New York, the Dutch traded for furs with the Iroquois and as far away as the Hurons. One of the goals of New France was to stop this drain to France in profits.

wanted to create the events, not be led by them. Furthermore, the feasting also began to include the drinking of brandy they had traded from the Dutch, and drunken revelry became more frequent. As their intoxication became stronger, so did their hostility toward the French, and La Salle began to fear that the knives they gave would become the very means of their demise.

Affairs degenerated still further with the arrival of a prisoner. They tied the poor, unfortunate wretch to a stake and made him endure every variety of agony his captors could conceive. None of the Frenchmen could bear to watch his torture, other than Galinée, who exhorted him to "endure patiently and carry up his sufferings to God." In a final attempt to save him, Galinée even offered to take the prisoner in exchange for the guide they were waiting for, but the Senecas would hear none of it. Eventually, after they had had enough of their "pleasure" the Senecas killed him and cut his body to pieces. One carried off his head, another an arm, a third some other member, which they put in the pot for a feast. Though they offered the French to partake in this repast, no one was willing to try.

Having witnessed the cruelty that the Indians could inflict, not only upon the white man, but captives of other tribes during the frequent wars, La Salle and Galinée feared for their lives as well. After a quick consultation they decided it would be best if they and the rest of their group leave and rejoin Dollier guarding the canoes. Caution and fear would always be twin companions of La Salle as he traversed the wilderness.

Their stay with the Senecas was not entirely unproductive, for they learned they could reach the Ohio by way of a nearby river (the Genesee). What seemed to be good news quickly changed when they also heard that this route would require a very difficult portage of seventy-two miles. This could mean the end of their plans before they even began, since they knew they would not be able to carry their canoes, provisions, and all their belongings on such a journey. They were told, however, that there was another route by way of Lake Erie, and this would require only a three-day portage to reach the river they sought. With their spirits revived at this news, they could wait no longer, and La Salle, with the missionaries left the Senecas.

Day by day, with nothing to impede their progress now, the small band of explorers made their way along the shore of Lake Ontario. As they approached its western end a new sound reached their ears, quietly at first, then ever increasing in intensity, until it became an overwhelming roar. They had come to the great outpouring of the Niagara River that connects Lake Erie with Lake Ontario. Galinée inquired about the thunderous sound they heard, and the Indians told him it came from a great falls higher up the river. They said that the river was about 120 miles long, and that the cataract, about thirty to thirty-six miles from where the river enters Lake Ontario, falls from a rock higher than the tallest pines, that is about two hundred feet.✤

✤ Galinee never saw the cataract, but in his *Récit* (Account) to Abbé Eusèbe Renaudot, he says he could hear it when still thirty miles away.

Though eager to see for themselves a cataract that created such a sound it could be heard thirty miles from its source, the current was far too swift to even attempt paddling their canoes up the river. Going by foot through the tangled forest growth and steep terrain was no less difficult. Reluctantly, they passed the Niagara and its wondrous Falls without exploring it. The period of good weather was beginning to end, and as they continued along the

Engraving of Niagara Falls.

southern shore of Lake Ontario, the voyagers increased their efforts to reach the village of Otinawatawa that lay near its western end.

Five days later, on September 22, they arrived at Otinawatawa. Here, as before in the Seneca village, they waited for the tribal chiefs to arrive and hold council. Much to their relief, the Algonquins were more amicably disposed than the Senecas, and did not detain them for long. The Ohio, they said, could be reached in about six weeks, and they were willing to give the voyagers a Shawnee prisoner as guide.

Just as they were about to set out, news came that there were two Frenchmen in a neighboring village only a few miles away. After all these months, completely cut off from the world they knew, the explorers did not want to leave without first speaking to one of their countrymen. The man they met with was Louis Jolliet, a young adventurer who had abandoned the idea of priesthood to become a fur-trader. Jolliet was just returning from a search for the rich mines of copper that lay beyond Lake Superior. In New France, the pursuit of gold and precious gemstones soon had given way to more realistic goals. Mines of ore were still being sought, but now it was for the baser metal of copper. The Jesuits, from their explorations, knew about these copper mines as early as ten years before Jolliet's expedition. As instructed by Jean-Baptiste Talon, Intendant of Canada, Jolliet was also to find a shorter way to transport the copper back to Montréal. Though he would fail to discover the copper mines, he did find that Grand River provided an easier route from Lake Erie to Lake Ontario, and it was this happenstance that brought him to the same spot, at the same time, as La Salle.

WHEN JOLLIET LEARNED that La Salle and the Sulpicians were attempting to reach the Mississippi River, he suggested they change their route and go by way of the Upper Lakes. He told them what he learned from his travels there and showed maps he had made, adding that in this direction were many tribes "in grievous need of spiritual succor." The latter was an added enticement to the Sulpicians who now favored this new course. It seemed to them an easier way to reach the river they wished to enter and had the added advantage that they already knew the Ottawa language of the Nations through which they would be traveling. La Salle, however, was either unable, or unwilling, to believe the source of the great Mississippi began west of Lake Superior and could be reached the way Jolliet suggested. He knew the river lay to the west and south, and he was not about to go still farther *north* in search of it. As for Christianizing more souls, that was the domain of the Sulpicians, not his. He did remind them that Jesuit missions were already established in these lands, and that they might not take too kindly to intruders in their midst.

At the end of September the two groups parted; the Sulpicians to bring Christianity to the Indians of the Upper Lakes, and La Salle, with a small group of men, to continue their exploration toward the Ohio and the Mississippi.

The missionaries went south on Grand River and in fourteen days came to Lake Erie, which Galinée described as "a vast sea, tossed by tempestuous winds." They determined that here they would spend the winter and set about to build shelter and gather food for the long, cold months ahead. Come spring, they planted a cross, proclaimed the land in the name of King

Louis XIV, and continued their journey. From the western end of Lake Erie they entered Lake Huron by way of the Detroit River and Lake St. Clair. Finally, where the waters of Lake Superior exit, they gained the Jesuit mission at Sault Sainte-Marie. They were made welcome at first, but soon found out that La Salle's predictions were true. The rival Jesuit missionaries did not want their help. There was nothing for the Sulpicians to do but leave and make the long journey back to Montréal. They made no discoveries, nor brought any of the native tribes closer to the True Faith, but to their credit, Galinée and his Sulpician brothers, with patient endurance, accomplished a remarkable arduous journey through 2,000 miles of wilderness. Their efforts provided the geographic information from which the first map of the Upper Lakes was made.

The exact course La Salle took is not chronicled as clearly as that of the Sulpicians, but it appears that when he parted from the missionaries he found an Indian guide who led him to a river not far from Lake Erie. Somewhere, in the flat, low-lying country where the river was but a mere trickle that meandered, split, and disappeared altogether into marshland, the explorers lost their way. The situation was not entirely hopeless, for they met some Indians who said the water eventually rejoined into a proper riverbed. Those who thus far accompanied La Salle were too fatigued to continue, and one night they all abandoned him to make their way back to the nearest civilization.♣ La Salle, with unyielding determination, continued his journey alone.

With the Shawnee guide, a native of the Ohio country, and thus familiar with the region, directed La Salle to travel along the southern shore of Lake Erie. There, in a matter of only fifty miles he came to a point opposite Lake Chautauqua. With an eighteen to twenty-one mile portage, he arrived at Lake Chautauqua and used it to bridge the gap to the Allegheny River, by which he could reach the headwaters of the Ohio. Living on the wild game he hunted, picking fruits and berries, and occasionally augmented with food given him by the Indians along the way, La Salle descended the river. At the rapids near today's Louisville he stopped

♣ According to Abbé Faillon, a Sulpician priest in Montréal, the deserters made their way back to La Salle's seigniory on the St. Lawrence River. They derisively gave the name La Chine to the site, since the river supposedly was to lead them to China.

his search and returned home. La Salle never claimed he made it to the Mississippi River during that expedition, only that he *approached* it. What he *did* assert, in a letter to Count Frontenac, was that "In the year 1667, and the following ones," he made several voyages with many expenses, in which he discovered the first lot of land to the south of the Great Lakes, and "among others, the Great Ohio River, and followed it to a place where it fell from very high in the vast marshes."

Three years of journeying, filled with hardships, disappointments, and frustration ended, and La Salle had nothing to show for it. He neither penetrated to the Mississippi, nor was he able to discover whether the mighty Mississippi River emptied into the Vermilion Sea (Gulf of California) or the Gulf of Mexico. More than that, his goal of finding a navigable way through the continent to the Pacific, and beyond to Cathay, was left unfulfilled. Back at La Chine, with empty dreams and empty pockets, La Salle found himself in an awkward situation. In need of money to finance the 1671 expedition, he had again borrowed funds from the Seminary, with the promise to return the loan by the next year in cash or furs. He could hardly push his goodwill with the Sulpicians by asking yet another time for their support. La Salle returned to traveling the woods and rivers north of the St. Lawrence in search of the beaver pelt, doubtless to make good his promise of repayment.

LA SALLE AND FRONTENAC

Just as La Salle's affairs appeared at their lowest, a new governor of Canada was appointed to replace Courcelle. Intendant Talon, La Salle's advocate, if in words only, shortly thereafter returned to France. Though Talon was no longer present in Canada, the goals he set, and initiated, continued to bear fruit. During his stay Talon had been determined to have the heartland of North America explored and annexed to the rest of the French colony. His ambition had been to present to Louis XIV a kingdom whose territory extended from Nova Scotia to the Gulf of Mexico. The few, far-flung missions of the Jesuits to the west, and the widely spaced, independent fur-traders,

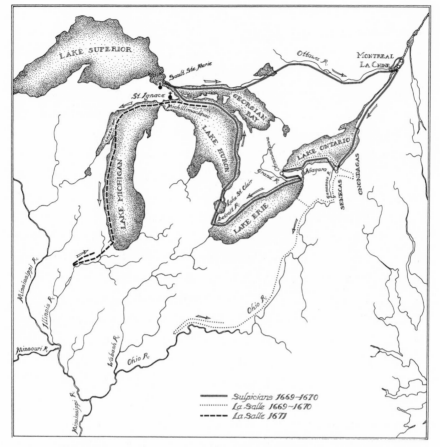

Route of the Sulpicians and La Salle in 1669–1670, and La Salle's route in 1669–1670 and 1671.

whose spiritual and commercial interests more often came before that of France, were not a sufficient possession of the land. Officially sanctioned and organized expeditions were needed that could result in a claim to sovereignty that would be recognized by the nations of Europe. Dominion of land in the middle of the continent, and control of its rivers, the only practical way of moving men and goods, would enable France to effectively hem in the English to the east, preventing expansion from this direction and keep the Spanish from moving northward, claiming *de facto* sovereignty. La Salle's exploration of the Ohio had been a beginning toward these ambitions.

Talon furthered his resolve to find the Mississippi, and thus claim all the land drained by it for France, when he chose Louis Jolliet and Jacques Marquette to lead an expedition in 1673. Though both men were Jesuits, Intendant Talon did not let his aversion to the Jesuit Order blind him in his desire to extend exploration in the west and expand the territory of New France.

Marquette had spent eleven years in France to become a Jesuit priest. The desire to work in far off lands, where he could create missions and convert the heathens to Christianity, was a goal he entertained while still a novitiate. He arrived in Québec in 1666, and two years later was assigned to the mission at Sault Saint-Marie (between Lake Superior and Lake Huron) to assist his Jesuit superior, Claude Dablon. It was here that Jacques Marquette heard from the Indians about a river called the *Missispi*. The following year he founded two new missions himself: one on the western shore of Lake Superior, called "the mission of Pointe du Saint-Esprit;" another, on the north shore of Michillimackinac Strait (between Lake Michigan and Lake Huron), called "Saint-Ignace mission."

Louise Jolliet attended a Jesuit school while in Québec and had taken minor religious orders. But being a missionary was not a particularly driving force in his life, and he renounced his priesthood. Instead, Jolliet became a merchant and a fur-trader. It was while setting up a trading post at Sault Saint-Marie that he met Marquette and convinced him to join in a search for the Mississippi River. When Jolliet next met with Marquette on December 8th of 1673, at the Saint-Ignace mission, it was with orders from Count de Frontenac, as well as Intendant Talon, to commence exploration of the Mississippi River, and determine into what body of water it flowed— the Pacific Ocean or the Gulf of Mexico.

Each man brought to the expedition his own special skills: Jolliet, the fur-trader and explorer, proficient in cartography, made maps of their travels; Marquette, "as chaplain and emissary to the Indians," was particularly adept with the native languages, and spoke several of the Algonquin dialects, in addition to the language of the Illinois Nation.

The following spring the two men set out. With five others as crew, and two canoes loaded with provisions and equipment, they made their way along the northern shore of Lake Michigan and into Green Bay, a large extension of the lake on its western side. Here, at its southern end, enters the

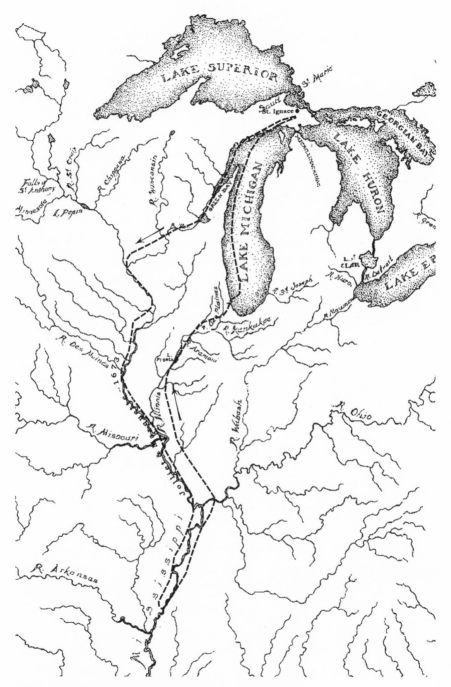

Route taken by Jolliet and Marquette on their 1673 expedition.

north flowing Fox River. Undeterred by reports from the Menomonie Indians about the "merciless savages" and "horrible monsters" they would encounter if they continued farther, the small group worked their way up the
rapids of the Fox River. At its head, a short portage brought them into the
Wisconsin River. Now the current augmented, rather than hindered, their
progress, and on June 17th of 1673 they entered the Mississippi River.

As THEY MADE their way down river, Jolliet took measurements of the
latitude with his astrolabe in order to make proper maps of their exploration, while Marquette filled his journal with notes about their encounters
with the Indians and detailed descriptions of the landscape and wildlife.
Time passed quickly and peacefully as the current propelled them south and
through the great prairies that bordered both sides of the river. Not until
they reached the land of the Peorias (a band of the Illinois Nation) did they
encounter any Indians.

When finally they did meet, each approached the other warily, but fear
and caution soon gave way to trust, and the Frenchmen were accepted,
treated to festivities and feasting. In part, the warm welcome given them
can be attributed to the increasing incursions into Illinois territory by the
Iroquois. They could ill-afford to wage war on their own with the Iroquois,
but with the French as allies, the balance of power could shift in their favor.
Marquette and Jolliet parted in the friendliest fashion, and with a young
captive given to them as a guide, continued their voyage.

Nearing the Missouri River, they heard the turbulent rush of current as
the turbid water poured forth into the Mississippi. Trees, and "floating islands of debris," swirled around their frail craft, threatening destruction. "I
never saw anything more terrific," said Marquette. Paddling onward, they
passed the Ohio River and 280 miles farther downstream came to the confluence of the Arkansas River with the Mississippi. Here, they halted and
determined to go no farther. Since their provisions and ammunition was
running low, and evidence of nearby Spanish settlements in New Biscay
stirred doubts about their safety, they thought it best to return home. Marquette wrote: "We felt that we were exposing ourselves to losing the fruit
of this voyage, of which we could publish no knowledge were we to fall

"Louis Jolliet and Jacques Marquette among the Peorias in 1673." Artist: Charles Hout, 1913. Charcoal drawing on paper, 21.7 x 36.0 cm. Collection: Musée du Québec, accession number 34.192. Photographer: Patrick Altman.

into the hands of the Spaniards, who no doubt would have held us captive, at the least."

By now it was clear to them that the Mississippi continued its southerly flow and entered into the Gulf of Mexico. They accomplished what they had set out to do. Marquette conjectured that the Missouri might be the way leading west to California and the Vermillion Sea (Pacific Ocean). "One day," he wrote, "I hope to discover the California Sea by following its course."

The return voyage was by way of the Illinois and Chicago rivers into Lake Michigan. The two explorers parted at Chicagou on Lake Michigan: Father Marquette going to stay with the Miamis; Jolliet to continue the voyage to Montréal to give the report on their expedition to the Intendant, Talon. In the five months of travel, Marquette and Jolliet covered over 2,500 miles of previously uncharted wilderness. Not only did they fill in the blank spaces on maps of the interior of North America, but they made it easier for their successors—notably La Salle—to continue the exploration which allowed King Louis XIV to claim to the entire Mississippi Valley for France. They achieved their remarkable feat with "considerable skill, caution, and diplomacy toward the Indian tribes of the region." When La Salle later arrived among the Illi-nois, he did not have to suffer a legacy of enmity toward the Frenchmen.

Louis de Baude, Count of Palluau and Frontenac, replaced Courcelle as governor. His goals for New France were as ambitious as Talon's. Like Talon, he saw the way of realizing his plans through La Salle. When Fron-tenac arrived in the winter of 1672, one of his first acts was to commission La Salle to visit the Senecas and invite them to a general congress of the tribes. He selected La Salle for this service because of the young explorer's stay with the Senecas and Onandagas the past two years. The English were in the process of persuading the Iroquois to make peace with the Ottawas, and France was fearful lest this would lead to fur trade with the English and Dutch. A treaty of peace was already in effect between the French and the warrior tribes of Five Nations, and to keep it, it was important to constantly maintain their fear and respect. Alliances and hostilities quickly changed, and New France could ill afford having its young settlements destroyed. The king's orders to Talon, when he was given his commission as Intendant in 1665, was to protect the colony from the Iroquois:

> . . . who are all perpetual and irreconcilable enemies of the Colony, having by the massacre of a number of French and the inhumanity which they exercise towards those who fall into their power, prevented the country being more peo-pled than it is at present and by their surprisals and unexpected forays always keeping the coun-try in check; the King has resolved, with a view of applying a suitable remedy thereto, to carry war even to their firesides in order totally to ex-terminate them, having no guarantee in their words, for they violate their faith as often as they find the inhabitants of the Colony at their mercy.✤

✤ In the end, calmer minds prevailed, and a more moderate policy was adopted, one that favored maintaining peace with the Iroquois, rather than initiat-ing any war. Eventually, King Louis came to this conclusion as well, for in 1677 he wrote to Frontenac saying: "You must work for the maintenance of peace and understanding between those peoples [Iroquois Nations] and my subjects." Though the remedy changed, the continual threat of violence remained.

When the river was sufficiently clear of ice to permit travel, La Salle made his way to the main village of the Onondaga where he gave

them presents, as was customary, and delivered Talon's message about meeting with the Iroquois. All the tribes were requested to send delegates to
Quinté (near the head of Lake Ontario) where the Sulpicians had a small
mission, and Frontenac would meet with their chiefs to reaffirm their treaty
of peace.

At the end of June, Governor Frontenac set out to visit Quinté. For this
journey he gathered nearly four hundred men, 120 canoes, and had two
flat-bottomed bateaux built, which were brightly painted and displayed
armament. As the fleet of boats neared Quinté, they all lined up in military order as though about to enter battle, in order to impress the Iroquois
chiefs with his Majesty's importance and power. With La Salle as advisor
and interpreter, Frontenac retained the Iroquois as allies of the French and
received from them permission to build a fort. Frontenac achieved what
he had set out to do. Through a delicate balance of intimidation, lavish
gifts, and appeasing speeches, he won the favor of the Iroquois. He provided for the safety of the missionaries who lived among the Iroquois
tribes, ensured the maintenance of peace between the Five Nations and
France, and caused the resumption of an active fur trade between the Ottawa tribe and Montréal.

FORT CATARAKOUI

When de Courcelles conceived the idea of building a fort at Catarakoui, he
laid his plans before chiefs of the Five Nations, saying that its purpose was
to give them a convenient place to come and trade their furs with the
French. This appealed to the Iroquois, and they approved the idea, little realizing the true reason was to have a place to store arms and ammunition
which could quickly be used against them if the need should arrive. Before
construction began, however, de Courcelles was recalled to France. Frontenac, as his successor, now with assurances of friendship and reaffirmed
permission for the fort, was in a position to begin construction.

Henry de Tonty saw in Fort Catarakoui—later to become Fort Frontenac—much more than strategic location and political importance, he had

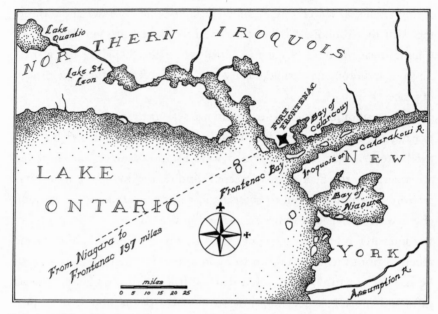

Location of Fort Catarakoui, later renamed Fort Frontenac, on Lake Ontario.

high praise for the countryside surrounding it. In his "A New Account of the Northern-America," presented to the French King, he wrote:

> *That fort lies within 120 Leagues from Quebec, about the 44th Degree of Latitude, on the Mouth of a Lake called likewise Frontenac or Ontario which is near 300 Leagues about, and has a communication with four other Lakes, much of the same extent. All those Lakes are Navigable, and Plentifully stored with Fish; the Mouth, or entrance of this Lake is defended by a Fort with four large Bastions, which might protect a great number of Vessels against the attempts of any Enemy. As M. La Salle had Erected, this Fort, the King had given him the Propriety there-abouts with their dependencies. The Country about it is so Charming, that it is impossible to describe its Beauties. The vast Meadows are intermixed with Woods and Forests, full of all sorts of Fruit-Trees, and watered with fine Brooks and Rivers.*

henry de Tonty

The ground the Sulpician missionaries owned, and initially planned for the fort, was deemed unsuitable and another site nearby at the mouth of the Catarakoui River was selected instead. Fort Catarakoui (presently Kingston, Ontario) was strategically placed to keep the Iroquois in check and prevent English and Dutch fur-traders from doing business with the Ottawas. It was the first of a long string of military posts and forts planned to serve the French in their westward expansion and territorial claims. Located at the head of Lake Ontario, it also provided access through the Great Lakes to the Mississippi, where gold and silver mines were thought to exist. With a vessel on Lake Ontario, and another fort and vessel on Lake Erie, France could control all the Upper Lakes.

Catarakoui had all the desirable elements for this first fort; good land for farming, forests for timber to construct the fort and build boats, and a well-sheltered harbor. The harbor particularly pleased Frontenac, for not only was it well protected from winds of any direction, but had a good mud bottom for secure anchoring and was large enough to hold a hundred ships. Once the site for the fort was decided upon, no time was lost in getting started. Within a day, trees were felled and land cleared to begin building. Four days later, the first fort at the gateway to the West stood completed. It was a relatively simple affair, with four bastions extending from each corner of the fort, surrounded and protected by a fence of pointed stakes and a broad, flat-topped earthen wall.

Fort Catarakoui lacked but one thing: it did not have the official approval of the king and the king's minister, Jean-Baptiste Colbert. There were those in the Colony who felt the fort was not worth the expense to maintain it, and freely expressed their opinions in letters to the Court in Versailles. Frontenac firmly believed that retention of the fort was essential for preservation of the fur-trade and security of the region; therefore he prepared a petition to the Court to defend his enterprise. At first, he chose his friends and merchants in Montreal, Sieur Bazire and Sieur Le Bel, to deliver the entreaty, but then changed his mind and sent La Salle instead. In a dispatch to Colbert, Frontenac said that if the king should decide to abandon this post altogether "he would go next year if it is necessary, to demolish the fort with as much joy as he had pleasure in seeing it built."

He need not have worried about carrying out his pledge, for Frontenac chose well in sending La Salle.

With the letters of recommendation from Frontenac, La Salle was well received by the Court at Versailles. Largely due to his power of persuasion, he gained from the king everything requested in the petition for the support of Fort Catarakoui. When La Salle returned to Canada the following year (1675), he was full proprietor of Fort Frontenac—as he now called it in honor of his friend and patron. Along with Fort Frontenac, which the king gave as an outright gift to La Salle, was twelve miles of adjacent territory, including several islands and smaller islets in the river. The seigniory included the rights to hunting on these lands and fishing in Lake Ontario and the rivers around. La Salle also came back with an elevated social status, for the king had raised him to the level of untitled nobility. The fort and letters patent of nobility were given to La Salle "in recognition of the number of years he spent in New France in the service of his country, and the discoveries he made while there." The reception La Salle received at Court also improved his financial condition. Close friends and relatives were eager to invest in the enterprise and provided much needed capital. They, as did the king, expected their money to be well repaid from profits in the fur trade.

These gifts to La Salle carried with them certain obligations. He had to reimburse Frontenac the cost of building Fort Catarakoui—a sum of 10,000 livres; maintain the fort and garrison in proper condition for its defense; at his own expense to clear the lands given him and to support twenty men for two years to assist in doing this; and to maintain (again at his cost) a priest to perform divine service and to administer the sacraments, until there were enough settlers to warrant building a church.✦ Naturally, La Salle was expected to pay the Crown all revenues and taxes customarily due it, and though he was governor of Fort Frontenac, he would be under the authority of Lieutenant-General Frontenac of New France.

✦ Livre—an old French currency, roughly equal to the present franc.

When La Salle returned to Canada he put all his energies into creating Fort Frontenac. He tore down the old fort and replaced it with one that was roughly four times the size. The basic plan remained the same, that is, a reg-

Plan of Fort Frontenac.

ular square, with four bastions, but he had them now faced with stone and mortar and surrounded by a wall three feet thick and fifteen feet high, on which nine small cannon were mounted. Since it was built on the a small peninsula of land, water provided a natural protection on three sides, while at the isthmus of land on the remaining side, La Salle had a moat dug. A garrison of eighty men, half of them soldiers, were able to defend the fort with its stores of grenades, rifles, and munitions. Devoting the same enthusiasm and effort to the building of Fort Frontenac as he did at La Chine, within a few years La Salle met all the king's stipulations. Buildings within the enclosure included a hundred-foot-long house made of squared logs, an officer's house, guard's house, blacksmith's shop, a well, and a cow-house.

Outside the enclosure, land was cleared and sown with winter wheat, which he found did as well here as in France. A barn was built to hold the harvest. Cattle, pigs, and fowl were brought from Montréal to add to the food supply. He had plans for next year to plant grapevines, an orchard, and all kinds of vegetables. Two villages comfortably co-existed beyond the walls of the fort; one of twelve French families, and the other about one hundred Indian families. La Salle hoped that the Indians who had become accustomed to living in the French manner would also adopt their religion and live as good Christians and good Frenchmen. In this short time he also managed to build four decked vessels; one of thirty tons, one of forty tons, and two of twenty-five tons. Plying the river and Lake Erie, they carried articles for trade with the Indians and brought back the pelts. Furthermore, they provided an extra measure of security for the settlement. Should there be an attack from the Indians, the ships could safely sail away at any time with the colonists, whereas the open canoe was always a vulnerable target that could leave only under cover of night.

All these accomplishments had their cost. First, there was the debt La Salle had to repay Frontenac, which had grown to 12,000 to 13,000 livres. Additional wages for laborers, supply and maintenance of forty-four men, victuals, clothes, canoes, and countless other items brought his total expenditures in the first two years to almost 45,000 livres. These were minor sums compared to the potential earnings La Salle could make in the fur-trade from this favorable location.

The promising fortune never happened; partly because whatever talents La Salle had, they did not include bookkeeping and balancing accounts. Also, undeserved malice came from two merchants of Montréal, Sieur Charles Bazire and Sieur Jacques Le Ber. In a letter to Colbert (November 12, 1674), Frontenac reported upon the recent success he had in preventing the Iroquois from trading with the Dutch, and siding with them in a war against the French. Frontenac said that once again he had won over the support of the Iroquois. He reported that Fort Frontenac had the effect that had been hoped for, in that it protected the missionaries and increased the amount of furs brought to Montreal by the Iroquois. Frontenac then went on to say:

> . . . representations have been made by Sieurs Bazire and Le Ber, who, along with the chief men of the country, are persuaded that its [Fort Frontenac] security, and the preservation of the fur trade, depends upon the retention of this post, have convinced me to seek a way to maintain it without costing the king any-

thing since in his present situation he can not take on any extra expense. And since I cannot carry it on at my own expense, as I have done for a year, I have put it into the hands [of Sieurs Bazire and Le Ber] . . . they will continue the enterprise.

Frontenac

Colbert accepted the proposal, understanding well that an increase in the fur-trade was "the only means of strengthening and enriching the colony." When La Salle returned from France with a new grant of proprietorship of Fort Frontenac, he was in control of a major part of the fur-trade in Canada. La Salle, formed a partnership with his lieutenant, La Forest, and Sieur Boisseau to profit from the fur-trade at Fort Frontenac. Le Ber and Bazire found the trade monopoly they recently enjoyed—with its profits—now usurped by La Salle. What had been a friendship turned into bitter enmity.

Other fur-traders in the colony joined with Le Ber and Bazire in their hatred of La Salle. They envied the monopoly La Salle enjoyed at Fort Frontenac and turned against him. Not only did they see their profits drained Fort Frontenac, but feared La Salle's monopoly was about to expand to include the territory of the Ohio and Mississippi valleys.

Opposition came as well from the Jesuits. Their antagonism toward La Salle resulted from a conflict of plans. Both wanted control of the valley of the Mississippi and the West; La Salle, to occupy, fortify, and trade; the Jesuits, to make spiritual converts, build churches and schools, as well as control the fur-trade to their benefit. Additionally, Frontenac had allied himself with the Sulpicians and Récollets in their disputes with the Jesuits. La Salle was too closely linked in friendship and in business with Frontenac, to whom the Jesuits were losing their power. The hatred for one spilled over to include the other.

La Salle spent two and a half years diligently transforming the old Fort Catarakoui into a vital, thriving Fort Frontenac. From the beginning, Fort Frontenac was planned to be but one of a string of forts extending into the middle of the continent. Now that he accomplished what he wanted at Fort Frontenac, La Salle felt it was time to carry out his plan of exploration and military domination of lands to the west.

On his return to Montréal in the spring of 1674, Jolliet stopped at Fort Frontenac where he met with La Salle. Though there are no documents to prove their meeting, all circumstances point that way. La Salle's later expedition followed a route evidently derived from information imparted by Jolliet. More than a mere adventurer who could spend innumerable hours recounting tales to La Salle about the new lands visited and the peoples met there, Jolliet was also able to put down on paper an accurate graphic representation of his discoveries. He was an experienced mapmaker, and with the astronomical instruments he carried on the expedition was able to give the exact latitudes of places they visited.

Jolliet's discoveries on the Mississippi must also have excited La Salle and spurred him on to take up where he left off three years ago. He needed to be free from demands made upon him by other men and the conflicts that hovered over him with increasing insistence at Fort Frontenac. He longed to once again be his own master as his canoe silently glided along the forest-fringed shores of the lakes and rivers, where the only sounds that met his ears were those of the cry of the loon and the whisper of wind through pines and firs. Even the howl of the wolf was preferable to the raucous shouting of quarrelsome men.

La Salle's commercial and military enterprise was in perfect accord with the duties proscribed to Count Frontenac by Louis XIV and Minister Colbert in 1672; Frontenac was "to transform a mission country into a Crown colony." By militarily occupying the whole of the Mississippi valley, three goals would be realized: the establishment of French settlements would extend the king's domain in New France and bring additional revenue; it would act as a barrier preventing any further westward expansion of the British colonies and prevent their access to the fur-trade so necessary to the survival of Canada; and it would control communication between the Indian tribes and sway their policies.

ROYAL SUPPORT

To put his grand plan into effect, La Salle needed more money. In November of 1677, he again sailed for France to gain Royal approval and to raise funds. Letters of support from Frontenac and strong friends in Paris made it easy for La Salle to present his plans to Minister Colbert. He described the lands he already discovered, adding some of what he had heard from Jolliet to enhance the vision. This region, he said, contained a bountiful supply of game and fish, had fertile soil for crops; the broad plains needed no felling of trees to till. Hemp and cotton grew naturally here and could easily be made into manufactured goods. Though everything needed to sustain life was found wild there in abundance, the earth could produce everything grown in France and in the same fashion. He told about the buffalo, which the Spanish call *Cibola,* that grow wild in vast herds, whose thick wool would make good cloth and hats. The hides of these beasts, he said, are better than those in France, and as proof he brought along a sample to show them. As for the Indians in this western land, they were, "in the main of a tractable and social disposition, and since they have the use neither of our weapons nor of our goods . . . they will readily adjust themselves to us, and imitate our way of life." In a few years they would become new subjects to the Church and the king. In short, nothing would prevent French colonies planted in these western lands from becoming strong and prosperous— much more so than in the poverty-stricken land of Canada, where the forests were unclearable, the land infertile, and snow covered the land for six months of the year.

When he completed his eloquent testimonial to the beneficence of the western lands, La Salle then proceeded to outline the dangers, difficulties, and expenses of such a venture, adding as a little further inducement to the king that if France did not take command, surely the English would. First, there was the difficulty vessels had in navigating the St. Lawrence River and the straits connecting the various Great Lakes. Before one even entered the lakes, there were three areas on the river where falls and rapids required a portage around them. Then there was the outpouring of the Niagara, with

The old Château de Versailles, designed for King Louis XIV by the architect Louis Le Vau, was an embellishment of the original hunting lodge of Louis XIII. This château was further enlarged from 1668 to 1670 by enveloping the older building with a second, and much larger, building. *Photo: courtesy of Réunion des Musées Nationaux / Art Resource, New York.*

its Falls, from Lake Erie into Lake Ontario which had to be passed if ships were to reach the Mississippi. Second, it would be difficult to get supplies and necessities to these new colonies that were so far away. Third, a great number of men would be necessary to man the garrisons and defend the colonists from the Indians, and this would be expensive. Fourth, the Iroquois, who were bold and warlike would be a constant menace to the far-flung French settlements, preventing communication between them, or worse yet, destroying the villages. The contradictions in his attitude toward the native tribes did not seem to concern La Salle. He qualified his assessment of danger from the Iroquois by suggesting it was not as great as others believed, and that he hoped to live well with them. If any group could be a threat to the plan, it would be the English, for they could prevent entry to Lake Ontario and Lake Erie, which were necessary passages for this enterprise. All these problems and difficulties, La Salle felt, were not insur-

"Wild cattle. Instead of hair, these cattle have a very fine wool, which is still longer on the females than on the males; their horns are nearly all black, much bigger than the horns of European cattle, though not quite so long. The head is of monstrous size. The neck is short and strong, with a great hump between the shoulders; the legs are big and short, covered with very long wool. Upon the shoulders and around the neck and horns there is a great black mane, falling over the eyes, and giving them a terrible appearance. The body is much larger than that of our cattle, especially in front, but this great bulk does not prevent them from running very swiftly, so that no Savage can overtake them in the chase, and they frequently kill those who have wounded them." *From: Relation of the Discoveries and Voyages of Cavelier de La Salle from 1679 to 1681.*

mountable, if taken step by step, and care was taken to provide a solid base by clearing much surrounding land.

La Salle described all that he had accomplished at Fort Frontenac and said he was now ready to start a new colony at the western end of Lake Erie. In reward for his efforts, he asked that his title to Fort Frontenac be reaffirmed and that he be allowed to proceed with the larger plan of discovery of western lands in New France. To start with, he would establish two other forts: one at the entrance of Lake Erie, by the Niagara River, and the other at the mouth of Lake Michigan. Both he would build totally at his expense. For his efforts, and the cost to him, La Salle asked that he be granted sovereignty over all the lands he discovers and settles, as well as ownership of all the cleared lands the Indians leave him, and to be made governor of all the country in question. He also asked that he be allowed twenty years to accomplish his tasks without having to worry about the land being taken away.

In return, La Salle was willing to make some concessions. He promised not to carry on a fur-trade in beaver with the Ottawas, or in Lake Nipissing, Lake Huron, Lake Superior, and Green Bay on Lake Michigan. This was all Jesuit territory, where their missions were located. La Salle knew that if he removed the business traffic of fur from the Jesuits, it would virtually destroy them, for their subsistence depended on it. Perhaps it was a conciliatory gesture toward the Jesuits, or maybe La Salle counted on the return of even greater profits from the buffalo than from the beaver. He may have been thinking of the gold and silver mines always rumored, but never found, that lay beyond the Mississippi. La Salle assured the minister that he would not do anything to endanger Canada, and that everything was with the approval and pleasure of Count Frontenac, governor of New France. The king replied to La Salle's petition:

> *Louis, by the grace of God, King of France and Navarre, to our dear and well-beloved Robert Cavelier, Sieur de la Salle, greetings. We have received agreeably the very humble petition made in your name, to permit you to work at discovering the western part of New France; and further we have willingly given our consent to this proposal, as there is nothing more than the discovery of this land in which it appears one can find a route to penetrate as far as Mexico . . . to which [enterprise] the application that you have given to have cleared the lands we granted you by the decree of our Council of May 13, 1675 and certified letters of the same date, to form habitations on those lands, and to make defensible Fort Frontenac, of which we have accorded you domain and governorship, gives us every reason to expect you will succeed to our satisfaction and to the advantage of our subjects of that country. To these considerations, and others that move us, we have permitted and do permit by these present, signed by our hand, to work at the discovery of the western part of our said land in the New France, and for the execution of this enterprise, to build forts in places you deem necessary, which we agree you will enjoy upon the same terms and conditions as Fort Frontenac,*

following and conforming to our certified letters of May 13, 1675 . . . on condi-
tion, nevertheless, that you achieve this mission within five years, in default of
which the present letters will be null and void; that you will do no trade with the
Ottawa savages and others who carry their beaver and other fur trades to Mon-
tréal; that you do everything at your own expense and that of your association,
to whom we granted the privilege of the trade of buffalo-hides. We mandate to
Sieur Count Frontenac, our Governor and lieutenant-general, and also Duches-
nea, Intendant of justice, police, and finance, and the officers of the supreme coun-
cil of the aforesaid country, to see to the execution of these presents; as such is our
pleasure.

Given at St. Germain-en-Laye, May 12, 1678

King Louis was obviously pleased with what he heard, for La Salle received even more than he had asked for in his petition; not just two but *all*
the forts he thought necessary were permitted, and would belong to him,
along with the adjacent land and monopoly in trade—the same rights given
him in his first petition for Fort Frontenac. Though he was restricted from
dealing with the Ottawas in beaver pelts and with other tribes who brought
their furs to Montréal, La Salle was given a monopoly in the hides and wool
of the buffalo, so plentiful in the plains. But the time limit allowed him for
his exploration, to built the forts and to create new settlements, was severely
restricted by the king—reduced from twenty years to five years, or La Salle
would forfeit everything.

From La Salle's petition and the king's letter in reply it would appear that
the two parties had entirely different goals in mind. Throughout, La Salle
emphasized the importance of settling new colonies, whereas the king
made it clear that he was giving La Salle permission to discover the western
part of New France because it would enable him to find a route "*that would
penetrate as far as Mexico,*" and makes no mention of colonization—only that
the land discovered should be secured by forts. La Salle refers to Mexico
only briefly in his report on the discoveries he has already made: the many
lands south of the Great Lakes, and rivers, including the great Ohio River
that he followed until it joined with another river coming from the north.
These waters, he said "discharge, according to all appearances, into the Gulf

of Mexico, and gives one the hope of finding a new communication with the sea, from which France could someday gain great advantages, as well as the large lakes occupying part of North America." The "to all appearances" portion was the conclusion reached by Jolliet, from his exploration in 1673, which La Salle alludes to vaguely as the result of his own discovery.

La Salle believed that the Mississippi River and the Gulf of Mexico could provide an alternate route for ships sailing back to France, loaded with the furs and goods, instead of having to go through the Great Lakes and the St. Lawrence River. He was very explicit in pointing out the difficulties of navigation on the St. Lawrence. But he did not mention that the waters of the Gulf of Mexico and the Caribbean Sea were Spanish territory and it was highly unlikely Spain would allow French vessels to slip through without seizing them and confiscating their cargo. La Salle's real objective may have been to establish a harbor or home port for French ships at the mouth of the Mississippi, or in nearby safe waters. This is what Minister Colbert obviously had in mind in other correspondence when he said "it was important to the glory and service of the *King to find a harbor for his vessels in the Mexican Gulf.*"

Evidently, La Salle's friends and relatives believed as firmly as did the king in the success of his enterprise, for when La Salle returned to Québec it was with most of the money he needed. His brothers and relatives "spared nothing to enable him to respond worthily to the royal goodness." The remaining funds, about 14,000 livres, La Salle procured by taking out a mortgage on Fort Frontenac and accepting loans using the pledges made in France as collateral; all which he hoped to repay from anticipated profits in the buffalo trade.

PART III

Beyond the Great Lakes to the Mississippi

While still in France attending to his affairs at Court and raising funds for the expedition, two men were introduced to La Salle whom he persuaded to join him in his quest. One was La Motte de Lussière, about whose background little is known. The other was Henry de Tonty, an Italian born officer and mutual friend of Prince de Conti, who became La Salle's life-long friend and staunchest ally. A military man, retired in France after the Sicilian wars, he was healthy, full of energy, and had the courage and determination to help La Salle carry through his plans. During the war, when his hand was partially blown away, Tonty took out his knife and completed the amputation on himself. Later, an iron hand, covered with a glove was attached to the empty stump. This earned for Tonty, among the Indians, the appellation of "iron-hand." Of all the people who associated themselves with La Salle, Tonty was the person whom he trusted the most.

These two adventurers, along with thirty other recruits for the expedition, all new to the demands of life in Canada, sailed with La Salle from La Rochelle, France on July 12, 1678. Two months later their ship reached Québec. The rest of the journey, from Québec to Fort Frontenac, was more difficult than usual; this time their canoes were loaded with tons of materials brought from France that were needed to construct two ships. Thousands of yards of cordage, iron castings, anchors, tools and bulky, heavy sails, plus the artillery needed to defend the forts, and all the merchandise for trade had to be unloaded, carried, and loaded again as they portaged their way past each rapids and falls on the St. Lawrence River.

Their group now was increased by one other person, Father Louis Hennepin, who came to Québec from Fort Frontenac to greet them. When the Récollet Franciscans in Québec (displaced by the Jesuits) were allowed to re-establish themselves there, four Récollets sailed to New France in 1675: Fathers Zénobe Membré, Christian Le Clercq, Luc Buisset, and Louis Hennepin. They established a friary in Québec, but their numbers remained small, and at the end of the year there were still only ten Récollets in all of Canada. Five remained in Québec, acting as priests, preachers, and confessors, while the rest were divided among the four other Récollet missions at Three Rivers, Isle Percée (on the Gaspé peninsula), Fort Frontenac, and Acadia. Father Zénobe Membré was not assigned to any permanent post, but visited the outlying stations, acting as coordinator, and keeping communications open. He later accompanied La Salle in all three of his exploring ventures in the role of chaplain and missionary companion.

Father Louis Hennepin and Luc Buisset were assigned to Fort Frontenac and remained there while La Salle was away in France. During this time, Hennepin decided to join La Salle in his grand scheme, feeling there was no better opportunity to indulge his passion for travel and to visit strange lands; a passion almost equal in intensity to his vocation of saving souls. In fact, he admitted that the chance to do missionary work and travel was one of the reasons he entered the Order of St. Francis. When not fulfilling his duties as missionary at Fort Frontenac, Hennepin took every opportunity to visit neighboring Indian settlements. During the summer, when the rivers ran freely, he would journey by canoe. Dressed in his course, gray gown with pointed hood, wearing a crucifix and rosary, and carrying a small, portable altar strapped to his back, Hennepin reached the outlying settlements to preach and say Mass.♣ Winter was no deterrent to his zealous endeavors, he traversed the frozen, snow-covered land

♣ Hence the appellation of "gray-robes" for the Récollets, which distinguished them from the "black-robes" of the Jesuits.

on snow-shoes. In 1677, accompanied by one of the French soldiers at the fort, Hennepin traveled to the western end of Lake Ontario, and from there, south, to the lands of the Onondagas and the Oneidas. Then he headed east, visited the Mohawk territory, and finally, completing the circle, made his way back to Fort Frontenac. He thoroughly demonstrated his ability to participate in La Salle's grand enterprise.

On the 18th of November, hardly a propitious time, since winter storms were already more the rule than the exception, the excursion started out— not as a unified group, but in three separate parties. Fifteen men, their canoes laden with 7,000 to 8,000 livres worth of merchandise, were dispatched to the land of the Illinois tribe who lived near the Mississippi River. As an advance group, they were to initiate friendly relations with the Indians by giving them presents and winning them with speeches. Until the rest of the group met up with them the following spring, they were to stockpile provisions necessary for the following season of exploration. Most importantly, they were to engage in trade for the buffalo hides, in which La Salle now owned the monopoly. Without this source of income, La Salle would be unable to repay his debts in France and in Canada, and the total enterprise would be doomed to failure.

At the same time, La Motte, Hennepin, and sixteen others set sail from Frontenac for the western end of Lake Ontario in the smallest decked boat built earlier, a Brigantine of ten tons burden. They were to begin building a fort at the mouth of the Niagara River. La Salle and Tonty stayed behind to settle the rest of their affairs, and then would join them there with more workers and supplies.

La Motte's little vessel, her hold crammed to capacity, and decks overcrowded with men, bravely set out on a cold, blustery November day. It might have been more prudent to wait for calmer winds, but they were so eager to start and reach Niagara before winter really set in that they did not let the weather deter them. When the ship reached open waters, they felt what the full effects of a northeast gale could have upon this inland ocean— for such is each of the Great Lakes—tossing their ship about in the short, steep seas. To gain some surcease, they clawed their way to the northern shore of the lake to gain the advantage of a lee shore. Even so, it was a cold, wet, miserable sail, giving all those aboard ample time to reflect on what they had committed themselves to—knowing that the most arduous part was yet to come. On the 26th of November they anchored in the mouth of a small river as refuge for the safety of the vessel and to rest from their ordeal. The harbor provided neither; the river froze over, locking the ship in its icy grip. It took them nine days, chopping with axes, to clear their way free of the ice. In seeking the relative comfort of a lee shore, they were now on the opposite side of the lake from their destination, prolonging the voyage even more by having to cross over to the south shore.

Their goal finally reached, they entered the Niagara River and dropped anchor, thankful that this part of their journey was over. La Motte and most of the men remained with the ship, while Hennepin and several others took a canoe farther up river to explore. When they had pushed their way against the torrent of water as far as possible, they landed, and continued the exploration on foot. Despite the difficulties of deep snow and dense, tangled, forest growth the ever-increasing roar of the falls goaded them onward. At last, they broke through to a clearing, and there before them lay the cataract that falls from a height of six hundred feet. On that December day of 1678, Father Louis Hennepin and his companions became the first Europeans to behold the amazing spectacle of Niagara Falls. Galinée, in his expedition nine years earlier, had heard about these cataracts from the Indians. They described to him how in the river above the Falls "the current very often sucks into this gulf, from a great distance, deer and stags, elk and roebucks, that suffer themselves to be drawn from such a point in crossing the river, that they are compelled to descend the Falls, and to be overwhelmed in its frightful abyss."✤ Galinée said that the thunderous roar from the falls was so great, he could hear it from thirty to thirty-six miles away.

Hennepin, historian for the venture, was as much impressed with the sight as were the Indians who had described it to Galinée, and wrote:

✤ Niagara Falls was mentioned by the Indians to Cartier when he ascended the St. Lawrence River in 1535. But Galinée's description of it in *Récit d'un ami de l'abb' de Galinée,* by Abbe Eusèbe Renaudot, is the first in written records. The Falls was given its first depiction on Champlain's map of 1632.

The waters which fall from this vast height, do foam and boil after the most hideous manner imaginable, making an outrageous noise, more terrible than that of thunder. The two brinks of it are so prodigious high, that it would make one tremble to look steadily upon the water, rolling along with a rapidity not to be imagin'd. Were it not for this vast cataract, which interrupts navigation, they might sail with Barks or greater vessels, above the four hundred and fifty leagues further, cross the Lake of Hurons, and up to the farther end of the Lake Illinois [Michigan]; which two lakes we may well say are little seas of fresh water.

Hennepin

FORT CONTI

A fort at the Niagara River was of utmost importance to the success of La Salle's plan. In order for the Iroquois to reach the western country to hunt and trade for furs which they could sell to the English and Dutch, they had to go and return by way of Niagara. A fort here, commanded by the French, would effectively block this route to the Iroquois—amicably in time of peace, but by force if required, in time of war—especially the Tsonnontouans (Senecas), who were the most numerous and most war-like. This would oblige them to do all their trading with the French. Additionally, La Salle aimed to build a vessel above the Falls of Niagara, which would enable the French to sail from Lake Erie all the way to Lake Superior and easily transport quantities of merchandise and furs. Dominating all the waterways west of Lake Ontario also ensured control over the interior region for the trade in beaver pelts, elk, and buffalo hides.

When the Indians, gathered at the banks of the river where La Motte's vessel lay, perceived his intentions, they objected to his building a fort. He tried to cajole them into accepting the idea, but at length had to reconcile himself—for the moment at least—to being satisfied with erecting only a

small, palisaded house to protect the munitions. The protesters were small
in number, since most of the Iroquois warriors were away to fight with a
Nation on the other side of Lake Erie, but La Motte and his group were in
no position to oppose them. Resolved to carry out La Salle's orders, La
Motte took Hennepin, and a few well-armed soldiers, with him to the village of the Senecas to try and gain their permission for the fort. It was the
very end of December now, and they had to travel by canoe halfway back
to Fort Frontenac to reach the Genesee River at Irondequoit Bay. From
there another five-day journey on foot lay ahead before they could reach
the village.

A council of forty-two elders, representing the entire Nation, gathered
to hear La Motte's request. Dressed in their ceremonial robes made of
beaver, wolf-skin, or of black squirrel, and holding a *Calumet* (pipe) in their
hand, they were an impressive group. Hennepin states: "The senators of
Venice do not look more grave, or speak with more majesty and solidity,
than those ancient Iroquois." Anthony Bradford, one of the French party,
who knew the Iroquois language well, acted as interpreter for La Motte and
informed the assembly of the reason for their visit. He had come on behalf
of the governor of Canada, to build a ship, a "great wooden canoe," above
the great Falls of the River Niagara. The French wanted the Seneca chiefs
to inform those of the other four Iroquois Nations about the ship and tell
them how beneficial it would be. Such a ship would sail the Great Lakes
and Mississippi River, and reach Europe by a shorter and much less difficult
way than having to negotiate the dangerous currents and rapids of the St.
Lawrence River. This would mean the French could transport and sell their
commodities to the Indians at a cheaper rate than do the English and Dutch
of Boston and New York.

This was not true, but La Motte hoped it would sound good enough to
be accepted. The same reasoning extended to the fort he wished to build.
The Iroquois owned axes, knives, and even guns, given them, stolen, or
bought, but they had no way of keeping them sharp and in good working
order. La Motte promised he would start a settlement at the mouth of the
Niagara, where a blacksmith and gun-smith would be kept at all times for
the convenience of the Iroquois Nations. He gave gowns, pieces of fine

cloth, axes, knives, and belts of beads as presents to the Senecas to help per-suade them in favor of his design.

The assembly listened to all the arguments patiently and with great civil-ity, but withheld their approval. They would still rather deal with the Eng-lish and Dutch, who they believed would give them the better rates. Weary and discouraged at their lack of success, La Motte and Hennepin returned to the River Niagara.

Their affairs now in order, La Salle, his lieutenant Tonty, and additional workers recruited for the expedition left Fort Frontenac to join La Motte. The forty-five-ton Barquentine, loaded with provisions and all the rigging needed to build the new ship on Lake Erie, fared no better at sea than did La Motte's vessel. The fault this time lay not with the condition of the weather, though it was already the very end of December, but in a poor choice of pi-lots. They barely avoided wrecking the boat off the Bay of Quinté, before they reached the mouth of the Genesee River. As La Motte and Hennepin had done earlier, La Salle went to the village of the Senecas where he called another council. This time, whether due to his greater eloquence and pow-ers of persuasion, or a better facility with the Iroquois language than La Motte's interpreter, he was able to persuade them to allow a fort at the mouth of the Niagara and a ship to be built beyond the cataract. The cheer-ing effect of this welcome news was short lived.

When they came to the Niagara River, La Salle left the ship with the pi-lots while he went to determine the best spot to build his new vessel. He returned to find that in his absence, the pilots had smashed the Barquentine on the coast. Ropes and anchors were saved, but several canoes, most of the commodities, and all the provisions for the settlement were lost.

In the meantime, La Motte's men at the settlement had become a discon-solate, argumentative group. Confined to their shelter by the winter weather, forced to keep each other's company, low on food, and little work to keep their hands busy and their minds off problems, small disagreements and dif-ferences of opinion quickly escalated to major quarrels and fights. It did not help, either, that their two leaders, the one spiritual, the other temporal, could not get along with each other. Adding to these problems was yet an-other, the Iroquois had become suspicious of the fort, with its stockpile of arms and ammunition. It appeared to them that it might all be a ruse, and the real purpose of the Frenchmen's presence was to wage war against them. Feelings ran so high that for a while the workers were obliged to stop construction and return for protection to the small palisaded house.

Nonetheless, La Salle continued with his plans and selected a site about six miles beyond the Falls, to start the ship's construction. On the 26th of January, the keel was laid. This project, as well, was continually beset with problems. The Indians were no more pleased about the vessel than they were about the fort and took every opportunity to show their resentment. One of them, pretending to be drunk, almost killed the blacksmith, who saved his life by swinging a red-hot iron at his assailant. After than, a much better watch was kept, especially when word got to them that there was a scheme to torch the partially built vessel. During the winter, the ship slowly took shape. The shipbuilders, however, fell prey to the same discontent that seized workers on the fort; prolonged cold, and lack of food, slowed their efforts. Father Hennepin tried in his own manner to stimulate the dispirited group; at services he exhorted them to continue their undertaking "for the Glory of God," and for "the advantage of our Christian Colonies." More likely, the greater effect he had upon them was his reminder that this ship would be the best way to free themselves of their situation.

Since all the provisions they had brought with them had been lost with the shipwrecked Barquentine, and the Indians would no longer sell their corn for money, La Salle left to obtain the sorely needed food for his men. It was February, a time when all the waters were frozen motionless, and a thick mantle of snow covered the ground. Accompanied by two companions, and a dog to drag the meager baggage on a sledge, La Salle undertook the arduous journey on foot two-hundred and fifty miles back to Fort Frontenac. Before he left, he placed Tonty in charge of finishing the vessel and gave instructions on how he wanted two blockhouses built at Fort Conti (as he now named it) at the mouth of the Niagara River. The small bag of roasted corn carried with him was all the nourishment available, and even that paltry supply was exhausted two days before reaching Fort Frontenac.

In his absence, work progressed on the new vessel under the watchful eye of Henry de Tonty. She already had a name, and the wood-workers were busy carving an image to hang under the bow, to match that name: *Griffin*. A mythological beast having the head and wings of an eagle and the body and hindquarters of a lion, the Griffin was believed by the ancient Greeks to guard the gold of Scythia in that far-off wilderness of Asiatic Russia. Here, on the Great Lakes it would guard another form of gold, the pelts and hides of beasts that inhabit the wilderness of New France. There was another reason La Salle had for giving it that name; a pair of Griffins, for supporters, or guards, was the heraldic device on Count Frontenac's coat of arms. It was his way of showing gratitude toward his benefactor. La Salle said of this ship. "he would make the Griffin fly above the Ravens," in other words, Frontenac would triumph over the "black-robes," the Jesuits.

Formal ceremonies were held at the launching of the *Griffin*; Father Hennepin blessed her, the *Te Deum* was sung, and with shouts of joy, accompanied by the firing of three guns, the *Griffin* slid down the ways to taste water for the first time. She was hastily anchored far enough off shore to prevent the threat of being set afire from becoming a reality. Then, for their own safety as well, her builders went aboard to keep out of reach of the Indians. Later, they towed the *Griffin* farther upstream to finish the rigging and wait for La Salle to return.

It was not until August that they finally saw their leader again; the long delay caused by financial problems. At Fort Frontenac, La Salle learned a few people had spread the word that his venture was doomed to failure, and he would never return. Aroused by these rumors, his creditors in Montréal and Québec had seized all La Salle's assets and furs. Not everything was gone, at least the advance party he had sent to the Illinois seven months ago was busy purchasing more furs and hides.

There was nothing La Salle could do, since the harm was already done, and he was determined not to let it prevent the journey for which he had planned so long and hard. He left Fort Frontenac, and early in August was back at Niagara, along with three additional Franciscan Récollets, all compatriots (Flemings) of Hennepin. The newly recruited Father Melithon Watteau was to stay at Niagara, at the warehouse above the Falls, to minister to the Senecas, while Hennepin, and the two other newcomers, Zénobe

Membré and Gabriel Ribourde would accompany La Salle to preach the Faith to the western tribes.

La Motte stayed with the expedition for several years. He started out with seemingly good intentions, but disagreements with the priests in the group and bad health from the hardships and miserable climate of Canada soon forced him to return to France. When he finally left, it was a relief to La Salle who felt that La Motte worked against him by "corrupting the morals of his men." La Motte disappears from the La Salle saga in the same obscurity that he entered; his final epitaph being in a letter by La Salle, who said "he served me very ill."

VOYAGE OF THE *GRIFFIN*

At first, La Salle was going to place *Griffin* under the command of Tonty so that he could return to Fort Frontenac and see if anything more could be done to improve his financial affairs. Then, remembering how the pilots had already wrecked one ship, and might even be in league with his enemies to do more damage, he changed his mind, and sailed on the first voyage of *Griffin*. On August 7th, 1679, the *Griffin* weighed anchor, and by a combination of sailing and towing, ascended the river to enter Lake Huron, to become the first sailing vessel to navigate the Upper Lakes. As her sails were hoisted, filled with wind, and began to move across the water, the *Griffin* was an impressive sight to the Indians standing on shore. At forty-five tons burden, she was the largest wooden vessel they had ever seen; the muzzles of her five cannons ominously peering from the gun-ports made her an intimidating sight as well. The winds were favorable, and the *Griffin* kept to a course west by south to cross Lake Erie. She quickly reached the strait that separates Lake Erie from Lake Huron, covering the three-hundred miles in only three days. For the thirty persons aboard, including the three Récollet missionaries, it was a time free of problems and conflicts.

As the *Griffin* traversed the narrow strait of Detroit, the countryside crowded close, giving everyone a chance to note the fertility of the land, and the abundant game it contained. Fine meadows on either side alternated with fruit trees, grape vines, and forests. Hennepin felt that "One would think nature alone could not have made, without the help of art, so charming a prospect." Part way along, the strait widened into a lake, which the Récollets named Lake Sainte-Claire (in use presently), then returned to its narrow self. Now the current was strong and the wind against them. As they approached the entrance to Lake Huron, they were bested by the rapid current, made all the stronger by the unceasingly blowing north wind. Unable to make any progress, La Salle sent his men ashore to tow the *Griffin* into the open water of Lake Huron.

Passage through Lake Huron was not as easy as it had been on Lake Erie. After passing Saginaw Bay, they were becalmed. In itself, this would not be a problem, other than causing delay, but they found themselves among a group of islands, with barely enough water under the keel to keep the *Griffin* afloat. When any breeze at all sprang up, La Salle attempted to find an acceptable anchorage to wait out the calm. Finding none secure enough, he headed the vessel toward open water—taking care to continually sound the depths, a task he now had to do himself, since the pilot was negligent in this duty. The frustration of the past two days of calm winds finally changed, but it brought no relief or joy, for now they had to contend with a furious gale. The violence of the wind forced La Salle to lower the main yards and topmast, where they were lashed to the deck, and head for shore to find shelter from the wind, or an acceptable anchorage. Finding neither, and with the seas now running dangerously high, they took all sail down and left the ship to her own devices, at the mercy of wind and wave. By the next morning the gale spent itself, and under more moderate conditions the *Griffin* sailed to the Strait of Michillimackinac. Here, where the waters of Lake Michigan discharge into Lake Huron, La Salle found a suitable anchorage. Nearby was the Jesuit mission of St. Ignace, where Marquette and Jolliet had departed on their expedition in 1673 to discover the Mississippi River. Now, they were hosts to La Salle and his party. A short distance to the north stood the other Jesuit mission of Sault Sainte-Marie. Both missions attended to the spiritual needs of the Hurons and the Ottawas. They also were very well placed to serve, in turn, the financial needs of the Jesuits, since all the

Indians west and north of these two places had to pass through on their way to Montréal with their trade furs.

Until now, the enterprise was successful. Then, just as the weather before had suddenly changed from calm to storm, storm-clouds of another kind appeared to threaten La Salle's endeavor. For whatever reason they may have had, some of La Salle's men misrepresented to the Indians the purpose of their visit, telling them they were here to seize all their furs by force and to make war on them. Moreover, it was here at Michillimackinac that La Salle found out the fifteen men in the advance party sent to establish trading with the Illinois had cheated him. Instead of using the goods entrusted to them to exchange for furs, they wasted the supplies on themselves. Many of the men deserted to become *Coureurs de bois*, carrying off with them more of the trade goods. Some had remained at Michillimackinac and these, to their deserved misfortune, were arrested. Others had fled to Sault Sainte-Marie. To recover what he could, La Salle sent Tonty, along with six other men, to seize whatever was left in their possession.

It was already September, and the weather started turning bad. Tonty had not yet returned, and fearing that winter was fast approaching, La Salle decided he could wait no longer. He had to start without Tonty, who could catch up with him later at the previously determined rendezvous. La Salle weighed anchor, set sail, and the *Griffin* entered Lake Michigan. They covered a hundred and twenty miles, then, at an island by the mouth of Green Bay, La Salle found the few, faithful remaining members of the advance party. During their stay among the Pottawattamies, a Nation of the Ottawas, they had done what was expected of them, and accumulated pelts worth 12,000 livres. They were happy to behold La Salle, for they had grown impatient and fearful, waiting the many months for their leader.

Pleased at the chance to recover lost profits, La Salle had the pelts loaded aboard the *Griffin* to be immediately sent back to Niagara and stored in the warehouse. With these in hand, La Salle hoped to obtain from his creditors the release of his property seized at Fort Frontenac, Montréal, and Québec. All the merchandise, and a variety of tools and utensils that could not fit in the five canoes in which he planned to continue the journey, were also placed aboard. Once the store of goods was safely unloaded from the *Griffin* at Niagara, she was to rejoin La Salle at the southern end of Lake Michigan, by the mouth of the St. Joseph River. On the 18th of September, the *Griffin* set sail and headed north toward Michillimackinac.

HARDSHIPS AND PERILS

With their canoes heavily loaded, they left the island of the Pottawattamies and began the long and weary journey to St. Joseph (Miamis) River—the rendezvous point with La Salle for Tonty and the *Griffin*. Autumn gales created dangerous seas which threatened to overturn the canoes. Though La Salle had relieved much of the burden by sending it back on the *Griffin*, he still had with him all the indispensable items to build the second ship and fort: tools for house and ship-carpenters, merchandise for trade, and munitions. They pressed onward, alternating between trying to keep afloat on the storm-tossed waters and to keep warm on shore against the snow and rain. Huddled together beneath their blankets, they tried to pull some meager warmth out of a small driftwood fire. Though it hardly seemed possible, their miseries grew worse. They had brought only a small supply of food with them, since after loading all the merchandise in the canoes, there was little room left. They hoped to procure provisions along the way. By the beginning of October all their food was gone and hunger, like a burning ember, gnawed at their stomachs.

After days of hard travel without a morsel of food, relief finally came when they reached another Pottawattamie village. Initial hesitation and distrust between the Indians and the Frenchmen were overcome, and a friendly relationship was established. They prepared a feast for La Salle, who in gratitude gave them ten hatchets, two dozen knives, and for the women, some glass beads. Their strength revived, the journey resumed, and the small fleet slowly made its way south. High winds and rough seas continued to trouble them. When they wished to land to rest for the night, they were forced to carry their canoes, with all the contents, up the high bluffs that ran close along the lake, otherwise the breaking waves on shore would dash everything to pieces. The food acquired at the last village was soon finished, and with no game in sight to shoot, hunger again consumed their attention.

Adding to the hardship that enfeebled even the strongest was the need to maintain a constant vigil. They were in the land of the Outtouagami tribe, and their first encounter nearly ended in disaster. During the night the Indians robbed the voyagers of their possessions. Determined not to let them get away, La Salle found a solitary individual whom he took as hostage. He then captured the most important man in their tribe, showed him the first captive, and let him go with a message to the others that if they failed to return all that was stolen, he would kill their comrade. Persistence, bold action, and diplomacy on La Salle's part averted open battle at the last moment, and peace was restored.

During feasts and dances the following day, the Outtouagamis pleaded with La Salle to remain and help protect them against the Illinois. The chief told him how an Iroquois, captured and burnt alive by the Illinois, confessed before his death that the French of Canada hated the Illinois, and it was they who fomented the war between the two tribes. La Salle and his men were told they would surely meet their end if they attempted to go among the Illinois. The news concerned him, for almost all the Indians he met along the way had told a similar story. Regardless of his anxiety, La Salle decided to continue with the voyage. He reasoned that perhaps the story was falsely concocted, a contrivance by the Outtouagamis to prevent their neighbors, the Illinois, from becoming too strong if they acquired firearms from the French. La Salle thanked them for their advice, and said he was not afraid of the Illinois, "he would find means to bring them to terms, either by friendship or by force."

On November 1st the party embarked and made their way to the north-flowing St. Joseph River, where it enters Lake Michigan. This was the place appointed as a rendezvous with Tonty, as well as for the *Griffin*. Much to La Salle's surprise, no one was at the St. Joseph to meet them, nor were there any signs they ever had been. He decided to remain until their arrival and wait for winter to start. La Salle's plan was to make initial contact with the Illinois during the winter, when they normally break up into smaller bands to hunt to better advantage. By approaching smaller groups at first, giving gifts, and showing his goodwill, it would be easier to gain their friendship. This would lead naturally to his forming an alliance with the entire Nation. It would also give him the opportunity to learn their language. In the meantime he set his men to work building a small fort and a house to protect the *Griffin* and store her goods.

FORT ST. JOSEPH

In the weeks that followed, ground was cleared, trees felled, and a permanent fortification built. Forty feet long by thirty feet wide, it was well reinforced with musket-proof logs. As further protection against attack, twenty-five-foot-high piles were placed to create pincer-shaped walls on all four sides of the fort. During the construction, La Salle noticed that a sandbar at the mouth of the river would make it difficult for the *Griffin* to enter. He sounded the river and marked the deepest part of the channel with flags and buoys. Then he dispatched two men to Michillimackinac to inform the master of the *Griffin* what to expect at St. Joseph, and to act as pilots to safely guide the ship into the new harbor.

On the 20th of November, Tonty and his men finally arrived from Michillimackinac; their long delay caused by the foulness of weather at this time of the year. The news he brought La Salle was disheartening. Though it was but a short passage for the *Griffin* from the island at the entrance of Green Bay to Michillimackinac, it had failed to arrive. There was no word, either, about the ship from the various Indians who frequently traveled back and forth along those shores. It was evident she was the victim of shipwreck. Yet La Salle continued to hope that even though tardy, she would safely appear. By the end of December, ice was already beginning to form on the river, and he could wait no longer. He left letters hanging from posts, informing the late arrivals about their departure, and gave instructions for the ship's pilot. Thirty men in eight canoes made their way up the St. Joseph River to its headwaters. Here, in a vast plain, intricately laced with marshes, the Kankakee River (one of the headwaters of the Illinois River) takes its rise. The distance between these two rivers required a short portage of only four and a half miles. Since the rivers were still open, the travel was not difficult, but progress was slow. Provisions were low, and much of their time had to be spent scouring the woods and fields for food. The meandering course of streams through the marshlands further impeded their advance. From the complex mosaic of water, reed, and alder, there was no way of determining the true course of the water's flow. Much of their way was through quagmires too dry to paddle a canoe through and too wet to walk upon. After following a serpentine stream all day long, the constant backtracking in search of the best channel produced a gain of only six miles when measured in a straight line. At night, their only bed was the sparse tufts of frozen ground. As best they could, they marked their route along the way and left letters hanging from branches of trees, just in case the other adventurers from the *Griffin* should finally come to join them.

Once La Salle and his group reached the open plains, they should have found ample food. Normally the prairie was abundant with deer, beavers, otters, turkeys, swans, and numerous other birds. Buffalo, in herds of two to four hundred were to be found grazing on the lush grasses. But at this time of the year there were no animals; all they saw of the once verdant prairie was a course, fire-blackened stubble, where the bleached bones and skulls of innumerable slaughtered buffalo stood out in stark contrast. In the fall of the year the Miamis, as was their practice, would surround a herd of buffalo and create a circle of fire in the dry grass. Some places were kept free of fire, and when these beasts charged through to escape the flames, the Indians would lie in ambush to kill them.

December was cold and gray as La Salle continued his journey down the Illinois River. On the first of January, almost four hundred miles from Lake Michigan, he reached an Illinois village, where he and his men might find surcease from their ever present hunger. They found no relief. The Indians had gone off hunting elsewhere, leaving the village deserted. Desperate for food, La Salle helped himself to a hidden cache of corn stored by the Indians to be used as seed for the following spring crops and as subsistence until the harvest. Without it, there was the risk his men would perish.

Four days later, where the river widened to form a lake, thin curls of smoke in the sky alerted La Salle and his contingent that they were approaching another Indian encampment. They soon came to an inhabited village of about eighty cabins. As usual, the initial encounter between the two groups was one of mutual wariness and distrust. La Salle overcame the suspicions, restored confidence, and developed a friendly interchange. After the rejoicing, feasting, and giving of gifts, La Salle called the elders of the village together and explained the purpose of his visit.

First, though, he apologized for taking their corn from the other village without permission. He knew how essential it was to them, he said, but their own needs compelled him. He would gladly pay for it now, with gifts of hatchets and other things, if the Illinois would let him keep what still remained of his supply. If, however, they wished him to return the corn, he would do so, and go to the neighboring tribe of Osages to purchase food. In exchange, he would leave with the Osages his blacksmith and forge to repair their hatchets and other tools. La Salle knew this would make the Illinois jealous, for they too had need of a blacksmith, and they would fear the Osages becoming too strong through association with the French. Thus, through subtle intimidation rather than demand or overt force, La Salle received from the Illinois all the food he needed.

Then he broached the subjects most important to him; the fort he wanted to construct here and his plan to navigate the great river of the Mississippi. In the same manner as with the corn, he played on their fears of attacks from neighboring tribes, particularly the dreaded Iroquois. He could not help the Illinois by openly waging war upon the Iroquois, for there was still a treaty of peace between them and the king. If, however, they allowed him to build a fort nearby, then, should the Iroquois attack, the French posted in it could protect the Illinois. He even promised arms and ammunition so that they could defend themselves, and would furnish them with all other goods they required. The only obstacle to the plan, he said, was the great distance and difficulty of bringing these things all the way from France, by way of Québec and Montréal. La Salle disclosed he would build a "great canoe" to journey to France by way of the Mississippi River; this, he explained, would make the route to France faster and easier. Furthermore, he could bring goods to the Illinois at a much cheaper cost. It was an argument successfully employed before, and it worked here as well. The Illinois gave

La Salle their approval to the fort, and promised to help him in whatever way they could.

Not only did La Salle receive assurances about the ease he could sail his ship, unimpeded, the full length of the Mississippi to the open sea, but learned that no Europeans had a settlement at its mouth, or nearby on that part of the coast. This was important information, for it meant there would be no Spanish ships to thwart his endeavors. The Illinois knew from slaves they had taken in warfare from the region that no Spanish colonies existed there. Besides, if there were any settlements where the Mississippi entered into the Gulf of Mexico, they themselves would certainly be making the journey to the Gulf, which was only twenty days away, to trade with the Europeans.

All the concessions gained from the elders of the village and the information he learned about the Mississippi did not bring unalloyed joy to La Salle. Other problems, some concerning his own company, beset him. The men had suffered with La Salle through many difficult months, usually in fear of attack from hostile Indians, and always hungry. In this brief respite from their hardships, some of the men questioned their loyalty and duty. Father Hennepin, during services, encouraged the dissidents to remain cheerful and steadfast. For the most part, his entreaties were ignored. The Illinois further eroded La Salle's men's confidence in the endeavor by falsely depicting all the dangers that lay ahead.

While the principal chief was away, Nicanapé, brother to the chief, contradicted all that the elders told La Salle about the safety and beauty of the Mississippi. He said that the Mississippi had never been descended without everyone perishing. "Savage tribes," who line its banks, would slaughter the Frenchmen, and the water contained monsters and serpents that would draw them under. Falls and precipices from which their canoes could not escape, and violent currents, would draw them down into a subterranean gulf, no one knowing where it went.✤ La Salle was not alarmed, he recognized it as an attempt by the Illinois to keep him from departing. But some of his men were so frightened by

✤ An echo of Plato's *Phaedo*, in which he explained that all the waters pierce the earth to a sea called Tartarus at the center, and that all the rivers, lakes, and oceans are drawn into this "primary and original mass of water."

what they heard that their fears overcame calm judgment, and one night, six of them took flight, deserting La Salle. They preferred to risk death by starvation over the unknown dangers that lay ahead.

The Illinois, as well, were swayed by rumors. A visiting Miamis chief secretly met with the elders of the Illinois and told them not to listen to anything La Salle had to say. His true purpose, the chief claimed, was to furnish arms and ammunition to their enemies, and that the French were acting as spies for the Iroquois. The Illinois would soon be caught in the middle of these forces aimed at their destruction. With the well-supplied fort in their midst, there was no way they could escape ruin. The danger of lies of this sort was that they played so well upon the natural suspicions of the Illinois. It took all of La Salle's gift of persuasion to allay their fears.

Even the missionaries in the expedition succumbed to the malaise of despair that like a dense, damp fog, tangibly hung in the air. All their efforts to bring the True Faith to the native peoples had very little effect. Father Hennepin reluctantly concluded that the Illinois, like most other Indian nations in America, would not accept the morals of the Gospel until time and commerce with the Europeans made them more sensible to the charms of Christianity.

La Salle now had to turn the diplomacy that came so easily to him upon his followers to prevent more desertions. First, he urged the remaining men to be more true to him than the faithless fugitives, and not to be alarmed by the falsely depicted dangers. He said he would take with him only those who of their own free will chose to continue the venture. The others who wished to remain could do so and return to Canada the following spring, without any risk. If they left now, however, "forsaking him like cowards in a conspiracy," they would be punished when they arrived in Québec, for as he reminded them, they were still under command of the king. La Salle knew that to prevent his men from being influenced any more by false rumors, he had to separate them from the Illinois. It would not be easy getting them to leave the relative comfort of the encampment in the middle of winter and start another fort. He persuaded them by saying that in the likelihood of an Iroquois attack during the winter, the Illinois would be unable to resist, and would flee. The French, however, encumbered with all their belongings could not move rapidly, and would be left alone to face the wrath of the Iroquois. Their only hope lay in leaving now and finding a site farther downstream where they could build a fortress in an easily defensible spot, strong enough to resist an Iroquois attack.

La Salle already had selected such a place. Below the widening of the Illinois River (now called Lake Peoria) was a hillock several hundred feet from the shore. The climb from the bank of the river was steep, and deep ravines on two other sides made the hill even more defensible. In the middle of January 1680, a great thaw opened the river below the Illinois village, and La Salle seized the opportunity to move to the new site.

FORT HEARTBREAK

Considering the work that lay ahead during the severest part of winter, when icy winds swept down from the north and froze the ground to the hardness of granite and blinding snowstorms prevented all movement, they accomplished a remarkable amount. They built a fort strong enough to repel any assault. Soldiers occupied two of the inner angles, where they would always be ready to defend against attack; the Récollets were in the third angle, and the magazine the fourth. La Salle and Tonty lived in a separate dwelling in the middle of the fort. According to Hennepin, the name of the new fort—Fort of Crêvecoeur (Heartbreak)—was a reflection of the despair felt by everyone because of their unending misfortunes and the extreme difficulties they labored under.

At the same time that they worked on the fort, they began to build the second ship—the one which La Salle aimed to sail down the Mississippi to the open sea. The keel was laid for a vessel forty-two feet long. As the days progressed, the men amassed a growing stockpile of timbers for the frames and sawn boards for planks. By the 1st of March, everything was ready for assembly, but then the work had to stop. All the ironwork and hardware, all the rigging and sails had been on the *Griffin*. By now, La Salle abandoned all hope she would appear; there could be no further denial of the loss of the *Griffin*. With it was the loss of all of La Salle's plans. Everything that he bought in France, transported by canoe from Québec to Fort Frontenac and on to Niagara, had to be replaced and transported all over again. Gone were the tools, merchandise, all the rigging, and all the other materials needed to build the other ship—not to mention all of La Salle's precious pelts. In all, it amounted to 60,000 livres.

La Salle resolved to start out as soon as possible for Fort Frontenac—1,500 miles away—to replenish the lost materials. He could not wait any longer, either for the *Griffin* or the approach of more favorable weather for travel. To delay the journey now could mean the setback of his enterprise for a year or more.

The cause of the *Griffin's* ruin lies secret, taken with her to a grave in the wave-stirred waters of Lake Michigan. Somewhere along the coast on the way to Michillimackinac, the pilot brought the *Griffin* to shore to lie at anchor, so the men could rest. By one account, when they started out again, the Indians warned the pilot about an impending storm, and of the dangerous navigation of the inshore waters. Advice that should have been well heeded, from those who knew their home waters well, was ignored. The *Griffin* sank beneath the storm-tossed seas, taking with her all those aboard.

Other rumors hovered around her demise. The Jesuits, in their jealousy toward La Salle and his Sulpician followers, were accused of piracy. Some said that it was the *Griffin's* own crew and pilot who purposely drove her hard aground and sank her, in order to make off with the pelts and peddle them for their own profit. This is what La Salle had come to believe. In a long letter (June 4, 1683) to La Barre, governor of Canada, he related how a young Indian who once worked for him told about seeing a white man, who looked like the pilot, and four other Frenchmen. They had been captured beyond the Mississippi, as the small group was making their way toward the Sioux. When taken, in their possession was a quantity of goods and pelts. La Salle was convinced that the white man held prisoner was the pilot of the *Griffin*.

Bacqneville de La Potherie, in his *Histoire de l 'Amerique Septentrionale*, proposed another possibility—one that has a strong feeling of veracity. The Indians were seeing their land gradually taken over by the French—missionary stations, settlements, and forts were more numerous, and extended in their geographic range. Now, here was a ship that by its size could easily transport a large quantity of goods, quickly and easily to help support these far-ranging colonists. With its firing power of guns and cannons it could rule the waterways of their territory. Stirred by the Iroquois, who were planning to renew hostilities with the French, the Ottawas saw the destruction of the *Griffin* as a means to impede further incursions of the French. Either under cover of darkness at night, or by guile during the day, they boarded the *Griffin*, overwhelmed her crew (who were murdered or captured), and set fire to the ship.

The Iroquois had attempted earlier to destroy the ship when it was being constructed. They frequently visited the site and had planned to set fire to the *Griffin* as it sat on the stocks. The French were forewarned, however, and kept a close watch. As soon as the *Griffin* was launched, she was anchored far enough offshore to assure her safety.

Whether due to incompetence or treachery on the part of the pilot; by jealousy on the part of his own countrymen, or wrath through fear, on the part of the Indians, the result was the same—it was a terrible setback to all of La Salle's plans.

Were it not for a fortuitous encounter with a solitary Illinois warrior, whom La Salle befriended, and a subsequent meeting with chiefs of the village, La Salle might have lost the courage to continue the task entrusted to him by the king, of expanding New France in the West. The elders confirmed what La Salle first heard, and wanted to believe, about the Mississippi. It was indeed navigable all the way to the sea. Neither falls nor rapids would be met, though there were occasional sand-bars and mud-banks where the river became very wide. He learned the names of the various tribes that live along its banks, and the tributaries that empty into the Mississippi River. All this was confirmed by a visit of some Osages, Chicasaws, and Akansa, who had traveled north to buy hatchets and other goods from the Frenchmen. They also said that word had spread about the coming of the Frenchmen, and they would be well received. This not only strengthened La Salle's determination to complete his discoveries, but helped allay the fears of those he would leave behind to guard Fort Crêvecoeur.

He entrusted Lieutenant Henry de Tonty to be in command of the fort, while Father Louis Hennepin (with two companions) was charged with descending the Illinois River to its mouth, and exploring the Mississippi for some distance. He was to acquaint himself with the tribes he found on both banks, and secure their friendship.

TOILSOME JOURNEY

On February 29, 1680, Father Hennepin, the missionary with an insatiable desire for travel, left Fort Crêvecoeur toward Michillimackinac, and La Salle, with an Indian hunter and four French companions, departed the next day for Fort Frontenac. All they had had to suffer before was but a prelude for what was about to come. The river, still frozen, made their loaded canoes useless. They expected, however, that once above the lake, the river's swifter current would create an open passage, so rather than leave the canoes behind, they built sleds and dragged them over the snow and ice. To their dismay, the river above Lake Peoria was still covered with ice, and La Salle and his men were required to carry the canoes and contents through twelve miles of snow-filled woods and over frozen marshland. During the occasional times they could use their canoes in stretches of open water, they were in peril from the masses of ice that continually swept by. Heavy snowfalls that alternated with drenching rains contributed to their misery. On the 18th of March, the river was again frozen solid, and they finally acknowledged the futility of their efforts. They hid the canoes on an island and set out on foot to cross the prairie. Snow-shoes were as useless on the snow-covered fields as the canoes were on a frozen river. This time of the year the snow, though deep, was just beginning to feel the warming effect of the sun in the lengthening days. With every step, heavy, wet snow clung to the shoes, its weight anchoring them to the ground.

After a week of slogging over snow-fields, wading through great swamps, and fording streams on crudely built rafts made from reeds and branches, the intrepid little group arrived at the fort built last fall on the St. Joseph River. There, awaiting them, was more bad news. In November La Salle had dispatched two men from St. Joseph to meet the *Griffin* and act as pilot, helping bring her to the fort. Though they made a complete circuit of Lake Michigan, covering both shores, there was no sign of the *Griffin*, or any word of what happened to her.

La Salle and his men continued eastward, through dense forests and thickets that tore their clothes to shreds and clawed at their unprotected bodies. Then, on March 28 their fortune appeared to turn. Until now, food was always scarce, and many days they were forced to continue traveling with nothing to eat. Suddenly, game was ample, and they feasted on venison, bear, and turkey. The welcomed treat turned out to be a mixed blessing, which they quickly realized. The plenitude of game was because the Indians did not hunt here: this was a borderland between five or six warring nations. The adventurers now had to always be on their guard to prevent being discovered and mistakenly slain before they were recognized as French. When on the prairie, they set the dry grass afire to conceal their trail—a stratagem they quickly abandoned because the smoke signaled their presence. A band of Mascoutins, on a warpath with the Iroquois took chase, and La Salle's men barely escaped after wading for three days through swamps. Thereafter, they slept wrapped in their blankets, without the smallest campfire to relieve the aching chill.

Constant privation and fatigue began to take its toll. Two men became so sick they could no longer walk, and two others succumbed to pneumonia. La Salle and the last remaining healthy man carried the infirm to the relatively comfortable haven of the settlement at Niagara. While there, La Salle arranged to send fourteen or fifteen additional men, along with arms, munitions, and supplies to reinforce those he left with Tonty at Fort Crêvecoeur. Together, they should have been sufficient to repel any attack upon the fort and the vessel.

As at Fort St. Joseph, there was nothing but bad news awaiting La Salle at Niagara. He learned that the ship *St. Peter*, sent from France loaded with goods to support his enterprise, was lost in a storm in the Gulf of St. Lawrence. Twenty thousand livres worth of sorely needed merchandise irretrievably lay on the ocean floor. Furthermore, of the twenty men sent from Fort Frontenac to maintain the fort, only four remained. Frightened by the persistent rumors that La Salle would never survive to return, the others had abandoned the fort and returned to France.

All the calamities and adversities strengthened La Salle's resolve to make it to Fort Frontenac. He left Niagara at the end of April, and on May 10th, reached his goal. After seventy-one days, and 1,500 miles of traveling, the toilsome journey was over.

Though the journey was over, La Salle's misfortunes were not. Before La Salle left for his exploration of the west, he had instructed his agent to repay all the money, in the form of pelts, owed to his brother Abbé Jean Cavelier—a sum amounting to roughly 15,000 livres. Too impatient to wait for his money, Cavelier seized all the furs belonging to La Salle, which were stored in warehouses in Montréal and Québec, and sold them. About 7,000 livres went to repayment of some creditors, but the bulk of it, 15,000 livres went directly into his pocket. Other creditors, still unpaid, brought their claims to court in an attempt to collect on the amount owed them. Jean Cavelier produced letters and statements that the amount owed him by La Salle totaled 29,154 livres (which included the 7,000 livres already paid). On October 23 of 1679, the court awarded to Cavelier the amount acknowledged as due him. The value of La Salle's furs did not cover all that was owed, and in 1680 those who were still unpaid had the rest of La Salle's property and effects impounded.

By La Salle's account, he lost many more furs in the previous year than those stored in the Montréal and Québec warehouses. In a letter to an associate in La Salle's fur business, he begged indulgence for the delay in producing profit, and promised it would be forthcoming in a year or two. The fault, La Salle explained, lay in the many losses and other misfortunes in the past couple of years. He wrote: "Five or six thousand livres in goods and beaverskins were stolen by five or six rascals, at the Illinois. . . . Two other men of mine, carrying furs worth four or five thousand livres, were killed or drowned in the St. Lawrence, and the furs were lost. Another robbed me of three thousand livres in beaver-skins stored at Michillimackinac." Other property and goods, worth tens of thousands of livres were either lost or stolen.

La Salle had managed to acquire a considerable amount of furs in those early years on the St. Lawrence and in his travels on the Great Lakes. In the end, whatever money he may have made in the fur-trade was lost. By 1680 his finances were in ruin, no credit was available in Québec and Montréal, and he had a brother whom La Salle thought treacherous, "doing whatever his worst enemy would have done."

Affairs were made all the worse when two men who had come from Fort Crêvecoeur, and awaiting La Salle at Fort Frontenac, delivered a desperate message from Henry de Tonty. Almost all the men left under his command had deserted, including the very necessary shipwrights, woodworkers, and the blacksmith.

If they had departed to find a safer and easier manner of life, their insubordination would at least be understandable. After all, nothing could have prepared these men for the life they freely chose on this frontier. Back in France, in the comfort of their home, it all seemed to be a glorious adventure, filled with excitement, a chance to prove their bravery, and perchance to gain a little profit. But the reality experienced at Fort Crêvecoeur was quite different. Filled with a vindictive wrath toward the fort and all it represented, they became vandals. They raided the storehouse and stole all the goods and ammunition stored there, as well as La Salle's total accumulation of pelts. As a final measure, they weakened the defenses of the fort by destroying its palisade. Tonty, helpless and defenseless, was left dependent on the neighboring settlement for provisions. Fort Crêvecoeur could not have been more aptly named; brought to existence in misery, it ended in deceitful acts. Not content with their deeds at Fort Crêvecoeur, on their eastward travel the villains demolished Fort St. Joseph, taking the pelts stored there, and pillaged the warehouse at Niagara.

While at Fort Frontenac, news came to La Salle that some of the defectors were seen on Lake Ontario, and he promptly took out in pursuit. Of the twenty men who left Fort Crêvecoeur, he managed to capture about half. These he sent back to Fort Frontenac to be imprisoned. Two others were killed, but the remaining men who were on the opposite shore of the lake managed to escape by heading south to New York. An unfavorable wind prevented La Salle from following, and he returned to the fort. His attention was more urgently needed by Tonty.

RETURN TO THE LAND OF THE ILLINOIS

La Salle had suffered unending disappointments and was the victim of many iniquitous acts of desertion and destruction; his physical endurance was tested to the utmost. Everything accomplished since his arrival in Canada in 1669 was destroyed. The string of forts designed to expand France's ownership of western lands and protect the new settlements there were now useless. Fort Crèvecoeur, on the Illinois, was devastated by those who fled it; Fort Conti, on the Niagara, was pillaged and demolished by the very same defectors, and Fort Miamis, at the lower end of Lake Michigan was plundered. The *Griffin*, intended to plow the waves of the Upper Lakes, her hold filled with a wealth in furs for La Salle and for France, no longer existed. La Salle would not be blamed for conceding defeat, and returning to France.

Financially, La Salle was in ruin. Long ago he had sold his seigniory at La Chine to pay for the first expedition. His holdings in Montréal, Québec, and Fort Frontenac were seized for debts. Whatever furs he managed to accumulate and stored in warehouses from the St. Lawrence to Michillimack-inac were either confiscated or stolen. All that he had left to show for the eleven years of struggle was a partially constructed vessel on the stock at Fort Crèvecoeur. Even that, left open to the ravages of weather and prey to rot, was deteriorating.

Through the influence of his friend and supporter, Count Frontenac, and with aid from relatives, La Salle managed to borrow funds to purchase materials needed to finish the ship at Fort Crèvecoeur. Determined to repair the damages and continue with the grand plan which king Louis XIV had granted him, La Salle left Fort Frontenac for Fort Crèvecoeur. On the journey, he took with him twenty-five men to replace those who deserted, and shipwrights to complete the vessel in which he intended to sail down the Mississippi. When they departed, forces of violent change among the Indian Nations were already in motion.

Earlier, Iroquois war parties ranged from Hudson Bay to Florida, from the Gulf of St. Lawrence to beyond the Mississippi. Within eighty years, over 600,000 souls fell victim to their tomahawks, arrows, and guns. Those least fortunate were captured; these poor souls were tortured and roasted alive over a fire. By 1680, the Iroquois had either subjugated or destroyed the tribes south of them. They also had destroyed the Neutral Nation and the Eries, their neighbors on both sides of Lake Erie. They could not move against the Hurons and Ottawas to the north because they were protected by the French, and the Iroquois treaty of peace with France was still in effect. That left only the Illinois and Miamis to the west to vent their unceasing hostility upon.

Their normal antagonism toward these Nations was reinforced now by a strong economic drive. The Iroquois had come to depend upon the purchasing power derived from their sale of beaver pelts to the English and Dutch. As a result, the depletion of the beaver population in the east was so great, that to fill the demand for their skins the Iroquois were forced to find a new source. The most accessible and easiest way to procure more pelts was to hunt the beaver further west, where they were still plentiful—in the land of the Illinois and Miamis.

Alliances and treaties, always shifting, now took on a definite form and purpose. While ranging the countryside to hunt, chance encounters between various tribes usually resulted in quarrels or minor skirmishes. This year, hostilities erupted into open warfare. The Iroquois declared war on the Illinois, their traditional enemy, and on the Miamis. The Iroquois Five Nations, with their 2,500 warriors, numbered less than the Illinois and Miamis combined, but made up for it in the fierceness and determination to eliminate their neighbors. Not wishing to fight a battle against the combined forces of these two Nations—a battle they might lose—the Iroquois devised a strategy to fight them individually. They sent emissaries to the Miamis, with the invitation to join their raid against the Illinois. There was hardly much appeal for the Miamis in aligning with the Iroquois, yet their enmity toward the Illinois was no less strong. In the end, they agreed, thus falling into the cunning trap, which postponed, but ensured their destruction later.

In August, the same month that La Salle left Fort Frontenac, the Iroquois were moving west to attack the Illinois. It's not certain whether rumors of impending war between the Nations reached the French before they started out, but that would explain La Salle's change in route. Instead of taking one with which he was familiar, he led the men closely along the northern shore of Lake Ontario. Near its western extremity, about one hundred and eighty miles from the fort, where the Humber River enters, they left the lake and ascended the river to its headwaters near Lake Simcoe. It was then necessary to portage the remaining distance to the lake, from where they could enter the eastern end of Georgian Bay by the Severn River. This passage, a more northerly way to Lake Huron than by Lake Erie, kept them a greater distance from Iroquois territory.

The numerous anchorages, and protection from north winds, formed by the string of islands (Manitoulin Islands) separating Georgian Bay from the main body of Lake Huron, gave them an easy and comfortable passage the full length of the lake. When they reached the headland that divides Michillimackinac Strait from the Sault Sainte-Marie, La Salle first went to Sainte-Marie to see if there were any remaining pelts belonging to him, but the deserters had left nothing. He needed provisions for the rest of the trip, and tried to buy corn from the Indians, but they refused to sell. They willingly offered to sell their beaver pelts, but according to his agreement with the king he was prohibited from doing so. In this region, Jesuits ruled the buying and selling of furs. Eventually, after a delay of three weeks, the Indians capitulated and sold La Salle the necessary corn. La Salle and his men then headed toward Fort Crêvecoeur to relieve Tonty.

The Iroquois, on the war-path, were already close, and the soldiers sent to Tonty never reached Fort Crêvecoeur. On their way, the reinforcements met the deserters, who told them that nothing remained of the fort and claimed Tonty was dead. Hearing this, and concluding their journey and efforts were fruitless, they decided to go no farther and retraced their steps. Even if the unfortunate, coincidental meeting had not happened, there was little they could have done to bring succor to Tonty. There were too few of them to defend the fort against any attack. Furthermore, Tonty was in the difficult situation where he was helpless to take action, even if he had sufficient soldiers. It would be unwise to declare his association with the Iroquois against the Illinois, when he was living in their midst, and dependent upon their hospitality. And he could not side with the Illinois against the Iroquois, without breaking the treaty of peace between the French and Iroquois. His only option was to remain clear of both sides as best he could and reach the safety of the mission at Michillimackinac.

Tonty, with his few faithful followers—the two Récollet Fathers, Gabriel de la Riboarde and Zénobe Membré, along with three other Frenchmen—started their journey up the Illinois River. At the great village of the Illinois, above Lake Peoria, they stopped for sustenance, and to rest. On the 10th of September, the village was suddenly panicked by news the Iroquois were camped on the bank of the Aramoni River, only six miles away. The Illinois were scarcely prepared; more than half their warriors were away fighting battles with other tribes, and they had taken with them most of the arms and ammunition. Only three to four hundred men were left to defend the village against the greater number, and better armed, Iroquois. During the night they sent their women and children in pirogues to safety farther downstream. Also loaded in the open wooden boats were all the articles precious to the tribe.

Nicanapé, who stirred up trouble among the Illinois before by accusing La Salle of being in league with the Iroquois, made the same claims again, saying "La Salle had come to their country to hand them over to the Iroquois to eat." This time, it appeared they should give credence to his announcements. While reconnoitering the enemy camp, the scout saw a man wearing a black jacket, with black hat and stockings. By the faint, flickering of the campfire the scout mistakenly assumed him to be a Jesuit. He brought this misinformation back to the village, and claimed La Salle was also there. The news spawned a frenzy of cries for revenge against the "French traitors"—unfortunately, the closest Frenchmen were Tonty and those with him. Only by Tonty's quick and resolute actions were their lives saved. He assured the Illinois that he was on their side, and as proof, offered to lead them against the Iroquois. Somewhat placated, they agreed, and prepared for battle.

The Illinois started their attack, but Tonty immediately saw they were outnumbered and had no chance of winning. He checked the assault and proposed they instead try to gain a treaty of peace. In spite of the bullets and arrows flying about him, Tonty, unaccompanied, walked to the lodges of the warriors. At first, the infuriated braves though he was an Indian, and before they recognized the mistake, stabbed him. When they realized what they had done, they helped staunch the flow of blood from his wound and allowed him to speak. As Tonty stood before the chiefs, he declared they should recognize that "the Illinois were under the protection of the King, and the Governor of Canada," and demanded "they should be left in peace." By themselves, the words were insufficient to stop the fighting, but when he added that there were twelve-hundred Illinois, and sixty Frenchmen (a bit of exaggeration that seemed appropriate for the circumstances) ready and armed for battle, the Iroquois, seeing they had already lost the element of surprise in their raid against the Illinois, agreed to a peace.

We too, the Iroquois said, are children of the governor, and we should unite and make peace. They sent Tonty back to the Illinois with this message and a necklace of porcelain beads as affirmation. The next day the Illinois came to a meeting-place where they received presents of necklaces and other wares. As Tonty described it in his memoirs: "The first necklace signified that the Governor of New France was not angry at their having come to molest their brothers; the second, addressed to La Salle [even though he was not present] was with the same meaning; and the third, accompanied with merchandise, [indicated] they bound themselves by oath to a strict alliance, that hereafter they should live as brothers." Whereupon they separated.

The Illinois believed in the sincerity of the peace, but Tonty was more cautious and told the Illinois "they still had everything to fear," and reminded them that "they were among barbarians who did not practice in good faith." You should best leave, he said, while you still can. Several days later, the Iroquois brought Tonty and Father Membré to a council and presented them with six packets of beaver skins. The first two packets, according to Tonty: "Were to inform Frontenac that they would not eat his children [meaning the people of other tribes], and that he should not be angry at what they had done; the third was to serve as a plaster for his wound; the fourth was oil to rub on his and the Récollet Father's limbs, on account of the journeys they had taken; the fifth, that the sun was bright; the sixth, that we should depart the next day for the French settlements." Tonty refused the gifts, kicking them away, and said he did not believe their words.

The next morning they were directed to depart; a request that seemed wisest not to refuse. And then, the Iroquois forces withdrew.

The retreat was only a trick, for when the Illinois returned to their village, the Iroquois reappeared to surround them. Knowing their enemy full well, the Illinois dared not stay, and after burning the lodges, fled to join the rest of their party downstream. The Iroquois quickly inhabited what was left of the village and built themselves a makeshift fort from the remains. Tonty and the Récollets stayed in their cabin, which was saved from the fire, and tried to effect a peace between the two Nations. Finally, realizing the futility of the endeavor and the precariousness of their position, they decided to leave. In October, Tonty and his small party of Frenchmen, ascended the Illinois River to Green Bay and refuge among the Pottawattamies.

In the meantime, La Salle was still waiting at Michillimackinac for additional men and tools to finish the vessel. A rope-maker, two sailors, and a blacksmith, with oakum, sails, and munitions were on their way with Sieur de La Forest from Fort Frontenac. They had been directed to take the usual route, Lake Erie and Lake St. Clair into Lake Huron, instead of the northerly one used by La Salle, in the slight chance they might meet with Tonty along the way. When there was no sign of the men and replenishments, and the two canoes dispatched to search for them had failed to return, La Salle decided to wait no more and set out to the Illinois to find his missing friend.

At the beginning of October, La Salle, with twelve men, headed toward the St. Joseph River. This year, the weather was so severe, with such strong winds and rain, that the journey took a full month. Finding no one at the fort, they continued south, and by the end of November reached the confluence of the Kankakee and Illinois Rivers. Everywhere along the way La Salle looked for indications that Tonty and his small group had passed this way; all he saw, instead, was the rage of the Iroquois as they overtook and massacred the Illinois. At the great village, he beheld charred stakes where the captured had been burned to death; the heads of most of the victims fixed to the top of the pole, to be devoured by crows. Gruesome as the task was, La Salle carefully checked every carcass, half-gnawed by wolves, and every cadaverous head, to see if he could recognize Tonty.

As he moved down-river, La Salle investigated the Illinois and Iroquois encampments for any indication of the Frenchmen's presence. He found none, nor was there any evidence of conflict; with each advancement of their foe, the Illinois had retreated closer toward the Mississippi. Then, at a camping place on the plain below Fort Crêvecoeur, the ferocity, and enormity of Iroquois cruelty lay before him. The Tamaroas, a tribe of the Illinois, had not escaped and suffered the consequences. Women and children were everywhere, their mutilated and burned bodies still tied to the stakes. Like pigs, children were roasted on a spit, and parts of bodies still remained in the kettles which had been placed over a fire. Again, a careful search of the remains failed to produce Tonty, and with mounting anxiety, La Salle departed.

When at last he reached the mouth of the Illinois River, where it empties into the Mississippi, La Salle felt he should go no farther and turned back. By the middle of December the river was frozen solid and their canoes were no longer of use. They made sledges to transport the four thousand pounds of possessions over the ice, and through the snow, in search of Tonty. At the junction of the Illinois and Kankakee Rivers, he ascended the Kankakee a short distance, but found no evidence of Tonty there, and concluded he must have followed the Illinois River instead. To lighten the load and hasten the search, La Salle left all his belongings, including the canoes, in a well-concealed spot, while two of his men stayed to guard everything.

DOUBTFUL FUTURE

La Salle and the remaining five men spent the month of January, the frigid heart of winter, with its severe cold, and unending violent winds, pushing their way through waist-deep snow to reach Fort Miami. Here, he found himself in the midst of the Indian conflicts and had to suspend his quest for Tonty and devote his time negotiating a peace.

Of utmost importance was the need to reconcile the differences between the Illinois and the Miamis; there was much at stake if the two Nations failed to unite in peace. La Salle's ability to protect his own settlement, and the Frenchmen living there among the Miamis, depended on it. Once the Iroquois finished exterminating the Illinois tribes, their attention would quickly turn to the destruction of the Miamis. If he could bring the Miamis and Illinois together, their combined strength would keep the Iroquois in check and prevent further attacks. If the Iroquois were not prevented from incursions into western lands, it would likely follow that the English would do so also, and this was equally threatening to French occupation. Without peace in Canada, La Salle could not carry out his grand scheme of expansion, settlement, and trade in the western lands of New France. Lying halfway between the established Canada of the north and La Salle's intended colonization at the mouth of the Mississippi, peace in the land of the Illinois was the bridge to success of a consolidated New France. In the following months, several events helped him to carry out this endeavor.

When the raiding Iroquois returned to their homeland, while passing through the Miamis territory they came upon several Miamis lodges, and captured the inhabitants who were there engaged in hunting. When the chiefs heard about what their supposed allies had done, they sent delegates to try to free their compatriots, offering beaver pelts in exchange for the captives. The Iroquois accepted the gifts, but did not return the prisoners, and the Miamis now began to see the error they had made in aligning themselves with the perfidious Iroquois.

At the same time, one hundred braves of the Kaskaskia tribe of the Illinois returned to the great village, where they witnessed the carnage and overthrow of the Tamaroas. Appalled, outraged, and wanting revenge, they took chase after the Iroquois and caught up with them near Fort Miami. Though the Illinois were far outnumbered, they made four attacks on their foe before retiring from battle and moving on toward Lake Erie to kill other Iroquois hunters. The losses on both sides were minimal, but it had a great effect upon the Miamis who were heartened by the Illinois bravery. The Miamis decided to join the Illinois.

The moment was now appropriate for La Salle to go among the Illinois and negotiate a treaty. On the first day of March, he set out on snow-shoes, taking with him fifteen men on his mission of peace. Along the way they came upon a camp of eighty lodges of the Outagoumi Nation, where they were well received. This in itself was comforting, but the greater joy came from the news they were given that Tonty and the Frenchmen had survived and were safely living among the Pottawattamies at Green Bay. Additionally, Father Louis Hennepin, sent to explore the upper Mississippi, had also returned without harm from the land of the Nadouessious (Sioux) and was in Montréal. La Salle now shed the burden of anxiety he carried with him, fearing the loss of those who had struggled so valiantly alongside him and shared his dreams.

He sent a canoe, commanded by La Forest, to let Tonty know he should go on to Michillimackinac and wait for him there. La Forest was to then go back to Fort Frontenac and bring additional supplies and men to Michillimackinac. With gladdened heart, La Salle proceeded to the Illinois and urged them to make peace with the Miamis. The two of you, as one, he said, would become "invincible and formidable to all your enemies." The Frenchmen who would come to live with you then would further ensure the peace. The Illinois accepted his proposals, and the council ended with the usual dancing and feasting.

Back at the village of the Miamis, La Salle called for a grand council. The elaborate ceremony, in which he gave them many gifts and used his power of oratory, now finely adjusted to the manners and usage of the Indians, concluded with their approval of La Salle's entreaties. The Miamis accepted the Illinois as their brothers and promised to live in peace with them. They also acknowledged the king of France as their master and were glad to have his protection. Alone, and against insurmountable odds, La Salle had resolved life-long feuds and restored peace among the many Indian Nations occupying French Canada. It was now time, he felt, to continue his discoveries and follow the Mississippi River to the Gulf of Mexico.

On May 25th, La Salle left Fort Miami to rejoin Tonty and collect the supplies awaiting him at Michillimackinac. The weather was fair, the voyage a quick one, and at last he was happily re-united with Henry Tonty and the Récollet Zénobe Membré. The other Récollet, Father Gabriel, he learned had been killed by some Kickapoos shortly after they left the great village of the Illinois. There was no way, however, that La Salle could begin another expedition to the Mississippi from Michillimackinac. La Forest was negligent and had not sent the supplies, as directed, leaving the three men with no choice but to paddle their canoe the thousand miles back to Fort Frontenac.

Despite all the disasters, miseries, wasted energies, and lost wealth, La Salle persevered. Father Membré wrote: "Anyone else would have thrown up his hand and abandoned the enterprise; but, far from this, with a firmness and constancy, that never had its equal, I saw him [La Salle] more resolved than ever to continue his work and push forward his discovery."

PART IV

Descent to the Great River's Mouth

A gainst insurmountable odds, La Salle was determined to descend to the mouth of the Mississippi River. Financial ruin, hardship to the utmost limit of human endurance, deceits by those he trusted, and incessant wars among the Indian nations could not prevent La Salle from pursuing his cherished goal. By creating a string of trading-posts and military forts at strategic points on the Great Lakes, and along the length of the Mississippi River, he would dominate trade in the west, and present to his monarch a New France that extended from the St. Lawrence River to the Gulf of Mexico. Reaching the mouth of the Mississippi and establishing a settlement there would not only guarantee recognition among the nations of Europe of France's ownership of this vast territory, but also provide French ships with a port on the Gulf of Mexico and easy access to the interior of America. If his grand enterprise was successful, it would add to the greater glory of France—and not immeasurably, to the wealth of La Salle.

The information brought back from Jolliet and Marquette's exploration left little doubt that the Mississippi River emptied into the Gulf of Mexico rather than the Vermilion Sea. It also showed it was not the hoped for Northwest Passage leading to the riches of Cathay. Yet, the possibility still existed that somewhere near the mouth of the Mississippi, there might be another river or stream, flowing westward, providing a navigable way to the Pacific Ocean.

La Salle faced the recurrent problem of getting the funds for this, his third expedition to the Mississippi. Again, Count Frontenac, ever his supporter, came to his aid and provided some of the capital, while the rest came from one of his wealthy relatives. There were, however, past debts that needed to be paid. He still owed money for his previous expeditions and for the building and maintenance of Fort Frontenac. In addition, mortgages were due that he had taken out on the fort and his seigniory there. By signing away some of his monopolies in the western frontier—monopolies that produced no income yet—La Salle was able to appease his creditors and finance the expedition.

As soon as La Salle returned to Fort Frontenac he made preparations for the journey. Accompanying him on the voyage were Henry de Tonty, his trusted partner and second-in-command; thirty Frenchmen, including his brother, Abbé Jean Cavelier, and the Franciscan Récollet, Father Zénobe Membré; as well as more than a hundred Indians. If necessary, La Salle intended to augment these numbers when he reached the country of the Miamis and Illinois.

In order not to repeat the problems and failures of his previous journeys, La Salle aimed to do things differently this time. He would always keep the group intact, instead of sending off small, advance parties to prepare the way. This way, there would be no loss of any possessions due to the malicious acts of those entrusted with them, nor would needless time be lost waiting or searching for those delayed in meeting at a rendezvous. There would be only a single leader of all the men—La Salle. Although the size of the expedition, and the length of the voyage, required large amounts of provisions, he decided not to burden himself by additionally carrying materials to build another ship. After the despair of losing the *Griffin* and destruction of the second vessel at Fort Crêvecoeur, La Salle postponed his ambitions to build a ship for plying the Mississippi. Traveling solely by canoe, he would shorten the duration of the voyage to the Great River's mouth. In his words, this time he "hoped to bring his undertaking to a happy conclusion."

Confident that his endeavor would turn out well, La Salle and his men plied their paddles along the now familiar northern shore of Lake Erie. They could hardly allow themselves the luxury of admiring the autumnal foliage, with its startling contrast of golden patches of poplar and birch, set amongst the dense, black-green of spruce and fir. Winter would soon arrive, and it was best to be as far south as possible. They left the lake at its western end and ascended the Humber River to its headwaters; there, it was necessary to portage all their baggage to Lake Simcoe, from where the Severn River gave access to Georgian Bay. It was October before they reached the bay, and the days—days that were filled with memories of a ruinous past—stretched on endlessly as the heavily laden canoes made their way along the shore toward Michillimackinac and Lake Michigan.

At length they came to the settlement of the Miamis on the St. Joseph River. Their canoes had not yet been wetted by the waters of the Mississippi, and of the original thirty Frenchmen, seven had already deserted. These, La Salle replaced with more Indians—some Shawanoes of the Ohio Valley and some Abenaki and Mohegan allies from New England, who moved to the village of the Miamis to gain protection from Iroquois brutality. They would not agree to joining La Salle, however, unless they could take their squaws and children with them. When the journey resumed on the 21st of December, there were fifty-four persons altogether, of whom "some were useless, and others a burden."

Instead of using a portage between the St. Joseph and Kankakee Rivers to reach the Illinois, as La Salle had done before, he instead chose to cross Lake Michigan to the Chicago River and from there portage to the Des Plaines River. At this time of the year all the waters were frozen solid and sledges had to be built to carry the canoes and all the belongings. These they dragged over the ice and through the snow all the way to the Illinois River—a distance of two hundred and forty miles. Even then, open water did not appear until they were below Lake Peoria. Along the way they passed the site of the great Illinois village, now a forlorn, abandoned relic, provoking more memories of disaster and sorrow.

Once the arctic grip of winter relinquished its hold on the rivers, and the waters were open to be freely navigated, the party of explorers made rapid progress. What current the river had was in their favor, there were no rapids or waterfalls to portage around, and no inter-tribal wars delayed them. At the end of January1682, they reached the confluence of the Illinois and Mississippi Rivers. Here, La Salle had to curb his desire to immediately enter the Great River and hasten to the Gulf. Not all in the group were equally adept at handling their canoes, and over a period of time, stragglers fell behind. He had to wait for them to catch up, in order to travel as a unified group as planned. Then too, the Mississippi was filled with masses of thick, floating ice that could not be evaded, and would easily split apart their frail birch-bark canoes.

Until the remainder of the party caught up and the river was safe for navigation, the Frenchmen made a small encampment ashore. There they built a fire from the supply of driftwood that lay about, killed and cooked the plentiful game, and patiently waited for the Boreal winds and congeries of ice to diminish. After a week's delay, they were able to safely re-embark. At last, after striving for thirteen years, La Salle entered the Great River of the Mississippi. In honor of Jean-Baptiste Colbert, minister to the king, he renamed the river *Fleuve Colbert*.

Tonty's memoir makes no mention of their encounter with the violent discharge of the Missouri River, an event that can scarcely be ignored. When Father Marquette passed the Missouri effluent nine years earlier, he wrote that he had never seen anything more frightful: "A mass of large trees, entire with branches, real floating islands, came rushing from the mouth of the Pekitunoui [Missouri] so impetuously that we could not, without great danger, expose ourselves to pass across."

Travel became easier as they glided down the slow-moving body of water, free of all dangers. They continued beyond the entrance of the Missouri River, where its chocolate-brown, mud-filled water vehemently burst into the Mississippi; past the Ohio River, used by the Iroquois to reach, and make war upon the nations of the south; finally coming to a halt at the Third Chickasaw Bluff, near the present-day city of Memphis. Here, about one hundred and eighty miles from the Ohio River, there was another pause while they had to build a fort and search for a missing man.

Pierre Prudhomme, officially in charge of arms for the expedition, became separated from the rest of the group while hunting and lost himself in the woods. Fearing that he had been attacked and killed by the Indians, La Salle set some of his men to building a small stockade, while others sought their missing companion. Six days later, the would-be rescuers still had not found him and became apprehensive when they came upon two members of the Chickasaw tribe. Thinking that the missing man might have been captured by the Chickasaws, La Salle sent gifts and messages of peace to their village in order to obtain his return. The Frenchmen were assured that they had not seen the man they were searching for, but that peace would be received by the elders, with all kind of recognition. Three days later, Prudhomme was found floating down the river on a log, half-dead from starvation, and brought back to the camp. In gratitude for a safe return, La Salle christened the fort with his name—Fort Prudhomme. Too weak to continue the journey, Pierre Prudhomme and a few other Frenchmen were left in charge of the new fort, while the rest of the party resumed the voyage.

The weather improved, and seemingly in conjunction with the beneficence of a warming sun and budding spring, the peoples they encountered along the banks of the river—tribes of the Arkansas, Tensas, Natchez, Coroas, and the Oumas—opened the warmth of their hospitality to the travelers. In all the villages, they were entertained with ceremonies, dancing, and feasting. There was the usual presentation of gifts, for which La Salle received in exchange an abundance of provisions. The festivities were heightened by the Frenchmen who put on their form of ceremony for the Arkansas Indians. In the middle of the village they erected an immense cross, and in canonicals, offered prayers, sang hymns, and displayed all the splendor of religious rites. The missionaries attempted to teach the Indians the way of the cross and how to achieve salvation by adopting their religion. Father Membré believed he made some headway in Christianizing the Indians and wrote: "During this time they showed that they relished what I said by raising their eyes to heaven, and kneeling as if to adore."

With the same fervor displayed by those converting the Indians to the True Faith, La Salle thrust upon them allegiance to a new temporal leader—King Louis XIV. The arms of the king of France were attached to a post or tree, the *Te Deum* was sung, and with shouts of *Vive le Roi* (Long live the King), La Salle took formal possession of the land.

At the village called Ostouy, they met with the same friendly reception and were given guides to safely conduct them to the neighboring tribe of the Taensas, three hundred miles below the Arkansas. As they neared the end of their journey, two incidents marred the otherwise uneventful trip. One was an encounter with the hostile Quinnipissa (a tribe of the Choctaw), who, when approached by some of La Salle's men with signs of peaceful intent, let fly a barrage of arrows in response. The impact of one of these barbed weapons, which could be shot with almost the velocity and precision of a rifle bullet, would easily pierce their birch-bark canoes, not to mention drill a lethal hole in a human body.

La Salle had no intention of engaging in battle and ordered his men to withhold their fire, paddle to the opposite side of the river, and hastily flee from the peril. It was apparent that even if they were to show their superiority in combat and kill a number of warriors of this inhospitable tribe, there was another day to be reckoned with. The Quinnipissas could not be avoided on the return trip homeward; then, La Salle's men would meet an enraged tribe, eager for revenge. Any attempt later to establish a peaceful relationship would be difficult.

Six miles down river they came upon the ravaged village of Tangibao. For an hour, in silent contemplation, the procession of canoes passed by the smoldering remains of dwellings; the stench of decaying bodies from a brutal massacre, and demoniac torture, filling their nostrils. No one needed reminding that the apparent peace in this part of New France could quickly and easily be shattered. Colonization in the southernmost part of France's empire would be as arduous as among the Iroquois in the north.

THE GREAT ENTERPRISE
ACCOMPLISHED

The next four days were free of mishap, as the turbid current slowly propelled their descent of the river. Signs began to appear that the journey was now nearing its end. The shores were low and marshy, with no landmarks, and the water began to take on a brackish taste. On the 6th of April the band of explorers were upon the broad delta of the Mississippi, where the river divides into the three channels by which it enters the sea. Here, about nine miles from the mouth, they made camp. The next morning La Salle divided his fleet into three groups to explore each of the three channels. Mr. Dautray, one of La Salle's trusted followers, who had assisted him in his search for de Tonty in 1680, was assigned the eastern branch. Tonty and Father Membré were to take the great middle channel; while La Salle took the western channel. It was assumed that the middle channel would be the shortest, and that Tonty and his party would reach the ocean before the others. Accordingly, they were to wait there until Dautray and La Salle were finished with their exploration and could join them. No more welcome sight could have greeted them than to finally behold the open sea.

Safely reunited, La Salle listened to reports about the other two channels. All reported the same findings; that is, the channels were very fine, wide, and deep. Then, all the canoes ascended the western channel to find dry and solid ground upon which to camp. The next morning, the 9th of April, on a slightly elevated knoll, they all assembled for the ceremony that culminated a journey of over two thousand, five hundred miles. A massive pillar was erected, and upon it was painted the arms of France, with the legend:

Louis the Great, King of France and Navarre,
reigns the 9th of April, 1682

There were rounds of musket fire, shouts of "Long live the King!" and together they sang the *Te Deum*, the *l'Exaudiat*, and *Domine salvum fac Regem*. Beneath the pillar they placed a lead plaque bearing on one side the arms of France, with the Latin inscription: "Louis the Great reigns 9th of April, 1682," and on the other side "Robert Cavelier, with Lord Tonty—ambassador, Zenobio Membré—Recollét, and twenty Frenchmen, first navigated this river from the country of the Illinois, and passed through this mouth on the ninth of April, sixteen hundred and eighty-two."

In a loud voice to the gathering throng, La Salle proclaimed: "On the part of the very-high, very-powerful, very-invincible and victorious Prince Louis the Great, by the grace of God King of France and Navarre, fourteenth of this name, today, April 9, 1682, I, by virtue of the commission of His Majesty, which I have in my hand, ready to present it to whom it could belong, have taken and do take possession in the name of His Majesty and successors of his crown, of this country of Louisiana, seas, harbors, ports, bays, adjacent straits and all its nations, peoples, provinces, cities, boroughs, villages, mines, ore-bearing earth, fishing waters, salt-water rivers, rivers, included in the extent of the said Louisiana, from the mouth of the great Saint-Louis River from the east coast, formerly called the Ohio, Olighinispou, or Chukagoua, and that with the consent of the Chaouesnons, Chicaachas [Chickasaws] and other peoples living there with whom we have made alliance, as well as along the Colbert River, or Mississippi, and rivers which discharge from its origin in the country of the Sioux or Nadouesious, and with their consent and that of the Ototantas, Islinois, Matsigamea, Akansas, Natchez, Koroas, who are the most considerable nations and who abide there, with whom we have made alliance by us or people from our side, up to its mouth in the sea or Gulf of Mexico, around 27 degrees elevation [latitude] from the North Pole to the mouth of the Palmes, on the assurance we have had from all these nations that we are the first Europeans who have come down or gone up the said Colbert River. A protest against all those who would like in the future to undertake to seize all or each of the said countries, peoples, grounds, hereby specified, to the detriment of the rights that His Majesty has acquired here with the consent of the said nations, of whatever and of all occasion will be, take as witness those who hear me and request of it an act from the notary present in order to serve as reason."

All was duly noted and recorded by Jacques de La Métairie, official notary for the expedition, and signed by witnesses of the expedition.

La Salle's deep religious convictions impelled him to add that he would not acquire any country for his monarch unless he could establish the Christian religion and plant a sign of it here; whereupon an immense cross was erected next to the pillar. They performed rites of the Catholic Church, and everyone sang the hymns of *Vexilla Regis* and *Domine salvam fac Regem*.

"La Salle Proclaiming the French America" *Photo: courtesy of the Dallas Historical Society, Dallas, Texas.*

The civil ceremony and religious service thus concluded, once more there was a salute of firearms and shouts of *Vive le Roi!* With these acts France acquired all the land drained by the Mississippi River and its tributaries—a region of over one million square miles. Jolliet and Marquette had led the way when they explored the Mississippi to Arkansas, but it was René-Robert, Sieur de la Salle, who in reaching the outpouring of the Mississippi into the Gulf of Mexico, gave to the King of France a land three times greater than France itself. In honor of King Louis XIV, he named the country "Louisiana."

After formal possession of the land was taken, there was little desire to linger there. The low-lying, swampy coast held scant appeal, and provisions were running low. The reedy banks of the river prevented their setting foot ashore to hunt, but they sustained themselves by killing and eating the plentiful beasts of the river—the crocodile. This dreadful looking creature was totally alien to the experiences of the Frenchmen, and only the utmost necessity compelled them to add it to their diet. Father Membré was astonished that such a large beast should emerge forth, like a chicken, from an egg. Another aquatic giant, the Paddlefish (*Polydon spathula*) provided them food. This incredible looking fish, North America's largest freshwater fish, has existed for over 300 million years. With a body shaped somewhat like a tuna, it has as its most distinguishing characteristic a greatly elongated snout resembling a canoe paddle. Marquette and Jolliet saw them during their expedition and fully described their unique appearance. Fortunately for La Salle and his men, at this time of the year the Paddlefish were spawning, and close inshore where they were easily killed by axes and swords, so precious powder and shot were not wasted.

The fear engendered by the crocodiles, that they would attack their canoes, was matched by fear of yet another danger. Certain that they were close to the Spanish settlements in Mexico, they wished to depart before they had that foe to contend with and turned the bow of their canoes upriver. Keeping as close to the shore as possible to avoid the river's current, the voyagers returned toward the source of the Mississippi.

Again they passed the stricken village of Tangibao, a place obviously unsafe to halt, and continued toward the land of the Quinnipissa tribe. Experience

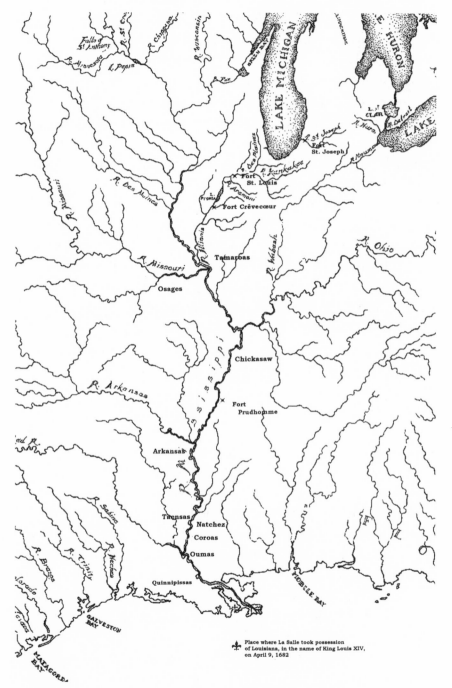

Place where La Salle took possession
of Louisiana, in the name of King Louis XIV,
on April 9, 1682

1681/82 Expedition. Expedition of La Salle to the mouth of the Mississippi River.

with these treacherous scoundrels was sufficient warning that the quicker they were beyond them, and reached the Natchez (where on the way down they had stored a cache of grain), the better. Provisions were so low, however, that they were forced to try to gain alliance with the Quinnipissas. As before, the show of peaceful intent by the Frenchmen gained nothing but another attack. This time, La Salle could no longer withhold his fire, and he vigorously repulsed the warriors. He smashed their canoes, and would have continued the fight by destroying their village were it not that it would have used up too much ammunition.

With the current against them, the flotilla of canoes moved more slowly now, yet the adventurers relentlessly pursued their course. Time spent in the fever-breeding swamps, however, had taken its toll, and La Salle fell dangerously ill. By the time he reached Fort Prudhomme, he could no longer bear the canoeing and decided to interrupt his journey. Father Membré remained behind to help restore La Salle to health, while Tonty and the others continued onward to Michillimackinac. La Salle would rejoin them when he was sufficiently recovered. But it was not until September, forty days later, that he was well enough to make the journey.

As La Salle passed Fort Crêvecoeur, now in ruins and desolate, he resolved to rebuild it. Fort Crêvecoeur was intended as the center of New France in the West; a base for storage of furs, and their transport to France by way of the Mississippi, as well as a primary defense against Iroquois incursions into the land of the Illinois. La Salle did not plan to remain in New France another winter, so he charged Tonty with the task of rebuilding the fort. In a letter to a friend in France, he said: "in my present condition, this [staying the winter] would be an act of suicide on account of the bad nourishment I should have all winter." In Michillimackinac, however, he altered his plans upon receiving warnings that the Iroquois were again planning to attack the Illinois and other western tribes. La Salle decided to rejoin Tonty and aid him in strengthening the defenses at Fort Crêvecoeur, for if it were destroyed, it would be the end of his Grand Enterprise.

At Fort Crêvecoeur, the two men reconsidered the site and felt it was not as defensible as originally thought. Instead, they chose another location farther upstream. At *Le Rocher* (now known as Starved Rock) they built a new fort, giving it the name of Fort St. Louis. On top of a steep cliff, a hundred and twenty-five feet above the water, La Salle and Tonty erected storehouses, dwellings, and a high timber palisade that surrounded it all. Accessible from only one direction by a steep, narrow pathway, it was virtually impregnable to attack.

La Salle's leadership, and his ability to inspire faith and trust in the Indians, generated the growth of a new settlement in the valley below the garrison. The Illinois, now protected by the French, returned to this, their favored dwelling place. The Miamis from the Kankakee River, the Shawnees from the Ohio, and Abenakis from Maine (driven westward by English harassment, as exiles from their native land) swelled the population to twenty thousand, including four thousand warriors. Threat of attack by the Iroquois ceased, and the settlement prospered under a new, albeit unstable, peace. La Salle, through his rights granted by King Louis XIV, reigned as feudal lord over all. As yet, though, his monopolies yielded no profits for himself, or his backers.

Those who accompanied La Salle on his journey to the sea had high praise for the country they saw. Father Zénobe Membré wrote: "The great river Mississippi is very beautiful in all places, without any fall or rapid from the Arkansas to the sea. . . . The blessings of the earth come there so happily that at the end of April the Indian wheat [corn] was in bloom at the Coroas, and the blossoms as high as poles. It is here the country of canes, laurels, and palms; there is an infinity of mulberry trees, of which we eat the fruit every day from the beginning of May. In fifty days the wheat ripens." Henry de Tonty agreed with Membré in admiration of the fruitfulness of the land, with its abundance of buffalo and other game.

For all the accolades bestowed upon this new land, not everything was ideally suited to La Salle's grand enterprise. Although the Mississippi was open to navigation from the Gulf of Mexico, the many windings of the river prevented large vessels from sailing above the village of the Natchez. There was no reason, however, wrote Tonty, that pirogues or flatboats could not be used to carry furs from the country of the Illinois down toward the sea, and then transferred to a ship.

AN INGLORIOUS SEQUEL

Rather than the enthusiastic response one might expect by the news of La Salle's great achievement, there was instead a cautious holding back by some persons, disbelief by others, and outright resentment by a few. The eminent Father Superiors of Montréal and Québec saw the opening of new lands as a fine opportunity to bring the Gospel to countless more heathens. They were not willing, though, to hasten and create new missions in such far away places. The missionaries were practical enough to realize that it could not be done without the king's involvement. Unless he established French colonies to help support and sustain the missions, the enterprise was doomed to failure. The Father's response was to bide their time and patiently wait for a response from the king. They would be ready to go to the new lands in the West "as soon as the Lord makes overtures toward it." Whether the country was established, or their wishes accomplished mattered little, provided the Lord was glorified.

Abbé Tronson, Superior of the Community of St. Sulpice, summarized the diverse feelings about La Salle's discoveries, when he wrote: "M. de La Salle had made a great discovery. He was in a very fertile, populated country, and went down by the river of the Illinois from Mississippi to the Mexican territory. Several say that this discovery could do harm to Canada, and others [say] that it is useless. All of them nevertheless, do not agree, and there are some who believe it very advantageous. As he had undertaken it by order of M. Colbert, he gave an account of it to the King. We shall see in very short time what success it shall have." He also commented in a letter to the Abbé of Belmont, that: "Louisiana has not had great popularity here . . . there's not much around of La Salle's discovery." The truth of La Salle's discovery was being appraised; people waited for confirmation of the voyage and to see whether things were as he represented them. It took two more years, and word that the king had heard him and was well pleased, before those in New France shed their doubts about the great achievement of La Salle.

Count Frontenac, always the staunchest supporter in La Salle's explorations and settlement of the western lands, no longer was able to come to his aid. During the expedition, disagreements between Frontenac and the Intendant, Duchesneau, grew more rancorous. Their respective powers, which were never clearly defined and which overlapped in some areas, became public battles for control. News of this soon reached the king. Both persons were relieved of their duties and recalled to France.

In place of Count Frontenac, his Majesty assigned an old naval officer, Le Febvre de la Barre, as the new governor and lieutenant-general of New France. The policies set by La Barre for Canada were directly opposite those of his predecessor; partially the result of the king's instructions, and in part due to his own avarice. King Louis XIV was no longer interested in expanding France's empire in the west, preferring instead, that efforts be directed toward cultivating the land already in their possession. He directed La Barre to withhold any further permission "to make journeys of discovery towards the Sious and the Mississippi." This was not applicable to La Salle, who was allowed to continue his explorations if they appeared to serve a useful purpose.

In his new post, La Barre allied himself with the Jesuits, who were rivals of La Salle and jealous of his success in the beaver trade. That his predecessor, Frontenac, sided with the Franciscans, and was a close friend of La Salle, induced La Barre to move against La Salle. He wrote letters to Colbert, spreading malicious rumors that La Salle had not reached the mouth of the Mississippi and was misrepresenting himself and his discoveries to the king. He extended his hostility by sending false reports to the king about La Salle's honesty and claimed that La Salle had deserted Fort Frontenac. Even the reports of La Salle's discoveries were said to be untrue. His only intention, reported La Barre, was to remain in the land of the Illinois and create his own profitable empire—an empire already in danger of downfall by abandonment of the French, and attack by the Iroquois.✚ "By exposing the Illinois and Miamis in the west to incursions by the Iroquois," he said, "he was about to involve the colony in war."

✚ A newly established Fort of Chicago, on the banks of that river, by the Jesuits, was an additional thorn to La Salle's enterprise, for it diminished revenue from the sale of furs away from Fort St. Louis.

Seeds of La Barre's malicious falsehoods were planted at Versailles and took root. The king responded to his new governor: "I am convinced, like you, that the discovery of the Sieur de la Salle is very useless, and that such enterprises ought to be prevented in future, as they tend only to debauch the inhabitants by the hope of gain, and to diminish the revenue from beaver-skins." It was all that La Barre needed to justify, in his own mind, the seizing of Fort Frontenac, and all the property belonging to La Salle.

For nearly a year, La Salle remained at Fort St. Louis, administering to the settlement and watching over his profits from the fur-trade. At the same time, in Québec, La Barre was quickly stripping him of all he owned. He seized Fort Frontenac on the pretext that La Salle failed to maintain and defend the fort, as the king required when granting him the property. His possessions were sold, with the proceeds going to La Barre.

When Louis later learned the truth, he sent a stern letter to La Barre, in which he rebuked him for his falsehoods. "I am satisfied," he said "that Fort Frontenac was not abandoned, as you wrote to me it had been," and told La Barre to return Fort Frontenac to La Salle, as well as all other of his belongings that he had seized. To ensure compliance, he let the Intendant of Canada, De Meales, know that La Barre was "to surrender . . . without reserve, all that belongs to La Salle." La Forest, La Salle's lieutenant, was dispatched from Paris to take command of Fort Frontenac, as well as Fort St. Louis of the Illinois. Without Fort St. Louis, the whole purpose of a settlement at the mouth of the Mississippi for trade and colonization was meaningless. La Barre's attempts to discredit the discoveries and actions of the explorer were silenced.

The Iroquois, prompted by the Dutch and English traders to wage war on the Nations of the western lands, posed a problem to La Barre. If successful in their conquest of the Miamis and Illinois, they would gain control of the fur-trade in the interior of America, and profits would be diverted from the French Colony—and the pockets of La Barre—to Albany. This would bring financial ruin to Canada. Yet it would also cause the much desired undoing of his rival, La Salle. In the end, personal interests and rivalry took precedence over La Barre's concern for the larger entity of New France. At a conference with the Iroquois, he arranged in exchange for a peace at the towns along the St. Lawrence River, permission for the Iroquois to plunder Fort St. Louis and kill La Salle. Later, when recalled to

France, he vigorously denied these accusations. Emboldened by his successes, La Barre sent an officer to Fort St. Louis with the message that he was now taking possession of the fort, and La Salle, relieved of his command, was to return to Québec. In his place, Chevalier de Baugis, an officer in the king's Dragoons, would take control.

Unable to obtain the supplies and men needed to support Fort St. Louis from an impending attack by the Iroquois, a defeat that would mean the end of his great enterprise, La Salle left for France to seek justice and recompense from the Court. He would inform the king of the importance of supporting Fort St. Louis, and the need to strengthen France's hold in North America by establishing a colony at the mouth of the Mississippi River. Additionally, he planned to ask that Fort Frontenac, Fort Miami, and Fort St. Louis all be returned to him.

Placing Henry de Tonty in charge of Fort St. Louis, La Salle set out in a single canoe, with two Indian companions, for Québec, and from there sail to France. Along the way he met De Baugis and the fleet of thirty canoes filled with traders and soldiers, headed toward Fort St. Louis. There was too much at stake for La Salle to risk losing the entire enterprise solely to save his control of this one fort, and when he reached Fort Chicago, dispatched a note to Tonty telling him to accept the authority of De Baugis. With De Baugis as commander, and Tonty reduced to merely a representative of La Salle, the two shared in the charge of Fort St. Louis. Without stopping at Québec to try and resolve the numerous conflicts with La Barre, La Salle immediately sailed for France, where he landed at La Rochelle on January 7, 1684.

PART V

Geographic Knowledge Expanded

THE GULF OF MEXICO

Before La Salle left Canada, he dispatched a letter from Michillimackinac, which preceded him to France. He described his descent of the Mississippi and emphasized the importance of that
river as a means to easily transport goods—primarily buffalo-skins and
beaver-pelts—from the interior of the continent. A colony established at
the mouth of the Mississippi was not only essential to his economic interests, but would support the claim by his monarch of possession of the territory of Louisiana. In this letter, one hears for the first time, additional
reasons for the new French colony.

He wrote that the fertility of the land, and temperate climate, would
make it easy to sustain a colony on the Gulf of Mexico, and went on to say:
"Seven or eight rivers of considerable size discharge [into the Mississippi],
of which there are five flowing from New Biscay and New Mexico where
the Spaniards have found so many mines. One would be able from there to
annoy notably—*and even ruin entirely*—New Spain." Stated simply, this was
but a murmur of what soon would rise to a crescendo in proposals for the
conquest of New Spain.

Such ideas, however, did not spring anew from the pen of La Salle. In

1678, the king's minister, Colbert, testified that "It was important to the glory and service of the King *to find a harbor for his vessels in the Mexican Gulf.*" Presumably, the purpose of a harbor on the gulf was to protect French vessels in their right to free navigation in the Gulf of Mexico and legitimate trade in the West Indies. Colbert went somewhat beyond this, though, when he said he wanted a base "where the French could establish themselves and harass the Spaniards."

There were designs upon the Spanish, other than attacking their ships at sea. When King Louis gave permission to La Salle to discover the western part of New France, it was as much to "find a route to penetrate as far as Mexico," as it was for colonization. The expedition of Jolliet and Marquette had already suggested that the mouth of the Mississippi was close to Spanish settlements in the West. It was the fear of being captured by the Spanish and put to death, or worse yet, being made their slaves, that settled their decision to end the exploration and return to Canada. They had already determined that the Mississippi entered the Gulf of Mexico, and not the Vermilion Sea, or even into the Sea of Virginia (Chesapeake), as had been conjectured by some. To continue the voyage to where the river entered the sea, and lose their lives doing so, would not add anything further to their discovery, but only deprive France of the knowledge they already gained. The king envisioned the possibility that one of the rivers entering the lower Mississippi might provide a route where the gold and silver mines in New Biscay, the most northerly Mexican province, could be reached and seized.

When La Salle was in France in 1678 to gain the king's approval to explore the western part of the continent, he met two men who now would play a role in furthering his plans. Eusèbe Renaudot and Abbé Claude Bernou were influential in France and had powerful connections with the court. Renaudot was greatly interested in the new discoveries in North America. As editor of *La Gazette de France,* the first French newspaper, he had a ready-made vehicle with which to express his views, and his contacts with important nobles gave him direct access to the king. Abbé Bernou, a French priest in the employ of Cardinal d'Estreés, had similar interests in exploration, geography, and the development of French colonies. Both men shared an intense dislike for the Jesuit Order and took every opportunity to discredit their works. By promoting the accomplishments of La Salle, and the Récollets, they saw the means to diminish the importance of the Jesuits in New France, and at the same time further their own special interests.

Abbé Bernou envisioned a plan whereby New France would be split into two separate colonies; one, in the north, with its already established settlements—tied to France through the St. Lawrence; the other, the territory of Louisiana, with the Mississippi River and Gulf of Mexico as its connection to France. If this happened, Bernou thought it might even be possible to persuade the church authorities to make him the bishop in the newly created Louisiana territory.

At the same time La Salle sought his commission, Bernou was actively engaged presenting to the court the proposal of a Spaniard named Diego de Peñalosa. Born in Peru, Peñalosa served as administrator in the Spanish colonies of South America. While governor of New Mexico he was recalled to Mexico City to face trial by the Inquisition. In 1664, Peñalosa was tried and found guilty of blasphemy and heresy. It cost him his career and his property. Moreover, he was exiled forever from New Spain. When the Spanish court rejected his claims to remedy the injustices, he resigned his allegiance and left for France to live in exile. Spurned by the very government he devoted his life to, Peñalosa vented his ire with plans to retaliate; under the auspices of a different monarch, he would attack New Biscay.

Failing to interest Charles II of England in his scheme, Peñalosa enlisted the aid of Bernou to present it to Seignelay. It found a more receptive audience with the French king's minister. Peñalosa planned to recruit 1,200 freebooters (buccaneers) from the French settlements at the western end of Saint Dominique (Hispaniola). Instead of preying on Spanish vessels as they passed through the Caribbean islands, they would create a French settlement at the Spanish town of Pánuco by the mouth of the *Rio Bravo* (Rio Grande) river. Here, they would carry on trade with neighboring tribes and search for the gold and silver mines known to exist in the area.

Occupation was only the first step in Peñalosa's plan. When the king was ready, the French, having now acquired a thorough knowledge of the geography of the region, would strike out to conquer New Biscay, with its rich mines. He doubted the Spanish would put up much resistance, since there were only four or five hundred Spanish men in the area capable of bearing arms. They could not expect support from Mexico City, nearly 750 miles away, for it would take at least three months for reinforcements to reach them. He further believed that the Indians and half-breeds there would sooner side with the French in any revolt, as "they are much more humane than the Spaniards." With the French colony nearby at Saint Do-minique, easy communications and support for the new colony at Pánuco was assured.

Numerous letters, memoirs, and proposals went back and forth between Peñalosa, Abbé Bernou, Renaudot, and Seignelay about this design to con-quer New Biscay. La Salle also was writing letters about *his* plan to create a French colony at the mouth of the Mississippi River. It occurred to Bernou that perhaps the proposals of both these men could be united into a single plan, since from what he heard, the mouth of the Mississippi was not far from that of the *Rio Bravo*. Once New Biscay was conquered, all of New Spain would be open to an easy takeover. Even if it went no further than the occupation of New Biscay, France would at least have strong bargaining power in any future treaty of peace with Spain.

The king's secretary, François de Callières, arranged a meeting between Peñalosa and La Salle to discuss the possibility of joining their two enter-prises. But La Salle had learned his lesson well after the disastrous results of shared responsibilities with others, and declined to coordinate his ambitions with another man.

Until now, La Salle had no difficulty finding the necessary funds for his expeditions. There were always friends, relatives, and speculative business partners willing to invest, with the anticipation of a good return in profit. La Salle's enterprises were of an almost unbelievable proportion: by canoe and on foot he traveled thousands of miles, under extraordinary hardships, through uncharted wilderness; with steadfast determination he created a string of forts and settlements in the western lands; and with the same zeal, he maneuvered a peace between the Iroquois and Illinois tribes, through his ability to inspire confidence. As a businessman, though, he was a com-plete failure. How much of his losses can be attributed to personal inepti-tude and mismanagement and how much the result of jealous competitors who schemed and stole from La Salle are debatable. Whatever the cause of his financial failures, they were know about and discussed on both sides of the Atlantic. Consequently, in 1684 he found no one in Rochefort, La Rochelle, Paris, or even his native city of Rouen, willing to finance his proposed settlement among the Taensa Indians above the mouth of the Mississippi. This left King Louis XIV as the only possible support left open to La Salle.

With the help of Renaudot, he prepared a proposal to submit to the Minister Seignelay. Titled *Mémoire sur les Affairs de l'Amerique,* it incorporated some of the ideas of Peñalosa along with his own. Spain and France were already at war in Europe, but if it expanded to North America as well, then, his settlement among the Taensas would place France within easy reach to invade the nearby New Biscay. La Salle assured Seignelay that he could raise an army of 15,000 Indians; all he required from the king was a single ship, containing sufficient arms and provisions for three hundred Frenchmen.

In February of 1684, Renaudot and La Salle produced a new memoir with a slightly different approach. It suggested independent attacks from two forces that would support and reinforce each other. La Salle would "attack that part of New Biscay that lies next to the river he discovered," and Peñalosa would follow with a seaward invasion on Pánuco. Later, a third memoir, titled *Report of La Salle on the Enterprise he proposed to the Monseigneur the Marquis de Seignelay against one of the Provinces of Mexico,* was presented to the king.

In this lengthy document, only the first two paragraphs discuss establishing a new colony in the territory of Louisiana; the remainder borrows heavily from Peñalosa's plan, expands upon it, and details the execution of La Salle's proposal to conquer New Biscay. His discovery of the mouth of the Mississippi guaranteed France's right to possession of the mid-section of North America, but to ensure it could not be contested by other nations, it had to be occupied. The territory covered an immense amount of land, but La Salle did not doubt the survival of his proposed colony 180 miles north of the mouth of the Mississippi River. He felt that its fertile soil and temperate climate would produce all the commodities of life, and only one or two posts were needed to regulate the entire continent. Furthermore, enemy attacks by ground were rendered improbable by the very remoteness of the terrain, and attack from seaward was equally difficult. Ships could be easily repulsed if they tried to sail against the current, on a very defensible river.

He affirmed that the settlement would offer an advantageous post for commerce, from which France could well profit in the exchange of merchandise. At the first rupture of peace—already eminent—the settlement would be ideally suited to attack New Biscay "the northernmost province of Mexico, situated between the 25th and 27 degree 30 minutes latitude North." La Salle believed that this province was close to the Mississippi River, and could easily be reached by way of the Seignelay River (Red River).✢ The mouth of the Seignelay River, he stated, enters the Mississippi about three hundred miles above the place where it discharges into the Gulf of Mexico, and "we have gone up it more than sixty leagues, always traveling west." If La Salle did travel the 180 miles west on the Red River, as he claimed, it is not mentioned in Membré's official report, and Tonty, in his memoir, says only that "they camped at its mouth."

✢ The name "Seignelay" was applied to the Illinois River, as well as to the Red River.

To conquer New Biscay he requested only one ship with about thirty cannon, and the power to take two hundred men from France that he judged appropriate to his plan. Sailing equipment aside, he would require provisions for six months, several cannon to protect the fort, arms and necessary munitions, and enough to pay his men for a year. In addition, he specified the need for: pickaxes, hoes, hones, shovels, axes, hatchets, and cramp-irons for the fortifications and buildings; 5,000 to 6,000 lbs. of iron, and 400 lbs. of steel of all sorts; a forge with its appurtenances, besides the tools necessary for armorers, joiners, coopers, wheelwrights, carpenters, and masons; two surgical supply boxes provided with medicine and instruments; two chapels and the ornaments for the almoners; a barge of forty tons in pieces, or built with its appurtenances, and refreshments for the sick.

Fifty men already in the country, plus fifty buccaneers from Saint Dominique would augment the two hundred he planned to take with him. He had no doubt that 4,000 Indians from Fort St. Louis would come down to join him, and that this number could be increased by as many as 15,000 from other tribes "who offered to follow him wherever he would lead."

He proposed to split his army into three parts. Two parts, composed of fifty Frenchmen, fifty Wabenakes, and 2,000 other Indians, would attack at the two extremities of the province, thus forcing the Spanish to divide their forces. Then, with the rest of his army he would enter the middle of the country, where "all the wretches who suffer in slavery" would join him. Attacks along the coast, led by Peñalosa and his freebooters from Saint Dominique, would create an additional diversion of Spanish forces, leaving the interior of the province deprived of help.

The memoir reminded the court that France had neglected Hudson Bay and the New England Colonies, leaving them to fall into the hands of England. It should serve as a lesson, it said, not to leave this colony, once begun, with all its advantages and profitable things, to be abandoned to Spain. This enterprise "would appear infallible . . . never has anyone undertaken such a high-minded consequence with so little risk and expense."

Thus, a scheme of the most bizarre nature and scope, based on misconceptions about the geography of Mexico and the termination of the Mississippi River, was placed before the court of the king of France. Did La Salle really believe he could accomplish all that he promised? Probably not. But this was his chance to gain the necessary capital to salvage his financial losses, redeem himself in the eyes of his compatriots, and justify the hardships and struggles he endured for over fourteen years. He had reached his goal, the mouth of the Mississippi, and did not want to lose everything—even if it meant adapting his plans to the desires of others. La Salle doubtlessly had little intention of conquering New Biscay, let alone an entire Spanish empire in the western hemisphere, but if feigned desire toward that end is what it took to gain acceptance of his own enterprise, then he would incorporate into his proposal what Peñalosa actively promoted at the same time.

That he firmly believed the mouth of the Mississippi was very close to the *Rio Grande,* was merely a convenient coincidence. The closeness of the silver mines, from which Spain received more than ten million per year, probably had some influence on La Salle's thoughts. It may have occurred to him that here was an opportunity for a source other than for pelts, with which to ride himself of debts and increase his wealth. As for the interests of Abbé Bernou, if the proposal was accepted, and Louisiana was settled and prospered under the guidance of La Salle, then perhaps he might be raised to a station of greater ecclesiastical glory.

There was little doubt in the mind of Seignelay as to how the king would react to his proposal on behalf of La Salle. Even before an official reply was given, he wrote to Sieur de Cussy, governor of Saint Dominique to start recruiting freebooters for a voyage that would depart from the island in October. He gave no explanation, other than that it was the king's wish, and that details would arrive with the additional forces from His Majesty.

On April 14 of 1684, La Salle received the commission he yearned for.

Commission for Sieur de la Salle
Versailles, 14 April, 1684

Louis, by the grace of God, King of France and Navarre, greetings. Having ordered to have made several enterprises into North America to place under our domination several savage nations and to carry to them the light of the Faith and the Gospel, we have believed we could not have made a better choice than Lord de la Salle to command in our name all the French and Savages he will employ for the execution of the orders with which we have charged him. To these reasons and others upon which we move, and being moreover well-informed of his affection and his faith to our service, we have commissioned and ordered, and do commit and order Lord de la Salle, by these present signed by our hand, to under out authority, commandeer as in the lands which will be newly subjected under our dominion in North America, from Fort Saint-Louis on the river of the Illinois up to New Biscay, as well as to the French and Savages he will employ m the enterprises with which we have charged him; to have them live together and in concord one with another, to contain people of war in good order and behavior following our rules, to establish particular governors and commandants in the places he judges suitable; until such other is ordered by us, to maintain commerce and trade traffic and generally do and exercise all that can be done as commandant for us in said lands and to enjoy the powers, honors, authority, privileges, preeminence, franchises, liberties, wages, rights, fruits, profits, revenues, and emoluments, as much as it pleases us. In doing this we have given you and do give by these witnesses, by which we mandate to all our subjects and people of war to recognize you, obey you and understand all things regarding your power. For such is our pleasure. In witness of which, we have set our seal in the presence of these witnesses.

News of La Salle's success spread quickly, both in Paris and across the Atlantic. Abbé Tronson, Superior of the Community of St. Sulpice, wrote to Abbé Dollier de Casson in Montréal about La Salle's commission. Tronson said that "He [La Salle] was well received by the King, who heard him, and was satisfied. His affairs are still very secret." To another confrere, Abbé Belmont, Tronson added: "If his enterprise succeeds; which some find hard to believe, he will apparently have enough to rid himself of his debts.

There still remained some who not only doubted the success of La Salle's future enterprise, but had a difficult time accepting what he already accomplished. Sieur de Machaut-Rougemont accused him of indulging in fanciful visions, and that his claim of going up the St. Lawrence River more than three hundred miles, crossing several lakes, and finally descending the Mississippi to reach the gulf, contained much of a fairy tale. He also criticized La Salle's knowledge of the Gulf of Mexico, especially since the departure from France would bring him to the gulf during the winter months. Rougemont pointed out that the strength of winds during this time, and their unfavorable northerly direction, would force La Salle to wait out the season in the Windward Islands before he could enter the Gulf. Others, he said, who have been there before, "have enough knowledge to know that the vessels cannot sail into that gulf except with grave danger, given the shoals which are there."

There is much truth in what Rougemont says about sailing conditions in the Gulf of Mexico during winter months, but he was certainly in error when he declared that "we already know enough about that gulf to know that there is no river [Mississippi] of that importance." The king's wish, and that of his minister, was more than enough to prevent further discussion of the matter, and arrangements were made to acquire vessels, enlist volunteers, and procure supplies. Though La Salle had requested a single ship, with thirty cannon, he received two ships from King Louis. The vessel *Belle,* a small barque carrying six guns was an outright gift to La Salle. A larger ship, the *Joly,* had thirty-six guns and was to act as an escort vessel to protect the ships enroute. After seeing the other ship safely to the Gulf, she was to return to France. With these committed to him, the explorer was able to expand his fleet by charting two other vessels; a small ketch, the *St. Françoise,* and a much larger vessel, the *Aimable,* for carrying cargo.

Encouraged by royal support, investing merchants loosened their purse strings, and creditors extended their loans. Once again, La Salle had gathered the necessary money for his enterprise. Specific details of his proposal were withheld, but it scarcely mattered; the potential for profit was sufficient. This time, there was the added inducement of the proximity of the silver mines of Santa Barbara in New Biscay to his future colony at the mouth of the Mississippi.

Volunteers for the expedition, many from the middle and upper classes, quickly joined. For them, the sense of adventure was sufficient reason. The rest were people of differing occupation, selected for their ability as iron-mongers, builders, farmers, and men proficient in the various tasks required to create and sustain a community. Women, some with children, others single, were included. Only fifty professional soldiers, plus as many freebooters as were to join later, were requested by La Salle. He fully explained in his proposal the reason for so few soldiers: 1—Necessity would quickly make them all soldiers if the need should arise; 2—Success would depend more upon his ability to command, even workers untrained in war, than on the bravura of those who know only how to obey; 3—The freebooters, and those already in the country, that is, the Frenchmen from Fort St. Louis, and all the Indians willing to follow him, are much more used to this type of warfare than what is practiced in Europe. Even old, experienced soldiers would find themselves as novices here; 4—It would only double the expense by taking two hundred soldiers, since additional workers still would be required; 5—The officers commanding the troops, would soon find that life in the wilderness was much more difficult than they had imagined, and become discontent. This would spread to the soldiers, who finding nothing to ease their hardship would "succumb to debauchery and libertinage." And finally, he said: "It would ruin the settlement to begin it with weaklings, such as almost all soldiers are, because, far from contributing to the advancement of the colony, they would endanger the best hopes by the disorder they cause there."

La Salle's very apparent animosity toward soldiers, together with the relatively small number of those he deigned to accompany him, speaks strongly that his sole goal was to colonize. If he truly intended to carry out an attack on New Biscay, he assuredly would have requested a different ratio of soldiers to workers. The king, and Seignelay, on the other hand, expected La Salle to attack Spanish ships in the Caribbean, capture her ports in the gulf, and conquer New Biscay. This conflict of purpose is but one of several that eventually led to the downfall of the entire enterprise.

Past quarrels between La Salle and his brother Abbé Jean Cavelier had been resolved, and he, plus two other priests of St. Sulpice, Father d'Esmanville, and Father Chefdeville, agreed to come along on the voyage. Like Abbé Bernou, Jean Cavelier saw the enterprise as a means of limiting the spread of Jesuit power and influence among the Indian nations of the immense territory of Louisiana, by making it a colony under the governorship of La Salle, separate from the rest of New France. If this were to happen, there would be an open position for a bishop—a position that Abbé Jean Cavelier was more than willing to fill.

Father Zénobe Membré, the Récollet who accompanied La Salle on his last expedition, was willing to again place his life in that explorer's hands. He brought along two others from his order: Anastase Douay, and Maxime Le Clercq. The Récollets were to devote themselves to bringing the Gospel to the Indian tribes in the new colony, while the Sulpitian's role in accompanying the expedition was to take care of the spiritual needs of the Frenchmen. All assembled at La Rochelle to embark on the voyage.

In an effort to keep the expedition's "true" objectives hidden from the Spanish, Seignelay wrote to the Intendant of Rochefort telling him that the king was dispatching a ship, the *Joly,* along with two hundred men to *Canada.* He counted on the spread of false rumors to counteract any suspicion the Spanish might have that the ships were headed for the Gulf of

Mexico. He let out little more than that the vessel would be under the command of Captain Beaujeu, an experienced naval officer, whose orders were also kept secret. Beaujeu's authority was restricted solely to the concern of the sailing of the ships. Even this much was diminished by instructions from Versailles that he "must not be difficult with La Salle on the subject of command . . . and do all that he desires." Provided the security of the ship was not compromised, La Salle had control over the destination, route to be taken, and the troops and personnel once they reached land.

It was an arrangement that suited neither party, causing hostility, and an exchange of angry letters. Beaujeu resented that he had to obey La Salle, a man he thought "has no character, and who has commanded only school-boys." The latter was an allusion to La Salle's early youth spent teaching with the Jesuits. Nonetheless, he promised to obey La Salle "without repugnance," but asked that he at least be given some guidelines that he could live with.

For a prideful man such as La Salle, who always required unquestioned control, the divided authority was equally distasteful. More than that, self-doubt gnawed at the conscience of La Salle; with this enterprise he had undertaken a venture for one purpose, yet under the pretense of another. Both his words and actions began to display that he realized he had committed himself to something he was not entirely sure about, but could not admit it to himself, or any other man. In contrast, Beaujeu's doubts were clearly expressed in a letter to Seignelay, when he said he sincerely believed in the futility of La Salle's enterprise, and that he expected to perish before ever seeing it succeed.

The combination of secrecy, ambiguity in orders, and conflicts in command created an attitude of distrust and confusion that hung heavily over preparations for the voyage. That Beaujeu's wife was devoted to the Jesuits fueled La Salle's distrust even more, and he began to suspect complicity of the captain with the Jesuit order, another of his foes, real or imagined. It was also conceivable, thought La Salle, that information about the voyage was being leaked to the Spanish by Beaujeu, and he retreated even deeper into his fears and furtive actions.

These were the uncertain conditions under which the destiny of the two men were linked in a voyage toward the Mississippi River, by way of the Gulf of Mexico.

INTO THIS CAULDRON of personal resentments, religious factions, and conflicting political aims, there was yet another element causing confusion and discord—the exact geographical location of the destination was not known. Indeed, almost until the time of departure, Beaujeu believed the fleet was headed for Canada. La Salle's goal was to land at the Mississippi and found his new colony in Louisiana. Since he was the only person on the ship to behold where that Great River emerged into a salt sea, the expedition depended upon his report of its location. Some explorers, such as Hernando de Soto, in his attempt to conquer the valley of the Mississippi, had come upon the river, but their knowledge of it was limited to isolated segments. Others had passed by the place where it discharges into the Gulf, without recognition and were unable to appreciate or understand the significance of the event.

Within a decade of Columbus's voyages to the West Indies, Spanish mariners extended their travels westward beyond that archipelago, exploring and charting the coasts of the Gulf of Mexico. Their expeditions centered on Central America, the coast of Mexico, and Florida; the northern shore of the Gulf was left relatively untouched. Tentative probing in this direction showed it to be a featureless, unfruitful-looking land, with an undesirable coast of shallow water that prevented close examination. More importantly, it gave no clue to possessing a potential for gold or silver mines from which any wealth could be extracted.

In 1512, Juan Ponce de León, then governor of Puerto Rico, set out to make new discoveries for his sovereign. With a fleet of three vessels, he went to explore lands to the northward, especially the island of Bimini. It was more than a quest for geographical knowledge that propelled him in this direction, for he had heard rumors that the island possessed a never-failing spring of running water which bestowed everlasting youth upon the person who drank from it. On the 2nd of April the fleet landed upon what was thought to be an island. Because it had a "lovely landscape, with many green groves," he named it *La Florida*. The name also fit well with the Feast of the

Resurrection, or Feast of the Flowers, which occurred several days earlier. Juan Ponce took possession of this land for King Ferdinand of Spain. He searched inland and along the coasts in both directions of the Flowery Land for the rejuvenating fountain before returning to Puerto Rico. The object of his desire was never found, but that did not diminish the strength of belief in its existence. Even though Ponce de León had coasted some distance along the east and west coasts of Florida, he never realized that it was part of the mainland. Apart from this one misconception, his exploration did produce a thorough knowledge of the Florida peninsula, its many offshore islands, reefs, and the swiftness of the Florida current that sweeps eastward between Cuba and Florida toward the Bahama Islands. All contributed toward a mapping of the region.

To the south, Vasco Nuñez de Balboa explored the coast of Central America. On foot, he penetrated the interior of the isthmus of Panama, where he heard from a local chief that beyond the range of the *sierras* lay a great sea, and the surrounding countryside was rich in mines with great quantities of gold. Ten years earlier, when Columbus sailed along the eastern shore of that isthmus, he too had heard of a sea to the west, whereupon in nine days, ships would come to the remote shores of India. With 180 men, and a number of Indian guides, Balboa pushed his way through the dense forest and across precipitous slopes to the summit of the Sierra de Quarequa. There, on the 25th of September, 1513, he looked down upon the great Sea of the South—the Pacific Ocean; an event ensuring that his name and deed would be remembered forever.

Three years later, Diego Velasquez, governor of Cuba, outfitted three vessels to search for western lands. As usual, the driving force behind the expedition was the greed for gold, silver, and pearls. Under the command of Francisco Hernando de Córdova, the fleet sailed for twenty-one days, until it reached the northeastern part of the Yucatan peninsula. There, they came upon temples built of stone and mortar, in which were found many clay idols and all manner of ornaments and figures made of gold. Their overwhelming joy in finding this rich treasure quickly changed to desperation when they were assailed by the inhabitants. Though the Spanish fought with the superior firepower of muskets against the bows and arrows, lances, and slingshots of the natives, they barely managed to escape with their lives and return to their boats.

The treasures they brought back were of inferior quality, and not of great value. Nonetheless, they were sufficient to excite Velasquez. His interest was increased by false tales told him by two captives of rich gold mines in their country. This prompted Velasquez to outfit another expedition to the Yucatan. In 1518, four vessels, with 220 men, commanded by Juan de Grijalva, sailed in search of the riches in New Spain. Their explorations ranged much farther than those of Córdova, covered both sides of the Yucatan peninsula, and extended northward along the coast of Mexico as far as the Province of Pánuco, near the Rio Grande River. The tribes they met were less hostile than those encountered previously, and they allowed the Spanish to view their ceremonies. Even to men hardened to the sight of blood and death on the battlefield, they were shocked and disgusted by what they saw. On the altars of the temples were bodies of boys who had been cut open, and their bleeding hearts offered to the abominable looking god Tetzcagtlipuca—god of hell. Sacrificed men with arms and legs chopped off, lay about, their blood besmearing everything around.

Revulsion over the religious practices in no way stopped the Spanish from bartering with the Indians. In exchange for green, glass beads and other trinkets, they collected as many golden ornaments and axes made of finely polished copper as they could. Then, since winter was approaching, their supplies were running out, and one of the boats was leaking badly, they headed back to Cuba.

Within a year, Diego Velasquez commissioned a third expedition—the largest yet. With Hernando Cortés appointed captain, the fleet of eleven vessels, and over five hundred men, sailed west. They made landfall at the island of Cozumel, at the eastern coast of the Yucatan. The subsequent travels Cortéz made inland, and the history of his meetings with Montezuma at Tenochtitlán (Mexico City), the capital of the Aztec empire, are too well chronicled to repeat here, nor do they further an understanding of the mapping of the Gulf of Mexico. What is relevant are the orders that he gave while he was being entertained by Montezuma, for two of his ships to continue northward and explore the coast of Mexico to the Rio Grande,

Juan Grijalva

near Pánuco. They covered the same territory as Grijalva had done the previous year, but went no farther.

Where Cortés first set foot on the coast of Mexico, about 175 miles from the capital, he built a new city and gave it the name of Villa Rica de Vera Cruz (the Rich Town of the True Cross). It became the principal port from which the plunder of Mexico was transported back to Spain.

Following the siege of Montezuma's great city, which the soldiers of Cortés left in complete ruin, and filled with innumerable dead bodies, the Spanish departed. The booty they extracted, "amounting to eighty-eight thousand *pesos* worth of gold bars," was sent to their sovereign. Diego Velasquez received twenty thousand *pesos* as his share.

When reports of the wealth that was pouring into the coffers of Spain, as well as the pockets of Velasquez, reached the governor of Jamaica, Francisco de Garay, he saw no reason why he too couldn't benefit from the conquest of New Spain. He requested permission from His Majesty to "make further discoveries on the river Pánuco, and to be appointed as governor of all the lands he should discover." At the time, King Charles was in Flanders and unable to grant the request. In his stead, governors managing the affairs of the Indies gave the authorization. De Garay had accompanied Columbus on his second voyage in 1493 and always maintained a strong interest in exploration and navigation. When he heard the description given by the pilot of one of Córdova's ships of the "gorgeous Mayan dress, and strange-looking pyramids," he took this to be signs that the outer limits of the Orient were near at hand.

RIVER OF THE HOLY SPIRIT

The geography of the eastern and western boundaries of the Gulf was rapidly being delineated on maps. But the northern coast, stretching nine hundred miles from the Apalachee Bay of Florida to the Pánuco River in Mexico, was still unknown. It was conceivable to de Garay that somewhere along this shore there was yet to be discovered that elusive passage between the Atlantic and Pacific Oceans, yielding a way to the East Indies and Cathay. To this end, he fitted out three ships, with 270 men, many well armed, and placed Alonso Alvarez de Piñeda in command of the fleet.

The explorers left Jamaica, headed toward Juan Ponce's "island" of *la Florida,* and followed north along its western shore. They found no strait giving egress from the Gulf and were forced to turn their ships westward. Along the way, they examined as much as possible, the country, rivers, harbors, inhabitants, and all that deserved to be noticed along the coast, claiming everything they encountered for Spain. After nine hundred miles of sailing, the fleet came to the river of Pánuco. They had reached the limits of exploration of the ships that Cortés had sent north. The circle of the Gulf of Mexico was not closed; other than the Yucatan Strait between that land and Cuba and the Florida Strait, there was no outlet. The realization of this ended all hopes of finding a sea-path from the Gulf of Mexico to Cathay.

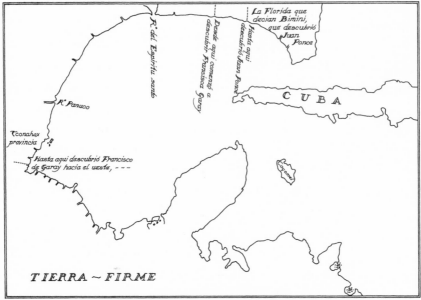

La Florida que
decian Bimini,
que descubrió
Juan
Ponce

R.ª del Espíritu santo

Desde aqui comenzó á
descubrir Francisco Garay

Hasta aqui
descubrió Juan Ponce

C U B A

R.ª Panuco

Tconahox
provincia

Hasta aqui descubrió Francisco
de Garay hacia el ueste, - - -

T I E R R A ~ F I R M E

Coasts of the Continent and of the New Lands ~ 1521

The map produced following Piñeda's voyage was the most accurate made to date of lands bordering the Gulf of Mexico. It became the prototype for all future maps of that region for the next 180 years. The configuration of lands is remarkably similar to that shown on present-day maps. Unfortunately, it erred in placing Mobile Bay, labeled as *Rio Espirito Santo*, approximately ninety miles farther west from its true position.

When Cortés heard that Piñeda's ships had landed at Pánuco, he wrote to the king and gave a detailed account, complaining this his territorial right was being usurped. He described the event with remarkable understatement. "They [Piñeda's men] met with a rude reception from the natives, on account of the bad management of the captains in trading with them" Actually, Piñeda's expedition nearly ended in complete disaster at Pánuco. One of his captains. Antonio Galuão reported: "the natives attacked them at every place. Many of them were killed at Chila [near the mouth of the Pánuco], where the natives flayed and ate those who fell into their hands, and hung up the skins in their temples to commemorate their valor." Some of Piñeda's men escaped in one of the ships and managed to reach Vera Cruz. From there, the half-famished survivors pushed onward to Villa Segura where they met Cortés. Though he treated them well, Captain Comargo and many of his men died shortly thereafter. Alvarez de Piñeda, with the remaining survivors of the Indian attack, set sail, and retraced their route to Jamaica.

One of Piñeda's pilots prepared a map incorporating the explorations of Alonso Alvarez de Piñeda, Juan de Grijalva, Francisco Hernando de Córdova, and Juan Ponce de León. He gave it to Garay, who forwarded it to the Spanish Regents in 1520, along with his petition to colonize, and become governor of the newly discovered land by Piñeda. The map demonstrates, he said, that the Gulf "bendeth like a bow, and that a line drawn from Yucatan to southern Florida would make the string to the bow." It also showed Florida as a peninsula attached to the mainland, rather than an island. This topographic correction is noted on the map as "Florida called Bimini which Juan Ponce discovered." The eastern and westernmost extents of Piñeda's exploration are marked, along with those geographic features deemed most important: Vera Cruz, Pánuco River, and *Rio del Espiritu Santo* (River of the Holy Spirit).

The expedition was doubly disappointing to de Garay. Piñeda not only proved there was no strait from the Gulf of Mexico leading to the Pacific Ocean, but showed that there was little in the way of wealth to be gained from the shores he explored. De Garay reported to Spain that he "thought the coast to be very lytle hospitable, because he saw tokens and signes of small store of golde, and that not pure." Undeterred by these setbacks, he pursued his claim to the right of governship of the Province of Pánuco— perhaps expecting to gain what he could from the mines nearby. In 1523, he left Jamaica with a fleet of thirteen vessels and an army of nearly one thousand soldiers. The enterprise was a total failure, and he died in Mexico City at the end of that year.

IT MIGHT SEEM SURPRISING, even incomprehensible' that an expedition with its primary purpose of exploring the character of a coastline, could miss entirely a feature as large and as important as the delta of the Mississippi River. Piñeda was not alone in making what appears to be such a grievous error. The very same navigational oversight occurred when La Salle later attempted to find the river when he approached it from seaward.

And in 1524, when Giovanni Verrazzano sailed the middle section of the east coast of North America in search of a route leading to the Pacific and Cathay, he missed the entrance to both Chesapeake Bay and Delaware Bay, before dropping anchor in New York's Upper Bay.

These may seem as blunders of the grossest nature, but to the mariner, knowledgeable about the inherent dangers of approaching an unknown and uncharted shore, they are evidence of a wise and cautious captain; one unwilling to risk his ship or place his men in danger.

Far at sea, with plenty of water under a ship, and surrounding it, storms are the greatest danger to contend with. But any well-built and properly manned vessel can safely ride out a storm at sea, no matter how tumultuous the wave and wind. It is when land is approached and the ship comes into soundings—the swinging of the lead-line reveals a bottom rising up to meet the ship—that causes the greatest concern. For it is here that hidden rocks and unforeseen shoals lie await, with seeming malice, to destroy his frail vessel.

On the Gulf of Mexico coast, and much of the eastern seaboard of North America, the shore is one long, unbroken, low, and featureless line, with shallow water extending many miles out to sea. As these explorers—Piñeda, Verrazzano, and La Salle—found themselves within soundings, and yet unable to see land on the horizon, their apprehension was increased. By keeping far enough out to sea to keep sufficient water under their boat's keel, it simply was not possible to see the shore, and consequently they missed the bay or river they were seeking. Rather than recklessly push forward, they merely exercised due caution.

PIONEERS OF THE MISSISSIPPI

There is no strong evidence, either on the first portion of the voyage or on his return, that Piñeda ever discovered the mouth of Mississippi River. The Spanish historian, Martin Fernández de Navarrete, relates in his *Coleccion de los viages y descubrimientos* (Collection of the Voyages and Discoveries) what little is known about Piñeda's homeward passage.

The expedition having gone east and west, and taking possession of the coun-
try in the name of the King, they turned back and entered a river of very great
volume, at the mouth of which there was a large town [gran pubelo] where they
stayed more than forty days, repairing the ships and trading with the natives, in
the most friendly and amicable manner. They traveled six leagues up the river
and saw forty towns on the shores. This was called the Province of Amichel:
good land, quiet, healthy, well stored with provisions and fruits: its inhabitants
wore many ornaments of gold in their noses and ears.

It might at first appear from the phrase "they entered a river of very great volume" that Piñeda could be accorded the first European to discover the Mississippi River. Unfortunately, the information is too general and could apply to almost any river. It was a commonly used expression by explorers, given for almost any river, regardless of size. Even a stream as small as the Pánuco was called "a great river" by Cortés.

Everything else in the description mitigates against concluding that Piñeda found the Mississippi River. La Salle declared that the channels of the river were deep and navigable, but this was a bit of wishful thinking, and truly applied to only very small vessels. A ship such as the size Piñeda commanded would have been unable to enter the Mississippi, let alone ascend it for a distance of eighteen miles. This is born out by the experience of d'Iberville, when in 1699 he sought a place for a French settlement there. His ships could not navigate the shallow water, and smaller boats had to be used to reach the site.

None of the other accounts from the early period of that region mention anything about the presence of a large town at its mouth or of forty towns crowded along the shores. In 1543, when the remnants of Soto's expedition made their way down the river, they found no towns on the lower part of the Mississippi.

All the evidence strongly supports the conclusion that the "river of great volume" entered by Piñeda was the Alabama and Tombigbee Rivers that flow into Mobile Bay. Within a year of his return, Spanish maps display Mobile Bay on the northern shore of the Gulf. It is the only prominent feature along that nine-hundred-mile-long section of coast; evidence of its importance to mariners on account of the easy access, good protection, and large bay for anchoring. The shape of the bay remained consistent on maps and is the same that one sees today. From 1521 onward, the "river of very great volume" is called *Rio del Espiritu Santo*—River of the Holy Spirit.

Though he may have been the first to enter, the name *Rio del Espiritu Santo* for the river flowing into Mobile Bay, came not from Piñeda, but a contemporary historian, Peter Martyr. In his *De Orbe Novo Decades* (Decades of the New World) Martyr relates that both the Panucus [Pánuco] and the River of Palms (somewhat more than ninety miles northeast of the Pánuco) maintain their integrity a long way out to sea. Mariners, he says, were able to replenish their freshwater supply from these rivers, even at a distance nine miles beyond their discharge. Martyr then adds: "The third river, which our men call the river of the *Spiritu Santo,* neerer to ye country of Florida, hath a more streight & narrowe channell, yet very rich and fruitfull countryes lying round about it, & well replenished with people." There is no way that the straight and narrow channels he describes can be correlated with the many serpentine wanderings of the Mississippi River at its terminus. And the pear-shaped bay into which the rivers discharge is the very antithesis of the Mississippi delta.

CHRONOLOGICALLY, THE NEXT EXPLORER to experience the outpouring of the Mississippi was the Spanish *conquistador,* Cabeza de Vaca. De Vaca was part of a royal expedition to occupy the mainland of North America and claim it as a possession of the Spanish empire. Under the leadership of Pánfilo de Narváez, the fleet left Spain in 1527 and landed near present-day Tampa, Florida. Narváez struck inland to subdue the natives, thinking he would soon become "Governor of Florida, Rio de las Palmas, and Espiritu Santo." But the ferocity of attacks by the Indians, combined with hardships in the unyielding wilderness of swamps and forests, took their toll. Those who weren't killed by arrows and axes, died from disease or starvation. After three months, all attempts at the original plan were abandoned, and the surviving men retreated to the coast. Their only desperate hope lay in constructing crude rafts, with which to make their way to the Spanish colony at Pánuco.

Gulf of Mexico – 1536

Titled "Gulf of Mexico–1536," this map appears to have been made by a Frenchman from Spanish sources. Details of the Florida coast lead to the conjecture that it was originally drawn from reports of the Narváez expedition. With the Bay of the Holy Spirit firmly established on the map, and known as a fine harbor with a good entrance, it was frequently designated by mariners for their rendezvous. Such was the case when Soto sent ships to Cuba to return with supplies.

Early French Map

The "Early French Map" may have been based on that drawn by the Portuguese cartographer Diego Ribero. Its date is somewhere between 1529 and 1544.

Sebastian Cabot – 1544

Sebastian Cabot's map of the New World, of which only a portion is shown here, incorporates information derived from earlier Spanish maps. Location of the Bay of the Holy Spirit is unchanged since the time of Piñeda's expedition twenty-four years earlier.

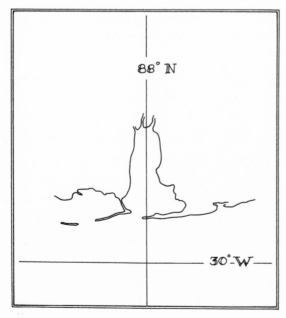

MOBILE BAY

Narváez reserved for his use the best-made raft, and kept with him the strongest of the remaining men. Then he abandoned the raft containing de Vaca, and three others, leaving them to their own devices and the will of the weather. Storms, currents, and a hurricane propelled de Vaca's raft far to the west, where it eventually landed on the coast in the vicinity of what is now Galveston, Texas. From there, he and his companions walked the almost unbelievable distance of two thousand miles, across Texas and Mexico, to reach the town of Culiacan, on the Pacific Coast. De Vaca lived with the natives for six years, until 1557, when he finally returned to Spain. In a published account of his experiences, he told how when their raft drifted westward, they encountered "a huge freshwater current, which pushed their boat to sea." The current was too swift to make any progress with their clumsy craft against this river in a sea. Unable to explore it further, they were left to only conjecture its source. De Vaca's encounter with the river in the sea failed to interest Spanish authorities, and it never found a place on the map.

Hernando de Soto was born into a Spanish family of relatively minor nobility. But after his travels in Peru with Francisco Pizarro's expedition in 1531–1534 to conquer the Incas, he returned to Spain a wealthy man and was rewarded by Carlos V with a knighthood and title of Marquis Don Hernando de Soto. In 1537 he was granted the right to invade and conquer the land of *La Florida* (a name the Spanish ascribed to all the southeast region of North America) and all the territory extending for 600 miles along the coast. Additionally, he was made governor of this immense region. For Soto, though, it was the possibility of gaining even greater riches, such as those of Pizarro in his Peruvian conquests, and Hernando Cortés obtained in Mexico, that spurred him on. The expedition left Sanlúcar de Barrameda, Spain, in 1538 in a fleet of ten ships—seven large galleons, one caravel, and two brigantines. The caravel and brigantines were much smaller, lightweight vessels, well suited for exploration of shallow, coastal waters. After a brief stop in Cuba to re-provision, his fleet, carrying 500 men (as many as 950, according to some historians) and 250 horses, sailed north and made landfall at present-day Tampa Bay of Florida.♣

♣ At this time, Soto was governor of Cuba, as well as *La Florida,* and Marquis of certain parts of lands "yet to be conquered."

The expedition then headed inland. Ever in search for that precious ore, that was always just beyond the next mountain range, or somewhere along a yet to be reached river—but always just out of reach—the expedition continued their search. As the explorers traveled northward, shortly after crossing the Suwannee River, an incredible serendipity befell them. They met with Juan Ortiz, a survivor of the ill-fated Narváez expedition. Ortiz joined their group and aided as a guide and interpreter.

Hardships of drought, alternating with periods of torrential rains that produced swollen rivers impossible to cross, cruelly cold winters, starvation, and disease—not to mention those who were killed in Indian attacks—took their toll. During that time they had fought their way through 4,000 miles of wilderness.♣

♣ For a detailed reconstruction of Soto's route see John R. Swanton, *The United States DeSoto Expedition Final Report,* published by the Smithsonian Institution Press in 1985.

♣ Near present-day Memphis, Tennessee.

On May 8th of 1541, while marching westward in the hope of finding a way to the Pacific Ocean, Soto discovered the Mississippi River.♣ It took nearly a month to construct four large rafts with which to traverse the river and continue west and across the Arkansas River. Another bitterly cold winter halted any further exploration until the following spring. Then, they turned south, hoping to regain the Mississippi River and find their way back to the sea. Somewhere near present-day Natchez, Mississippi, they reach their goal. But for Soto, it was the end of his journey. He contracted a fever, and on May 21st of 1492, Hernando de Soto died. To prevent the Indians from discovering the body, his men wrapped Soto in blankets, weighted him with sand, and sunk him deep in the mud of the Mississippi.

Before his death, Soto appointed Luis de Moscoso Alvarado to continue as leader of the expedition. Moscoso's course first took him west, then he turned southwest in the hope of reaching Spanish settlements in New Biscay. By the time he reached the Brazos River in Texas, the futility of this approach was apparent; no Spanish settlements were found, and their provisions were running low. Moscoso and his men turned back to Soto's burial place on the Mississippi and remained there for the winter. In spring, the remnants of Soto's expedition built seven boats and sailed down the river to the Gulf of Mexico.

The importance of being the first white men to behold were the Mississippi River poured forth into the Gulf of Mexico was of little interest to them and scarcely noted; their concern was one of survival and reaching Spanish settlements. They followed along the coast, occasionally stopping to re-provision and take on fresh water. It is possible they even entered Matagorda Bay and the bay of Corpus Christi. Fifty-three days of sailing finally brought them to their goal. On July 2nd, 1543, they reached the Pánuco River in Mexico.

Although Hernando de Soto can be credited with discovering the Mississippi River, within the four years of his wanderings he had no conception of the full extent of that great river's length, nor any knowledge of where it emptied into the Gulf of Mexico—his contact with it confined merely to an isolated segment. The same can also be said for Moscoso Alvarado.

DIVERSE BEHAVIOR

The behavior of La Salle, compared with that of other explorers in similar circumstances in the Gulf coast region, was markedly different. La Salle was granted authority by Louis XIV to explore and colonize for France the vast middle section of North America. Likewise, Pamphilo de Narváez was authorized by *his* sovereign, Carlos V of Spain, to explore and claim for Spain all the territory between *La Florida* and *Rio de las Palmas* (*Rio Grande*) in Mexico. Both men set out to bring glory to their country by expanding its territory, thereby bringing additional wealth to the Crown. As well, both men had their own, personal goals for financial gain: La Salle, through monopolies in the peltries trade of beaver and bison; Narváez, seeking more directly, gold. La Salle and Narváez shared in common the traits of fortitude and bravery, along with a domineering, and unrelenting energy. There the similarities end.

Frederic Ogg, in his *The Opening of the Mississippi,* characterized Narváez as "an adventurer of very mediocre character and ability, but of unlimited cupidity." There is little in this assessment to contradict. In 1528, Narváez's expedition landed on the coast of Florida. After three weary months of travel through the Gulf states, they were forced to realize no gold was to be found here. Not only did they fail to gain the precious metal, but they made no great discovery and gained no geographic knowledge. What they *did* gain was an all-consuming hatred from the Indians toward the Spaniards. Forced by starvation and the threat of immediate death at the hands of the region's hostile inhabitants, Narváez and his men were forced to return to the coast and flee on rafts hastily constructed from the few remnants of their possessions. Within the few months of exploration, Narváez had lost fifty of his men. And before they could take to sea in their frail, homemade craft, another forty lives were lost to disease and starvation, or slain in Indian attacks.

Far from providing an escape, all but five of the men, which included Cabeza de Vaca, perished only a mile and a half from land when their rafts capsized. Narváez deserted his men in an attempt to save his own life.

When Hernando de Soto embarked from Havana, Cuba, in 1539 to invade and conquer *La Florida,* it was with an even greater expeditionary force than that of Narváez eleven years earlier. Armed with more than 500 men and 250 horses, Soto's men plunged into the wilderness of land north of the Gulf. Like Narváez, Soto's goal was gold, and like Narváez, he had a haughty, domineering attitude toward the natives he met. Treachery, torture, and the taking of captives who were put in chains to act as guides, made the Indians more hostile than ever. In the most memorable battle at Mavila (Mabila), on the Alabama River in 1540, Soto slaughtered as many as 6,000 Indians and left their town in ashes. It was not, however, without the loss of Spanish lives, of whom about eighty-two were killed.

By the following winter of 1540–1541, half of his men and more than half of the horses were dead. And on May 21, 1542, Soto died of a fever near present-day Natchez, Mississippi. His appointed successor, Luis de Moscoso, and the few remaining members of the expedition, made their way down the Mississippi River to eventually reach safety at Spanish settlements in Mexico.

In marked contrast to these earlier Spanish explorers, La Salle's demeanor among the Indian Nations earned him their respect, not their hatred. In many meetings, they sat and listened to his proposals for peace and the building of French settlements within their lands—and acted favorably upon his requests. If seeking their regard, and making all possible efforts to maintain the peace—a peace between the Iroquois and French, as well as reconciling the differences between the various Indian Nations—contained a strong element of self-aggrandizement, it at least can be said for La Salle that he did not leave behind him a trail of death and destruction. He came to colonize, not to conquer. He accomplished his task by words, not with armed troops. He traversed a country every bit as difficult as that of his Spanish predecessors, and in the harshest of climate; encountered Indian Nations as much warlike as the others had; and he did it all with but a scant handful of men—losing none.

PART VI

A Cartographic Dilemma

I t is one thing to discover a new land, or the course of a river such as La Salle had done, and quite another to appropriately mark the location of that discovery that it may be placed on maps and returned to at will. Mindful of this need, La Salle carried with him the navigational instrument and almanac tables required to fix the latitude of important geographic points in his exploration. With an astrolabe he had calculated that the Mississippi River entered the Gulf of Mexico at the 27th degree of latitude. There was an error, however, in his calculations; one that eventually caused his death by a deed most foul and treacherous.

How he came to make such an error is not known. His detractors claim it was no mistake at all, that La Salle purposely falsified the information. They say he claimed that the mouth of the Mississippi lay much closer to the Spanish territory of New Biscay than it actually was in order to gain a more favorable ear from the king. Historians have accused him of deception by giving a false location of the mouth of the Mississippi River in order to make the grand scheme of invading Mexico sound plausible. Others place such deceitful acts upon the writings of Abbé Bernou and Renaudot, but claim that La Salle equally shared in the blame by countenancing the deception.

At that historic moment on April 9, 1682, when La Salle took possession of the territory of Louisiana for France, he proclaimed in a loud voice for all to hear that "the land extended from the mouth of the great Saint-Louis River from the east coast, formerly called the Ohio . . . and along the Colbert River, or Mississippi, and rivers which discharge from it, from its origins in the land of the Sioux . . . to its mouth in the Sea or Gulf of Mexico, around 27 elevation from the North Pole." The events of the entire journey, to its culmination at the mouth of the Mississippi were recorded by La Métairie, notary for the expedition, and submitted as an official report (*Procès-Verbal*). La Métairie, La Salle, F. Zénobe Membré, Henry de Tonty, plus nine other members of the expedition all signed the *Procès-Verbal*. It was given to Count Frontenac, who place it into the hands of Monsignor Colbert, who presented it to the king.

Father Zénobe Membré's official report confirms La Salle's calculation of the latitude of the mouth of the Mississippi and extrapolates its longitude from the geographic relationship of that river to other known rivers. He left one copy, or the journal upon which it was based, with his superior at Québec in November 1682. Another copy (of the journal) he presented to the French court early in 1683. In part, it reads:

> For 350 leagues he [La Salle] had followed the Mississippi River, which retains a width of about a quarter of a league as far as the sea. It is very deep everywhere, not having reefs or anything that hinders navigation, although the contrary has been published in France. It empties into the Gulf of Mexico beyond the Bay of the Holy Spirit between the 27th and 28th degree of latitude, and at the place where some maps put the Rio de la Madalena, and others the Rio Escondido; it is about 30 leagues distant from the Rio Bravo [Rio Grande], about 60 from the Rio de Palmas [San Fernando River], and about 90 to 100 leagues from the Rio Panero [River Pánuco], where lies the nearest settlement of the Spaniards on the coast. The Sieur de la Salle, who always carries an astrolabe on his voyage has taken the exact latitude of this mouth.

Membré was explicit in placing the mouth of the Mississippi considerably west and south of the Bay of the Holy Spirit (Mobile Bay).

Even the mendacious friar, Louis Hennepin, in his *A New Discovery of a*

Large Country in America, published in 1697, asserts the latitude of 27 to 28 degrees as the location of the river's mouth. Largely a plagiarized account from Father Membré's narrative (*Relation of La Salle's Expedition to the mouth of the Mississippi in 1682,* published in 1691), Hennepin pretends as his own the voyage and exploration of the lower Mississippi. At that time he was not yet discredited, and his account served to reinforce in the minds of others the calculations at which La Salle had arrived. Father Hennepin wrote:

> *I don't pretend to be a Mathematician, but having learn'd to take the Elevation of the Pole, and make use of the Astrolabe, I might have made some exact Observations, had M. la Salle trusted me with that Instrument: However, I observ'd that the Meschasipi falls into the Gulph of Mexico, between the 27th and 28th Degrees of Latitude, where, as I believe, our Maps mark a River call'd Rio Escondido, the Hidden River.*

Hennepin

Other accounts gave different latitudes for where the Mississippi discharged into the Gulf of Mexico. Henri Joutel, in the preface to his journals, claims to have heard La Salle say that the mouth of the Mississippi lay somewhere between 28° and 29° N latitude. Joutel justifies the discrepancy on the grounds that when the expedition split up, following different channels, the channel La Salle took exited into the Bay of the Holy Spirit where the latitude, as he found it there, was between 28 and 29 degrees. The other channel, Joutel believed, exited farther to the southwest, between the 27 and 28th parallel of latitude. An even greater variation was given by M. Tonty in *his Account of Monsieur de la Salle's last Expedition and Discoveries in North America* (1698). There, the mouth of the Mississippi was placed between 22° and 23° N latitude. According to Joutel, this was obviously an error on the part of the printer or transcriber, for on the map that accompanies the book the said mouth is shown at 26.5 N, and, he says, "there is reason to believe he [Tonty] errs in that too."

Among the learned men of France and Canada, who had an interest in the geography of the New World, the subject of the course of the Mississippi and its place of exit into the Gulf of Mexico was much debated. In his memoir of 1684, La Salle reported to Seignelay that the discoveries made by him (which some still doubted) were sufficiently established by the *Procès-Verbal*. La Salle was called upon to defend what Membré wrote concerning his discovery. Abbé Tronson (Superior of the Community of St. Sulpice), in a letter to Abbé de Belmont, wrote: "I have corresponded much with M. de la Salle about his discovery. . . . He claims to have entered the Gulf of Mexico not by the Bay of Saint-Esprit, [Bay of the Holy Spirit], but the 27th degree of latitude, and by the same meridian [longitude] of Pánuco, which is at the end of the Gulf, and much farther from that Bay." Confirming this, Henry Tonty, in a letter written from Michillimackinac on July 23, 1682, said: "Like the Loire, the Colbert [Mississippi] River maintains its width as far as the sea, for a distance of 350 leagues. It has no rapids. We were farther south than the 29th degree, having left the Bay of the Holy Spirit on the northeast, at the left side. M. de la Salle believes that the mountains of St. Barbara [at New Biscay] are 80 leagues from there."

The instrument La Salle used to determine latitude—the astrolabe—was a simple one, without optics or need of any calibration. Developed in the Middle Ages, it consists of a perforated disc made of bronze or brass (to give it weight) and held by a ring at the top. A sighting bar, called the alidade, is affixed to the center of the disc and can be moved in a complete circle. La Salle aimed the alidade at the heavenly body (sun or star) and aligned it by sighting through holes or notches in plates at each end. He then read the altitude of that body, in degrees, directly from a scale inscribed around the circumference of the disc. This, in conjunction with printed tables of declination of the sun enabled him to calculate the latitude.♣

♣ The latitude of the observer is calculated using the simple formula of $L = D + Z$. Latitude equals the declination of the sun (or other heavenly body), plus the observed zenith distance. At the moment the sun reaches its highest altitude in the sky (relative to the observer)—its meridian passage—a sighting is taken. The zenith distance is the complement of the altitude; thus, the observed altitude is subtracted from 90 degrees. To this is added the declination of the sun for that day. This number can be anywhere from 0°, when the sun is at the equator during the vernal or autumnal equinox, to 23.5° N when it is at the summer solstice (Tropic of Cancer), to 23.5° S when it is at the winter solstice (Tropic of Capricorn).

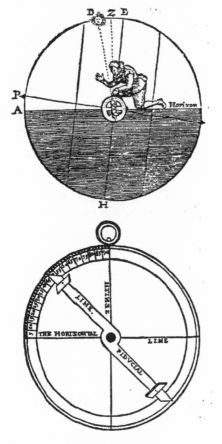

Mariners Astrolabe

Establishing longitude was much more difficult than finding latitude and continued to elude navigators until well into the eighteenth century.

In order to locate the position of any point on the surface of the earth, the two coordinates of latitude and longitude are required. But in La Salle's particular circumstance, the geographic features of the place he intended to return to by ship did not require knowing longitude. Even with the various latitudes, ranging from 26.5° to 29°—a difference amounting to a hundred and fifty nautical miles—the mouth of the Mississippi still had to be *south* of the northern coast of the Gulf of Mexico.

The configuration of the Gulf of Mexico is roughly that of a rectangle. Its east and west sides, respectively defined by the west coast of Florida and the east coast of Mexico, run north and south; its northern coast is nearly a straight line running east/west at 30° N latitude. Maps of the period, Spanish as well as French, correctly depicted the geography of the Gulf and placed its northern boundary at the appropriate latitude. The longitudes for the coasts of Florida and Mexico were not nearly as accurate. But for La Salle's purpose, being able to return by sea to the mouth of the Mississippi, this did not matter. His calculation of 28° N latitude proved, or so he thought, that the Mississippi did not discharge its water into the Gulf along the northern coast, but along the Mexican coast, somewhere close to and north of the *Rio Pánuco* (Rio Grande). To reach it, he only had to follow the northern shore of the Gulf westward, until it started to trend north-northeast by south-southwest, and automatically he would arrive at the proper longitude. Then, keeping his course due south, following the shore until he came to 27° of latitude, he would arrive at his destination.

From the very start it was believed, not only by La Salle but others on the expedition, that when they reached the mouth of the Mississippi they were much farther west than the Bay of the Holy Spirit. Their proximity to New Biscay was affirmed by all, and misplacement of the terminal portion of that river cannot be considered, as some historians have done, to be an evil plot by La Salle to purposely delude the king. Ironically, it was not the inability to determine longitude, but an incorrect calculation of latitude that caused La Salle to misplace the mouth of the Mississippi and later sail beyond it for a distance of 350 miles.

Until 1682, the termination of the "Great River" into the Gulf of Mexico was only an assumption—albeit a correct one—based on the explorations of Jolliet and Marquette in 1673. Throughout their journey, Jolliet kept notes and made sketches of the land through which they passed. Then, in one of those fateful acts of chance, after the successful completion of a long and perilous journey, he lost everything. He had paddled his canoe over 2,500 miles, passed through forty-two rapids, and escaped every peril from the Indians. When all danger seemed over and he was within fifteen minutes of arriving at Montreal, the place he had departed from, his canoe was overturned by an errant current. Two men lost their lives and he him-

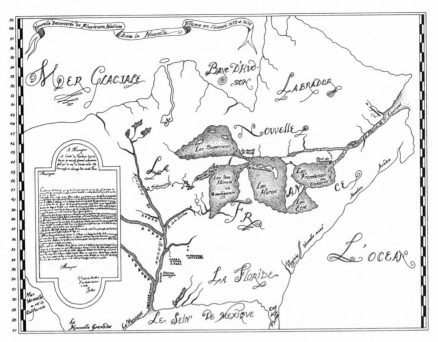

Nouvelle Decouverte de Plusieurs Nations Dans la Nouvelle France en l'année 1673 et 1674 (Reproduced by Gravier). Immediately after Jolliet returned to Montreal he made this, the first map of the Mississippi River to be based on firsthand information. Later, Jolliet produced several different versions.

self barely managed to escape. However, boxes containing his journals and sketches were casualties of the disaster.

Intendant Frontenac had ordered the expedition, with the goal of pushing the possession of new lands for France beyond the Lakes. Jolliet desired to let Frontenac know as quickly as possible the results of his discoveries, and despite the misfortune, prepared for him a map drawn from memory. He gave it the title of *Nouvelle Decouverte de Plusieurs Nations Dans la Nouvelle France en l'année 1673 et 1674,* and in the cartouche he appended a letter to Frontenac. Jolliet expressed his pleasure in being able to present the map, which for the first time showed the position of the Upper Lakes (Lake Superior and Lake Michigan) "on which one navigates across Canada or North America, more than 1200 leagues, from East to West," and of his discovery of the Mississippi River. In honor of the man who promoted the expedition, he bestowed the name of Baude (the family name of Count Frontenac) upon the Great River, and the name of *La Frontanacie* upon the Valley of the Mississippi. This river, he wrote, "flows through the most beautiful country that can be seen." Jolliet admired the extensive prairies, diversity of the groves and forests, the wonderful variety of fruits, game, and fish, along the river's length and claimed it "compared most favorably to anything in France."

Exploration of the Mississippi by Jolliet and Marquette ended at its confluence with the Arkansas River, but it was far enough for them to ascertain that it emptied into the Gulf of Mexico and not into the Vermilion Sea (Gulf of California) or the Sea of Virginia (Chesapeake Bay), as some believed.♣ With their goal accomplished, and fearing the danger of approaching too close to the Spanish, they retraced their journey. In his letter, Jolliet

♣ Coincidently, the farthest point of their journey was very close to where Hernando de Soto encountered the Mississippi and perished.

went on to speculate that perhaps there might even be a way to reach the Pacific Ocean by way of one of the tributaries of the Mississippi. He drew attention to the possibility:

> By one of these big rivers that come from the West, and discharge into the Baude River, one will find passageway into the Mer Vermeille [Red Sea, i.e. Gulf of California]. I saw a village that was only five days away from a nation that has trade with those in California. If I had arrived two days sooner I would have spoken to those who had come, and had left five hatchets as a present.

L. Jolliet

The entire course of the river, from its origin in three lakes west of Lake Superior to its discharge into the Gulf of Mexico, is displayed on his map. Although merely a sketch prepared from memory, Jolliet is careful to show all major tributaries of the river and the location of portages required to pass from one river into another. However, he erroneously connects the Ottawa River with Georgian Bay by way of Lake Nipissing. He corrected this in subsequent maps. The Missouri River is unnamed (Marquette calls it Pekitanoui), but five Indian villages are marked along its length, and the

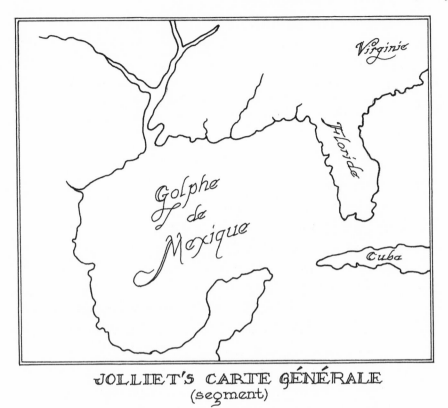

JOLLIET'S CARTE GÉNÉRALE
(segment)

Carrying the full title of *Carte generalle de la France Septentionale la descouverte du Pays des Illinois, faite par le Sr. Jolliet*, the map is dedicated to Colbert, minister to the king. The total map, of which the above is only a segment, covers the North American continent from Hudson's Strait to Mexico, with both the Atlantic and Pacific coasts.

one closest to the Mississippi is labeled "Messouri." Along the Arkansas River are also shown five Indian villages, including that of the "Arkansea Sauvages." Jolliet names the Arkansas *Rivière Bazire,* after Charles Bazire, a merchant of Canada who in 1673 supported Frontenac's plan to build Fort Catarakoui. Jolliet's draftsmanship was of sufficient quality, that in 1697, after returning to France, he was appointed royal hydrographer; a post he held until his death three years later.

Though Jolliet and Marquette never went beyond the mouth of the Arkansas River in their travels, they knew the Mississippi terminated into the Gulf of Mexico, and Jolliet showed it thus on his earliest map. On the map it discharges, neither by way of multiple channels (as La Salle later found) nor into any bay—but straight into the sea. Lacking entirely is the one prominent landmark historically always present on the northern coast of the Gulf—the Bay of the Holy Spirit. Its approximate location is taken up by three non-descript, and unidentified rivers. In subsequent maps he prepared, such as the *Carte Généralle,* the Mississippi is shown pouring into a bay which though unlabeled, has the general appearance of the Bay of the Holy Spirit.

The French cartographer, J.B.L. Franquelin, who preceded Jolliet as royal hydrographer, made maps of the rapidly expanding nation. While in Canada (1674–1697) he continually created new maps as exploration pushed the boundaries of New France increasingly to the west and south. In a work from 1682, Franquelin shows the progress of discovery of the Mississippi River. Only the upper portion is depicted, which ends a short distance beyond the point where it is joined by the Ohio River. The continuation is left blank, as that was all the information available to him at the time. But if one were to extend the river's course southward, it would empty into the Bay of the Holy Spirit. The following year, after La Salle returned to Quebec and Franquelin had first-hand information from the explorer, he made a new map (generally referred to as Franquelin's Great Map of 1684) which displayed the full course of the Mississippi River.

Father Louis Hennepin, as well, showed on the map that accompanied the first edition of his *Description of Louisiane* (Paris 1683), the Colbert (Mississippi) River ending shortly below the Arkansas River. Beyond that, the territory is occupied by the label *La Louisiane.* However, Hennepin (or his cartographer) indicates by a dotted line that the river continues its southerly course to enter into the Bay of the Holy Spirit before discharging into the Gulf of Mexico.

Before his expedition in 1682, La Salle believed that the Mississippi discharged into the Bay of the Holy Spirit. In a letter to Count Frontenac (October 31, 1678) praising Tonty and describing the start of Fort Conti at Niagara, he emphasized the importance of the waterway connection of the Great Lakes with the Mississippi, "from which it only remains to descend the

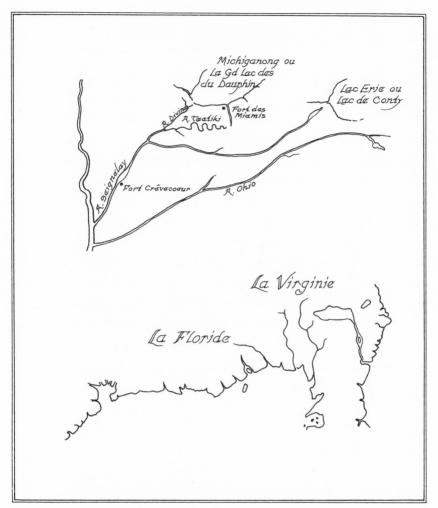

Michiganong ou
La Gd Lac des
du Dauphin

Lac Erie ou
Lac de Conty

Fort des
Miamis

R. Divine

R. Teatiki

R. Seignelay

Fort Crêvecoeur

R. Ohio

La Virginie

La Floride

FRANQUELIN'S MAP OF 1682

Carte de l'Amérique septentrionale et partie de la meridionale . . . les nouvelles descouvertes de la Riviére Mississipi, ou Colbert

great river of the Bay of St. Esprit, to reach the Gulf of Mexico." When La Salle arrived back in Quebec in 1683, he brought with him new geographic information as the result of his discoveries. Cartographers were then faced with the task of accommodating what La Salle had learned about the Mississippi, with their previous knowledge, in order to create a more accurate representation of America. Heretofore, maps displayed the Mississippi either as entering directly into the Bay of the Holy Spirit, or implied that a continuation of its course would bring it to that place. Now, the cartographers learned that the Mississippi entered directly into the Gulf of Mexico by way of three channels. It did not first enter into any kind of bay and certainly not into the Bay of the Holy Spirit. Nothing that La Salle described matched what was already known about that bay and its headwaters. To produce more accurate maps of the New World, cartographers took the new information provided them and integrated it into the previously accepted geography. La Salle's discoveries formed the basis of the changes and additions to the topography of America as depicted on the maps. He was an authoritative source, even with the controversies that seemed to always surround him. But he was not the only informant. In the narratives and journals of other explorers, cartographers found evidence to confirm his discoveries and additional reasons to shift the course of the Mississippi on their maps so that its mouth discharged into the Gulf, farther west, along the Mexican coast.

Such is the power of the line over the words that once the Bay of Spiritu Santo was discovered by Piñeda, and its location firmly established too far westward on maps, it remained that way, impervious to change, for the next 183 years.♣ Rather than reassess their information about the Bay of the Holy Spirit, cartographers chose to shift the mouth of the Mississippi.

♣ Not until 1703, with the publication of Claude Delisle's map *Carte du Mexique et de la Floride*, was the Bay of Spiritu Santo moved to a more accurate position and the way made for a correct location of La Salle's discovery of the lower Mississippi.

In the 1697 edition of Father Hennepin's *A New Discovery of a Vast Country in America,* an accompanying map shows the full course of the Mississippi, as it terminates into the Gulf of Mexico. The contours of the North and South American continents remain nearly identical to those on his earlier map of 1683. The most important change is a shifting of the placement of the mouth of the Mississippi. No longer indicated by a dotted line as entering into the Bay of the Holy Spirit, it is deflected sufficiently westward to discharge instead into the Gulf close to the border of Mexico. This was accomplished by introducing a large, sinuous course in the river, starting above the mouth of the Arkansas River and drifting westward. The Bay of the Holy Spirit, unchanged from its original location on the earlier map, is clearly over two hundred miles east of the Mississippi. To further confirm the new westerly meridian for the mouth of the Great River, it is placed near the mouth of the Magdalan River. Father Zénobe Membré, in his journal, asserted that the Mississippi discharged into the Gulf "beyond the Bay of the Holy Spirit, between the 27th and 28th degree of latitude, and at the place where some maps put the *Rio de la Madalena*." The nearby Magdalan River is extended northwest to almost come in contact with another river (unnamed) emptying into the Vermilion Sea, thus cartographically depicting the stories heard by Jolliet and Marquette of their proximity to the Spanish in New Biscay.

By virtue of a single toponymic change—removal of the label *La Louisiane*—Hennepin rescinds France's claim to ownership of the entire valley of the Mississippi. The land simply becomes an unowned region separating English territory and Spanish Florida to the east from Mexico or New Spain in the west. New France is thereby diminished and relegated to the land north of the St. Lawrence River and the Great Lakes.

With the new information provided by La Salle, Franquelin completely revised his earlier map and produced one showing the entire course of the Mississippi. Titled *Carte de la Louisiane ou des Voyages du Sr. de la Salle et des pays qu'il a découverts depuis la Nouvelle France jusqu'au Golfe Mexique les années 1679, 80, 81, et 82,* it more simply is referred to as "Franquelin's Great Map." As on Hennepin's map, the Mississippi is depicted flowing south until it reaches a point just below the Ohio River. If extended farther south it would enter Mobile Bay, but instead, it takes a sharp turn westward, continuing in that direction until it merges with the Rio Grande. Then, united with the Rio Grande, the Mississippi reverses its course to flow southeast to enter the Gulf of Mexico. On Franquelin's 1684 map, the Rio Grande enters the Gulf directly, through a single channel. In the map he produced four years later, it enters with multiple channels through a delta projecting into the Gulf, as described by La Salle.

General confusion about the geography of the region was compounded by the same river having several names, as well as one name being applied to different rivers. Father Membré stated in his journal that the mouth of the

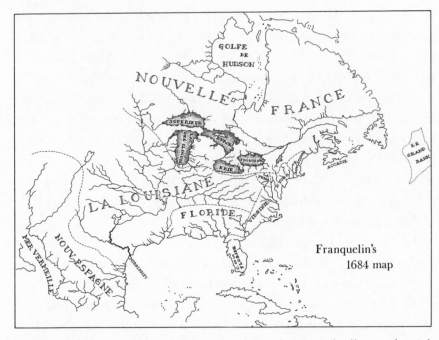

Carte de la Louisiane, ou des voyages du Sieur de la Salle et des pays qu'il a découverts depauis la Nouvelle-France jusqu'au Golfe de Mexique, les années 1679–80–81 et 82. Map of Louisiana, or the voyages of Sieur de la Salle to discover the land from New France as far as the Gulf of Mexico, in the years 1679–1682. By Jean-Baptiste Louis Franquelin, 1684, Paris. Later maps by Franquelin of New France and Louisiana retain most of the features of his 1684 map, but contain corrections of several errors.

Mississippi lay far to the west, "near the *Rio Bravo* [Rio Grande], where lies the nearest settlement of the Spaniards on the coast." The river discovered by de Soto, was called by the Spanish, *Rio Grande del Norte.* The French, however, kept the original name of Mississipy, or some appellation honoring a worthy Frenchman. It is easy to see how *the Rio Grande del Norte* and the Rio Grande of Mexico were thought to be their own "Great River."

None of the above, taken individually, was sufficient for mapmakers to shift the position of the terminal portion of the Mississippi. But taken collectively, and in conjunction with the very strong declarations of La Salle, who had, no less, the admiration of the king, there seemed to be every valid reason to place the mouth of the Mississippi far to the west, if not directly into the Rio Grande, at least nearby, before it entered the Gulf of Mexico.

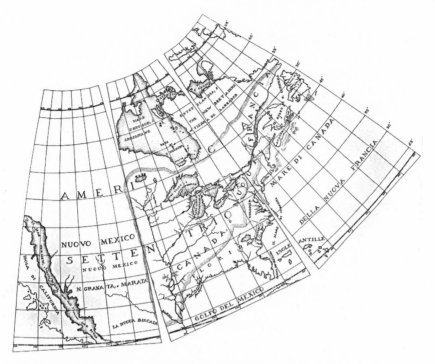

North America by Vincenzo Maria Coronelli, 1688. From the printed gores in the Library of Congress, Washington, D.C. *Reproduction: Courtesy of the New York Public Library*

Undoubtedly, the most impressive new representation of the North American continent and the Valley of the Mississippi is that found on the immense globe commissioned by the Cardinal of Estrés in 1680 for Louis XIV and constructed by the Venetian cartographer Vincenzo Coronelli. In the years it took to execute his work, Coronelli lived in Paris, where he used documents, texts, and maps provided to him by Abbé Bernou. These included manuscript maps from the National Library, which Coronelli used to depict the Great Lakes and the St. Lawrence River. For the region of New Mexico, Bernou supplied a map and manuscript prepared by Count Peñalosa, ex-governor of New Mexico, and Father Estevan de Perea, caretaker of the ordination of St. Francis in that same country. Coronelli not only incorporated Peñalosa's map into his own work, but in a long legend, reproduced the title of the document and gave credit to Peñalosa.

Bernou's attempt to bring Peñalosa and La Salle together to join their respective proposals to Seignelay had a secondary purpose. He wanted the combined knowledge of these two men in order to "produce a map of North America, perfect and complete." For that vast region between the St. Lawrence and New Mexico—the Valley of the Mississippi—Coronelli used the texts of Zénobe Membré, as well as La Salle's own *Relation des descouvertes* for his cartographic endeavors.

The monumental task undertaken by Coronelli was finally completed in 1688. Filled with a wealth of detail about the rivers, their tributaries, and Indian villages, enlivened with illustrations of the native inhabitants, and carrying long textual legends, it was nonetheless substantially the same geography as shown by Franquelin four years earlier. Coronelli, however, made two important changes. Rather than the Mississippi uniting with the Rio Grande to discharge into the Gulf as a single river, he kept the two separate and placed the mouth of the Mississippi about ninety miles farther north. This was in keeping with the report of Membré. Coronelli also restored New France to a single, large entity—calling it *Canada, ou La Nouvelle France,* with *La Louisiana* an integral part of it.

French explorers had journeyed the full length of the Mississippi, and with La Salle's expedition the mouth of that Great River was reached. By international accord, this gave France the right to claim all the territory through which this river flowed, including the land drained by its tributaries. On that occasion on April 9, 1682, France gained a land equal in size to half of all of Europe. Added to her ownership of the St. Lawrence River and its tributaries, she now owned a significant portion of the entire North American continent.

Franquelin, on his 1684 map, boldly displayed this dramatic change in political divisions in the New World. English territories of Carolina, Virginia, Pennsylvania, New York, and New England were confined by the Alleghenies to the Atlantic seaboard. Spain was dispossessed of a large portion of the north coast of the Gulf of Mexico; her land now limited to New Spain in the west, and Florida, composed of that peninsula and the land east of Mobile Bay. The latter part was defined by those rivers that drained into the Gulf, but Franquelin was careful to place the dividing line between French and Spanish territory at the *middle* of Mobile Bay, thus ensuring

French access to that important harbor. The remainder of the continent became the grand domain of France. A line south of the Great Lakes divided
it into two distinct provinces, *Nouvelle France* to the North, and *La Louisiane*
to the south—just as the Abbé Bernou, Abbé Cavelier, and La Salle would
have it. Such was the re-shaped political geography of the New World as
France discerned it.

PART VII

A Bold and Glorious Venture

QUARRELSOME BEGINNINGS

On May 17, 1684, Captain Beaujeu arrived in Rochefort, France, to take command of the *Joly* and oversee its outfitting. Here, on the banks of the Charente River, by royal order of Louis XIV only seventeen years earlier, the city of Rochefort had been created to provide a Royal naval dockyard for the building, arming, and servicing of the king's seaforces bound for French colonies around the world. The Sun King also wanted it to be "the most beautiful settlement in his kingdom." Now, the *Joly* was being rigged, its hold filled with provisions and water and the requisite munitions put aboard for an anticipated six months' journey to Canada and back. There was little Beaujeu could do to facilitate the preparations, for he still waited to learn from La Salle the details of the journey. When La Salle finally arrived, instead of divulging his plans, he continued to remain as secretive as ever. Gradually, vague hints brought Beaujeu to the realization that the fleet was destined not for Canada, as he had been led to believe, but for the more distant and far more dangerous shores of the Gulf of Mexico—into seas ruled by the Spanish.

He realized the timing was altogether wrong for a crossing to the farthest

Corderie Royale (Royal Rope Works) in the port of Rochefort, where the anchor, all the rigging, and the cordage were made for the *Belle*. At a quarter of a mile long, it was the largest industrial building of the seventeenth century. Painting by Claude-Joseph Vernet. *Photo: courtesy of Réunion des Musées Nationaux/Art Resource, New York.*

end of the Gulf of Mexico. And supplies barely sufficient for a round-trip voyage to the St. Lawrence were woefully inadequate for an undertaking of nine months' duration. Any attempt on the part of Beaujeu to resolve these problems were met with cold indifference by La Salle who reminded him that His Majesty intended for Beaujeu to "execute without any contest, all that La Salle indicated and desired." Beaujeu had been put in command of the *Joly*, with authority only over the safe navigation and sailing of the vessel; all other aspects of the voyage, the preparatory arrangements, its route, destination, and what should be done once Louisiana was reached, were under the complete command of La Salle. If for any reason he should happen to die, Henry de Tonty was to act as his replacement. That Beaujeu lost virtually all power over the voyage except for the safety of his own ship was defeat enough; but to not even be a second choice upon La Salle's death deepened his humiliation.

Unable to personally reconcile his differences with La Salle, he wrote to Minister Seignelay to place before him the difficulties he encountered. First, there was the problem of the departure time. Beaujeu pointed out that it was impossible to have the ship in readiness to leave until July. Then, it would take another two months to reach Santo Domingo, where by necessity they would have to stop to take on more water. This would use up another eight days' time, and it wouldn't be until the beginning of September before they could depart from there for the Gulf. The contrary winds of Cuba would be encountered, and avoiding the Bahama current would increase the miles to be sailed, adding another month to the passage in the Gulf before they reached the port which La Salle claimed to have discovered. By then, Beaujeu said, the month of October is well advanced, and at that time of the year, storms, with northerly winds, would prevent their leaving the Mississippi for the return trip to France until the end of May.

Based on this time estimate, additional supplies would be needed for such a lengthy voyage. The *Joly* was not large enough to hold the required two hundred tons of stores, as well as all the food and gunpowder necessary for its armament. At the most the ship could only contain 140 tons. "If Mr. de la Salle had told me this in Paris, as you had ordered him to," wrote Beaujeu, "we wouldn't be in this mess; I would have suggested the ship The Fendant, which has a large hold and would've carried three-hundred men with enough food for a year, and all of Mr. de la Salle's gear. There'd even be some space left over."

The final indignity was the imposition placed on Beaujeu of providing for fourteen passengers, not including the Lord Minet, engineer for the expedition. Not only was he to make space for them on his already overcrowded ship, but they were expected to dine at the captain's table, with the fare of their choice—all at Beaujeu's personal expense. He did not have enough funds to comply with this request, but rather than cause further unpleasantness by outright refusal, as a conciliatory gesture he extended the invitation to have La Salle's brother, Abbé Cavelier, and his two nephews dine with him. The offer was insufficient to placate La Salle, who became abusive, and said that "he distrusted men who offered so much and appeared so honest."

Beaujeu concluded his letter with:

You have ordered me, Monseigneur, to bring all the ease I could to this enterprise. I will contribute as much as I can; but allow me to make a great plea to you, since I have trouble submitting to the orders of La Salle, whom I believe a courageous man, but finally one who has made war only with Savages and has no character, whereas I have been ship Captain for thirteen years and thirty years I have served as much land as a sea. Aside from that, he told me Monseigneur, that you had suggested him for the command of Lord de Tonti in case he happened to die. Truthfully, that seems quite uncivil to me. In fact, since I have no knowledge of that country, going over the sites, I would be an extremely unskillful man if I didn't know as much as they did by the end of the month. I beg you thus, Monsiegneur, that I at least share the command with them, and that nothing happens in the issue of war without me or without notifying me about it. As for their commerce, I claim neither to want or have any knowledge of it. I still think this will be useful to the King's service, for if we are attacked by the Spanish, I can't persuade myself that people who have never made war can resist and make use of the advantages that the occasions and the experience give in trade. That is the favor I ask of you. I am, with respect, Monseigneur, your very humble and obedient and faithful servant.

De f Beaujeu

The Minister Seignelay's response was swift and curt. "You must not have well understood the orders I have given you, having no agreement with what regards you with what should happen on dry ground, and you should not be surprised that Lord de la Salle has the command of all that must be done on this voyage, and mainly of what regards the ground, since it is he who has made the discovery, and who is acquainted with the Savages of the area." In a somewhat placating gesture, but one that carried the sharp edge of warning, he said: "This command should not cause you any trouble, since it diminishes in no way the consideration that the King has for your services; and, on the contrary, it is a way to win more favor with His Majesty provided that you put it into your head to bring along all the talents which well depend on you and not to have any anger on the subject of the command, since otherwise there would be nothing that could sink this enterprise as certainly."

It was not enough to quiet Beaujeu's worries, and indeed they only mounted as new problems emerged. La Salle wanted all but seventy of the *Joly*'s soldiers to be turned over to him once they reached land. This, claimed Beaujeu, was not only against the instructions given him in Paris, but left him with insufficient men, even with the ten crew, to properly defend the ship on her return to France, especially since they would be sailing in waters that Spain claimed and defended as her own.

The amount of goods being stored aboard the *Joly* became an increasingly contentious issue. La Salle, not satisfied with filling its hold with an extra three months' of supplies and adding an additional one hundred men to the ship's compliment—a feat that far exceeded what had ever been accomplished before on the *Joly*—continued to add boxes and containers to such depths that they blocked entirely the action of the cannons and capstan. On top of all that, he proceeded to add another 20,000 pounds of goods belonging to a merchant named Cochy. This additional cargo was arms and ammunition given him by the king, and Cochy had taken out an insurance policy of 7 percent on it for the voyage to Louisiana. Beaujeu pointed out to Seignelay that there was already enough ammunition aboard to protect the ship, and how absurd it was to insure ammunition on a warship. But he could do nothing but try and make room for it. He managed the nearly impossible task by placing the containers in the 'tween-decks space, normally used as quarters for the crew. Consequently, the soldiers and sailors had to sleep on deck throughout the voyage, where there would be no rest, even when off duty, and exposed to the elements day and night.

La Salle continued his silence about the route. Only weeks away from departure and Beaujeu did not know which coast they were to close upon and who to choose as a pilot who had a familiarity with those waters. Whoever it would be, La Salle did not want him to be able to take the ship's bearings and possibly learn its destination. To which the captain replied that he would keep all the instruments needed to determine latitude securely put away. Even so, it would be impossible, he said, to keep people off the track. Simply by observing the length of shadow cast at mid-day by two flagstaffs, they could note a change in the latitude; as for that, he said, "there was no way he could possibly block the sunshine" in order to please La Salle.

Rancor between the two men was not a secret confined to themselves and Seignelay. Beaujeu confided in letters to his friend in Paris, Cabaret de Villermont, the difficulties of dealing with La Salle and of his ever-present suspicious nature. He constantly changes his mind, complained Beaujeu, saying one thing one day, another the next. "I think him a brave man, and true; and I am persuaded that, if this business fails, it will be because he does not know enough, and will not trust us of the profession." Beaujeu asked Villermont to please set the Abbé Renaudot straight about the character of La Salle.

Matters were only made worse by the interference of Villermont, no matter how well intentioned. He wrote to Renaudot, as requested, who, in turn, wrote to La Salle informing him about Beaujeu's letters, with their complaints about La Salle's ability, judgment, and manners. Furthermore, Villermont showed this correspondence to all his acquaintances. From Rochemont, in response to Villermont's request for information about the current events, Machaut-Rogemont (a fellow officer of Beaujeu) wrote that "he pitied the poor Beaujeu for having to deal with a human so poisonous." And concluded, saying: "Beaujeu has a nasty job; he'll really fool us if he succeeds. I don't see on what grounds he has done so much for a man who must regard him as only a passenger, not having shown that he has any other quality."

When Beaujeu learned that his very private confidences were being generally discussed throughout France, he complained angrily. He had asked that his letters be burned. Instead, without regard for the fact they were "scrawled in haste," Villermont indiscriminately forwarded them to others. The sad result was that it put Beaujeu in a less favorable position and only added more fuel to La Salle's already incredible distrust.

Beaujeu also began to realize that all these public disputes were burgeoning into something much larger than was prudent. In another, and more humble, letter to Seignelay (July 10, 1684) Beaujeu wished the minister to realize he was not trying to make matters difficult for La Salle, but "only to have peace and not slow things up." The problems, he said, are of La Salle's own making. "It troubles me, being devoted to you as I am, that they have engaged you in an affair, the success of which is very uncertain, and of which the author has begun to doubt." La Salle, he went on to say, "is a man who has undertaken a thing he is unsure about."

Another worry began to take hold—the possibility of being blamed for the failure of the expedition because he would not cooperate. This he addressed in writing as well. He feared that if the enterprise, whatever the real purpose was, failed, La Salle would cast the blame on others and it would fall equally on his shoulders. He asked Seignelay to "look things over beneath the surface . . . to take the trouble of informing [himself] about the character of that man," that you "may judge the future by the past."

Fear of failure, justified or not, had other consequences. Beaujeu was a career officer, looking forward to receiving a government pension, and it was up to Seignelay to fill those vacant positions. By now he firmly believed La Salle's enterprise was futile, and even considered the possibility he would perish before it ended. He asked, therefore, of Seignelay:

If I have done badly, sir, I beg you to consider my [good] intentions. . . .You know my service record and good will; I have nothing more to tell there. I ask also your protection for my family during my absence; and if I should die during this voyage, I have done business with powerful people, and if you do not balance their authority, by letters in my favor for my judges, I run the risk of losing in the business world all that I have already fairly earned. Do me the favor of seeing to Mrs. de Beaujeu when she asks you about it, and of believing me your very humble, very obedient, and very faithful servant,

De Beaujeu

Beaujeu, with perceptive clarity, put his finger on the main problem when he said that the words and actions of La Salle could be attributed to his own uncertainty about the success of the enterprise. This, combined with all the secrecy, ambiguity of purpose, and conflicts in command bred doubt and distrust between everyone. He harbored no illusions about any peaceable accord between himself and La Salle, but knowing that communication was necessary, promised to give La Salle, "a man who wants his pride . . . as much of it as he wants, and maybe more."

In the past eighteen years since La Salle first arrived in Canada, he alternately experienced success and disaster, friendship and deceit, starvation and prolonged anxiety. Now, he was finally about to embark on a voyage that would be the culmination of his long-held and cherished dream. He was soon to become master of his own empire—Louisiana—in New France, and with it attain financial security. As Francis Parkman wrote: "It is difficult not to see in this the chimera of an overwrought brain, no longer able to distinguish between the possible and the impossible."

Shortly before departure, La Salle wrote to his mother:

MADAME MY MOST HONORED MOTHER—

At last, after having waited a long time for a favorable wind, and having had a great many difficulties to overcome, we are setting sail with four vessels, and nearly four hundred men on board. Everybody is well, including little Colin and my nephew. We all have good hope of a happy success. We are not going by way of Canada, but by the Gulf of Mexico. I passionately wish, and so do we all, that the success of this voyage may contribute to your repose and comfort. Assuredly, I shall spare no effort that it may; and I beg you, on your part, to preserve yourself for the love of us.

You need not be troubled by the news from Canada, which are nothing but the continuation of the artifices of my enemies. I hope to be as successful against them as I have been thus far, and to embrace you a year hence with all the pleasure that the most grateful of children can feel with so good a mother as you have always been. Pray, let this hope, which shall not disappoint you, support you through whatever trials may happen, and be sure that you will always find me with a heart full of the feelings which are due to you.

Madame my Most Honored Mother, from your most humble and most obedient servant and son.

delasalle

WRETCHED VOYAGE

With the differences between the two leaders resolved, at least temporarily, the *Joly* left to join the other ships at La Rochelle. Since the end of the twelfth century, French ships departed from that great harbor to "split the waters, command the storms, ignore the anger of the winds, and travel beyond the sun." On July 24, 1684, another fleet was assembled and ready to take on the tempests of the Atlantic, for the greater glory of France and bring honor to the Sun King.

On a day of fine, settled weather, and fair winds, twenty-four of His Majesty's ships raised anchor and hoisted their sails skyward. As the wind filled the canvas, they set their stern toward the twin towers of Saint-Nicholas and La Chaine and headed out across the Bay of Biscay for Portugal's Cape Finisterre, that promontory so aptly named "lands end." They would all keep together until reaching the cape, then disperse toward their separate goals; some to sail for the St. Lawrence and Canada and others to the French colonies in the Indies. The four ships appointed for La Salle's enterprise were headed for the Gulf of Mexico and the mouth of the Mississippi River.

They had barely made 150 miles across the Bay of Biscay when the *Joly* buried her stem in a large wave and snapped her bowsprit. Sails were quickly lowered, and the rigging attached to the broken sprit cut to prevent further damage. There was no doubt the bowsprit had to be replaced, but the question was whether to proceed to the nearest port in Portugal or return to France for the repairs. The four vessels of La Salle's fleet headed back to Rochefort, while the other ships bound for the Islands and Canada held their course for Cape Finisterre.

La Salle, as was his usual wont, attributed the unexpected accident to sabotage; that it was further evidence of a scheme on the part of his enemies to prevent him from attaining his goal. More likely it was the result of the *Joly* being so overloaded with all the stores that she lost much of her buoyancy. Far down on her waterline, and sluggish, she couldn't respond quickly enough to the waves.

While repairs were being made, La Salle received word from Canada that

La Rochelle Harbor, painted by Claude-Joseph Vernet, was one of a series of fifteen paintings of French seaports commissioned by Louis XIV in 1753, and executed between 1754 and 1765. La Salle's fleet of vessels was launched from La Rochelle in 1684. Today, the harbor, with its fourteenth-century twin towers still standing, is primarily used by yachts. *Photo: courtesy of Musée de la Marine, Paris, France.*

the Iroquois were once again on the warpath, and Fort St. Louis on the Illinois was threatened. Fearing that La Barre would use this as an excuse to prevent La Forest from re-occupying Fort Frontenac and Fort St. Louis in behalf of La Salle, as he was instructed to do by the king, La Salle wrote to Seignelay. He told him that if necessary, he would leave his new band of settlers at the mouth of the Mississippi and immediately proceed to Fort St. Louis to rescue his colony there and ensure the safety of his store of furs. The possibility of having to divide his attention and energies between these two sites added one more burden to La Salle's already overladen conscience.

On August 1st, with her new bowsprit in place, the *Joly* and three other ships made a fresh start for the Gulf of Mexico. Chief persons aboard the *Joly* were Captain Beaujeu, La Salle, his brother the Abbé Jean Cavelier, two Récollet priests, the two Sulpitians d'Esmanville and Chefdeville, and Henri Joutel. The last named was a fellow native of La Salle's Rouen, who joined the expedition in the role of its official historian. Additionally, there

were the ship's crew, its soldiers, and the many workers and women recruited to start the fledgling colony. In all, the fleet carried about 280 persons, including the crew. The *Aimable*, commanded by Captain Aigron,
served as a cargo ship, carrying all the materials necessary to construct and
sustain the settlement. Thirty casks of goods destined for Santo Domingo,
where they were to be sold, filled the hold of the *Saint François*. The *Belle*,
given to La Salle by the king as a gift, was commanded by two masters, but
no mention is made as to her cargo.

This time the weather was fair and there were no mishaps. All went well
until they approached the island of Madeira. Then the smoldering resentments between the two leaders erupted. Beaujeu wished to put in to
Madeira and anchor so that the ships could take on water and fresh provisions. But La Salle would have none of it. He argued that they were barely
twenty-one days out from France and had all they would need aboard to see
them through to Santo Domingo. If they stopped now, it would be a loss of
eight or ten days to no purpose. Besides, he did not want to run the risk of
having the secret of his enterprise becoming known to the residents, who
might divulge the information to the Spaniards.

Neither Beaujeu and his officers, nor the ship's crew took kindly to La
Salle's notions, which prevented their having a brief respite from their con-
finement on the ships. One of the passengers, a Huguenot from La
Rochelle, attempted to intercede in behalf of Beaujeu's request, but for his
efforts only managed to increase the ire of La Salle, who retreated to the
solitude of his cabin.

With the decision made that there would be no anchoring at Madeira, the
ships held their course south to reach the trade winds, where they would
have an easy passage westward. Improved weather, the easy motion of the
ships under a steady breeze, and freedom from the chore of beating their way
against contrary winds restored everyone's spirits. They delighted in watching the flying fish as they took flight from a wave crest and soared above the
water—sometimes to land aboard the deck of the boat instead of back into
the sea. They did not let it pass them by that these acrobatic fish made fine
tasty morsels. Soldiers, sailors, and passengers alike were suspended in a
nether world; cut free from the cares they had left behind them, and not yet

arrived at the duties that lay ahead. They began to look forward to the ritual diversion offered when they reached the Tropic of Cancer.

Preparations were already being made on deck for the "baptizing" of those who had never before crossed the line, by dunking them in tub of water. The ceremony would be accompanied by an oath administered to perpetuate the same unto future neophytes. Following this, there would be a generous dispersal of refreshments, drink, and an exchange of money from those who preferred to buy their way out of the ordeal. Whatever the reason, whether it offended the sensibilities of La Salle's Jesuit training or simply that he was in a black mood and found a means to drive a thorn into the captain's already wounded esteem, La Salle stepped forward and prohibited all observance of the ritual. Superstition and tradition, the two pillars of a sailor's temple, were set askew by his command. Furious, Beaujeu was forced to cancel the festivities, and there was nothing the sailors could do but retreat in grumbling acquiescence. The mood was such, wrote Joutel, "that they would have gladly killed us all."

By the 16th of September they sailed past the island of Sombrero. Only a small, barren mass of rock, incapable of sustaining life, it marked the end of their Atlantic passage and entry into the Caribbean Sea. Throughout the entire voyage the fleet managed to stay within sight of each other, partly due to a reduction in the amount of sail carried by the *Joly* to allow the other, slower boats to keep up with her. Now, just when they were about to enter the "Spanish Sea" and most needed the strength in numbers and fire-power of the *Joly*, the ships became separated. The weather blew foul, and it already being the month of September, caused a growing concern that the winds presaged a hurricane.

Conditions aboard La Salle's ships were about the same as others of the period, that is, very nearly intolerable. The cramped accommodations offered no privacy. The sailor rarely had time to change his clothes—even if he had a second set—and the men quickly became infested with lice and infected with typhus, scurvy, and dysentery. Cabins of privileged guests, or even the master, were no better. They were "but sluttish dens that breed sickness."

When the *Joly* reached the torrid zone, many of the men were already ill. The infirmities were only made worse by the shortness of their water supply and the necessity for the men to sleep on deck, where they were exposed to the heat of the sun during the day and the rain at night. By the time the fleet reached the island of Santo Domingo, or Hispaniola, two of the men—a soldier and a sailor—had already died, and fifty persons aboard the *Joly* were seriously ill. Even the resolute La Salle, a man seemingly of iron constitution, succumbed to the malady. He was taken with a "violent fever," which the doctors judged "a long and dangerous illness, not only for the body, but also for the mind."

Beaujeu had predicted all this before the vessels even left La Rochelle and expressed in a letter to Seignelay. Not only were a large number of his crew unable to attend to their duties, but they could not even be treated. His personal surgeon, Lord Juif, and La Salle's surgeon were both sick and out of service.

Before reaching Santo Domingo, Beaujeu wanted to stop at one of the Windward Islands to take on fresh water. But he received from La Salle the same response, as to the like request at Madeira. La Salle said that his orders from the king forbade him to land at the Windward Islands. Though it meant risking the voyage, Beaujeu had no choice but to comply.

Shortly afterward, however, Beaujeu had the opportunity to make the decisions himself. As they approached Santo Domingo the weather became contrary. First the wind dropped altogether, leaving the *Joly* becalmed. Then, a storm of such strength came up that it scattered all the ships, leaving none in sight of their flag vessel. They called a conference aboard the *Joly* to decide whether to wait for the other ships to show up or go on ahead on their own. With so many sick men, and such an acute water shortage, the general consensus was to crowd on as much sail as possible when the wind abated and run for the nearest port on the French side of the island, *Port de Paix* (Port of Peace). It was the closest, and most convenient port, and they would wait there for the other ships. But when the wind blew fair, Beaujeu decided to take advantage of it. He sailed the *Joly* past *Port aux Paix*, which lay on the northwest shore of Santo Domingo and across the Bay of Goâve to *Petit Goâve* on the southwest end of the island.

At *Petit Goâve*, on the 27th of September, having spent fifty-eight days in their passage from La Rochelle, France, Beaujeu finally dropped anchor. Immediately, a canoe came out from the shore to greet the ship and to inquire as to her purpose. Upon seeing from her colors that she was a French vessel, they told the captain that Monsieur de Cussy (governor of the Island of Tortuge) was with the Marquis de St. Laurent (governor-general of the French West Indies) at *Port de Paix,* as was also the Intendant, M. de Bégon. La Salle, now sufficiently recovered to hear the news, was furious with Beaujeu, and berated him for sailing past *Port de Paix.* He was, of course, totally unaware that La Salle had very cogent reasons for wanting to put into that place. Arrangements had been made back in France to take on buccaneers from that port to add to La Salle's forces. And La Salle also planned to sell merchandise to the officials there in order to raise more money for the expedition.

There was nothing La Salle could do now but bear the setback with patience—a trait not high on his list of abilities. The passengers in the canoe were given a letter for de Cussy and the others to inform them that La Salle was in *Petit Goâve,* and could they please come meet him here, that they might assist him, "and take the necessary measures for rendering his enterprise successful." Meanwhile, the sick men were carried ashore, housed, and given treatment. The next morning, in thankfulness for a safe passage, they sang the *Te Deum.*

Those sailors still unaffected by any malady, celebrated the safe arrival in their own manner by heading for the nearest taverns and brothels as soon as they went ashore. La Salle's illness returned, and worsened. He was taken with a violent fever, accompanied by light-headedness, and given to delirious "imagining of things terrible and amazing." It left him totally incapacitated, a condition that lasted the better part of two weeks before there was any improvement. While he was recovering his health, Joutel and M. le Gros, one of the chief men of the company, managed La Salle's affairs, sold some commodities aboard the ship to help raise money, and nurtured him back to health.

One small glimmer of light shown through the pervading gloom hanging over the tired and sick men. Two of the lost ships, the *Aimable* and *Belle,* which had become separated from the rest of the fleet by the stormy winds, showed up and anchored next to the *Joly.* Just as quickly, the light they brought by the joy of their arrival was extinguished by the news they brought.

The third ship, *Saint-François,* while in shallow waters and unable to maneuver under sail, was captured by the Spaniards in two piraguas. The loss of this ship, with her men, was all the more grievous, for her hold contained provisions, ammunition, utensils, and tools for the settling of the new colony.

Cavelier de la Salle, Robert's brother, lay the blame for the unfortunate incidents and discontent of the crew on Beaujeu. In *his* account of the voyage (*Relation of La Salle's Last Voyage*) he said:

> If these unfortunate accidents damped the ardor of our adventurers, the conduct of mr. de Beaujeu . . . did so no less; and if your Lordship takes pains to examine, you will find that that officer, jealous of my brother's having the principal authority and the direction of the enterprise, so traversed it, that the failure may be attributed to him.

Le cavelier

As the days went by without any improvement in La Salle's health, there was growing concern whether indeed he might never recover. Many had placed their full trust, as well as their money, in an expedition which all its details were known to only one man, and that man, neither in sickness nor in health, would confide it to anyone. Fearing that La Salle might die, and they had best make their own plans if there was to be any hope of ever returning alive to their native France, the Abbé Cavelier and another Sulpitian priest named d'Esmanville approached Captain Beaujeu. They petitioned him to take command of the expedition and be fully in charge of all its affairs.

Beaujeu declined the request on two counts. One, if and when La Salle recovered, he knew that no matter what was done, nothing would please the man. He had heard La Salle say several times that they should not get involved with his business, or even talk about it. Aside from the personal reasons, he did not want to take on the responsibility for an affair which he believed to be ill-conceived from the start and led by a man improperly trained or experienced for the forthcoming demands. He recommended that they seek advice from the Intendant who was due to arrive from *Port de Paix* shortly. He did, however, act upon the need to provide for the people, most of whom were hired, aboard the *Aimable* and the *Belle*. Provisions supplied for a three-month voyage to the Mississippi were gone, and at best they would not be able to leave *Petit Goâve* until the 10th or 12th of November. What was left of the scant supply on the *Joly* was carefully metered out to the other ships. Since there was little hope of obtaining any degree of provisions on the island, Beaujeu ordered ovens to be built on the boat. In this way, they at least were able to bake biscuits with the remaining flour to increase the food supply until they reached the Mississippi. Beaujeu was reluctant to do any more than this, but stated in a full report to Seignelay about their passage, and condition at Santo Domingo, that he will send further news from the Mississippi "or die trying." He promised to regulate his actions according to the counsel and consent of the Intendant Bégon, M. de St.-Laurent, and de Cussy.

Under Joutel's care, La Salle slowly regained his health and began once again to take charge of affairs. It was clearly evident they had to leave Hispaniola as quickly as possible. With the passing of each day, more and more of their precious stores were being consumed. Many of the men, on which the future settlement depended, were dying or deserting. The tropical climate, so unsuited to their disposition took its toll through disease. And licentious behavior while ashore hastened the demise of others. As Joutel so succinctly stated in his journal, "The air of this place is bad, so are the fruits, and there are plenty of women worse than either." Many men were led to abandon the enterprise by stories they heard from the French buccaneers at *Petit Gouave,* of the land they were headed to being even more inhospitable and more dismal, and the awful mess in which they presently found themselves. To prevent the further loss of any men, La Salle ordered everyone aboard the ships and to remain there until departure.

In the meantime, Beaujeu had already started to seek out information about navigation in the Gulf of Mexico. From a French pirate called Le Sage, he heard that as a boy on a Dutch ship, he had been to the land they were headed for while looking for the Mississippi. They found it, he said, quite near the place depicted by La Salle. But they were unable to enter on account of the obstacles near its mouth. He also claimed that the Dutch ship had dropped anchor in the Bay of the Holy Spirit and had no trouble entering, as there were four fathoms at its mouth. Another captain, named Du Chesne, told Beaujeu that about six months ago, they sought and pillaged the village of Saint Louis de Tempico on the Rio Bravo (R. Grande). At that time, he thought he had seen the Mississippi.

These, and others Beaujeu spoke to, all affirmed his worst suspicions about the remainder of the voyage. From September until March, the Gulf of Mexico would be the least navigable, on account of strong northerly winds. Also that coast of the Gulf, with its shallow water and many shoals, is difficult to approach. These were the dangers of nature, but there were other kinds of dangers to deal with. The Spanish considered the Gulf of Mexico to be a Spanish Sea, and with their warships protected it from incursions by others. Ever since the reign of Phillip II, in the second half of the sixteenth century, Spanish decree forbid all foreigners from entering the Gulf of Mexico upon pain of death. Beaujeu was warned that there were as many as six Spanish vessels in these waters, carrying thirty to sixty cannon. In addition, there were other ships rowed by banks of oarsmen, such as the Galleys found in the Mediterranean.

Upon La Salle's recovery and arrival of the three government representatives from Port de Paix, all met aboard the *Joly* with Captain Beaujeu and Captain Aigron of the *Aimable* to lay out their strategy. Aiding them in matters of navigation were the two hired pilots from France, plus a French pirate familiar with the Gulf. After much discussion, they decided upon the following arrangement. First, rather than using the *Joly* as the leader of the fleet, the honor would go to the *Aimable*, the slowest and worst sailor of the squadron. She would carry the light that the others would follow. This way, they could be assured no ships would be left lingering behind, to be separated from the fleet. They would all be together in case of trouble with Spanish vessels. Second, leaving Petit Gouave, they would sail west, along the southern coast of Cuba, thereby benefiting from the lee shore of that island, and protected from any northerly blows. It had the further advantage of not having to sail against the strongest portion of the Bahama current. The velocity of this current, as it rushes through the gap between Florida and Cuba to eventually become the Gulf stream, was well known to them.

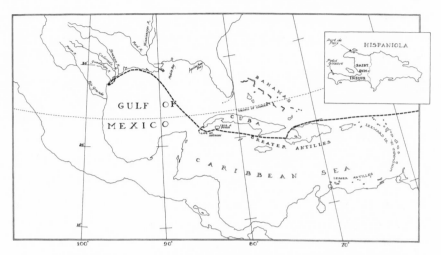

Route taken by La Salle's ships in 1684 in his return to the mouth of the Mississippi by sea.

When Juan Ponce de Léon, with his fleet of three ships, encountered this current in 1512, he wrote:

> . . . it was so swift that it drove them back, even though they had the wind strong. The two ships near the land, dropped their anchors, but the force of the stream was so great that it strained the cables. The third vessel, a brigantine, being farther out, either found no bottom, or was not aware of the current, which carried her so far from the shore that they lost sight of her, although the day was bright and the weather fine.

Though La Salle's fleet would be avoiding the brunt of the current by sailing west of Cuba, they still had to take it into account in their navigation.

Once Cape Saint Antoine, Cuba's westernmost point, was reached, they intended to drop anchor there in its shelter and wait for the most favorable winds and weather to make their passage across the Gulf to the Bay of the Holy Spirit. In all, considering their position and the time of the year, the course of action was well thought-out.

Before departing, there remained the one last task of procuring whatever food they could from the island for the remainder of the voyage. In this, the

Intendant was able to help them by arranging for the sale of 130 barrels of corn. Satisfied with the advice given about sailing the Gulf, and armed with a Spanish map of the Gulf of Mexico loaned by Du Chesne, it remained only to wait for fair weather to resume the expedition.

ACROSS THE GULF OF MEXICO

On the 25th of November, 1684, the fleet of three vessels hauled their anchors, hoisted sail, and set out for the southern shore of Cuba. The *Aimable,* leading the others, carried much of the cargo destined for the new settlement. Wishing to keep a close eye on his shrinking possessions, not to mention upon Captain Aigron, whom La Salle placed no more trust in than he did in Beaujeu, he chose to remain aboard the *Aimable,* rather than on the *Joly.* Accompanying him were Jean-Cavelier, his brother, the Récollet Fathers Zénobe Membré and Anastasias Douay, Father Chefdeville, and Henri Joutel. As soon as they were committed to making the passage, the weather turned fitful; periods of calm alternated with violent winds. Nonetheless, they were able to keep in sight of Cuba and continued their westward progress. Nine days later, almost at their goal of Cape St. Anthony, the wind dropped. They had come as far as the Island of Pines, near the western extremity of Cuba, and there they dropped anchor.

During the three-day stay at the Island of Pines, La Salle went ashore and shot an alligator, which he brought back to the boat. Some of the soldiers, those with stronger stomachs, ate the alligator, others much preferred the wild boar killed by one of the hunters. They all fed heartily on the fish that abounded in those waters. Here, for the first time, Beaujeu learned the exact destination of the expedition—the mouth of the Mississippi that lay in the acute angle of the shore of the Gulf, southwest of the Bay of the Holy Spirit.

No sooner had they embarked when the wind shifted, requiring frequent changes in their course. After four days of beating against head-winds and dealing with the calms and storms, the small fleet finally made it to Cape St. Anthony. There, they dropped anchor in fifteen fathoms of water, at the mouth of a creek. Once the weather turned favorable they again set sail. But when they were fifteen miles out, the impudent wind shifted against them. The next day the *Joly* came alongside the *Aimable,* and Beaujeu suggested that since the wind was still contrary they had best return to Cape St. Anthony. La Salle consented, and they returned to the prior anchorage.

While waiting for good weather once again, the men took the opportunity to fill their water casks from a rivulet they found in the woods. But a search for food was unsuccessful. Then, on the night of the 17th, an incident occurred that entirely diverted their attention away from reprovisioning and personal squabbles. A sudden wind came up, which caused the *Belle* to ride up over her anchor. This brought her into a collision with the *Aimable,* causing the loss of her spritsail-yard and spritsail-topsail-yard. The damages would have been much worse if the *Aimable* hadn't let out more cable. As it was, the *Belle* lost her mizzen-mast, her anchor, and about one hundred fathoms of cable.

On the 18th of December, a fresh start was made to cross the Gulf. At first, it seemed this attempt would fare no better than the earlier try. But after an initial bout with shifting winds, the weather finally settled in, and they began to make real progress. Nine days later, when there was a break in the clouds, they took an astrolabe sighting, which placed their position at 27° 14' N latitude. By this they judged they were not far from land and proceeded more cautiously.

The *Belle* was sent out ahead to see what she could discover, carefully taking soundings all the way. Finally, a half hour before sunset, the Belle found bottom at thirty-two fathoms and hoisted her colors as a signal for the other boats to come up to her. They sailed as a close group, and by midnight the water shallowed to seventeen fathoms. They held a conference to consider their plans and decided to keep a west-northwest course until they came into six fathoms. At that point they would alter course to the west and keep that heading until reaching land. The ship's boats would then be sent out to view the country.

The next day, the *Belle* being in the lead, put out her colors as a signal that she had discovered something. A sailor was sent up to the top of the main mast, where he sighted land no farther than six leagues away. According to their maps, and a dead-reckoning of their course, they should be approaching the Bay of the Holy Spirit. But no one on the ships had any first-hand experience with that bay, and the currents and frequent change in headings made them uncertain about their exact position. The pilot of the *Joly* agreed with La Salle's opinion that they were set farther east by the current than they had made allowances for. This led them to believe that the bay they saw was Apalachee Bay, the large bight of coast at the eastern end of the Gulf. By necessity, then, the Bay of the Holy Spirit lay still farther to the west. Accordingly, La Salle gave the orders to maintain their heading toward the northwest. They took care to follow the coast, always keeping it in sight, yet sufficiently far enough off to avoid its shallow banks.

On the first day of January 1685, they suddenly found themselves in only six fathoms of water, and they quickly dropped anchor before running aground. The current had brought them closer inshore than they realized. Shortly afterward, the *Belle* gave notice that she saw land twelve miles away. The *Joly* drew up alongside the *Aimable,* and between La Salle and Beaujeu they decided to send two of the longboats ashore to investigate. La Salle, with several others, took one boat, while Joutel and ten or twelve "other gentlemen" boarded the other. Since the *Belle* had the shallowest draft of all three ships, she was selected to accompany them as closely as possible, in case the wind should freshen and they were forced to make a hasty departure.

Several of those in La Salle's boat, which was in the lead, went ashore. The land they saw was "a spacious plain country of much pasture ground." There was no time to explore, for as they had anticipated, the wind suddenly came up, and they were forced to leave. But before regaining the *Belle,* La Salle took an observation of the sun and determined their position to be 29° 10' N latitude—still north of the latitude in which they expected to find the Bay of the Holy Spirit. What he did not realize, and had no way of discerning, was that in correcting their course to compensate for the current swiftly flowing eastward, he overestimated its strength and thus overcorrected for it. The error was compounded when they finally reached the coast and followed it westward. There, a countercurrent in the Gulf of Mexico swept them west along the shore, augmenting the westerly distance they traveled. The combination of these two placed their true position, not near the Bay of Apalachee or even that of the Bay of the Holy Spirit, but somewhere just west of the latter.

With their limited information about the Gulf's currents and the map they carried showing the Bay of Spiritu Santo (Mobile Bay) farther west than its actual location, it is a tribute to their navigational skills that they came as close as they had to their intended landfall. Ironically, if this landfall had been only a few miles farther east, they would have been on the eastern side of the Mississippi delta and conceivably "discovered" the mouth of that river. But whether he would have recognized it as the same river he descended in 1682 or believed it to be another river, stubbornly clinging to the belief that the Mississippi discharged into the Gulf at its western angle, is pure conjecture.

On January 2nd a fog enveloped them, and the ships lost sight of one another. Nonetheless, they cautiously continued on their way. When it cleared up the next day the *Belle* and *Aimable* were still together, but the *Joly* could not be seen. They fired a cannon and, in turn, the *Joly* answered, so although not visible, she could not have been far off. Relieved that the vessel intended to protect them from Spanish warships would soon catch up with them, the two ships resumed sailing westward.

Anchoring whenever the wind was against them, or the soundings too shallow to safely proceed, the *Aimable* and *Belle* slowly felt their way along the shore. At one time, the pilot of the *Belle* sent word that he spotted a bay which had a small island between the two points of land at its entrance. This agreed with the general description of the Bay of Spiritu Santo, and La Salle sent men ashore to investigate. Closer examination revealed that in all other aspects, it did not match what the charts showed about the bay. La Salle concluded that the bay they previously saw, and thought was Apalachee Bay, was some other, and instead, this was really Apalachee Bay. Observations, whenever they could be taken, continually placed their parallel of latitude farther north than where he expected to find the mouth of the Mississippi. This could only mean they must travel farther west to reach the desired goal.

It had been six days now, since the *Joly* parted company with the other ships, and she had yet to rejoin them. La Salle was not overly concerned, for he knew her to be a faster ship, and assumed that upon reaching the Bay of the Holy Spirit before them, would drop anchor and await their arrival. However, if she never showed up, there would be a real problem. Although all the supplies and tools for the new settlement were now with La Salle on the *Aimable*, the *Joly* carried all the soldiers and the cannon for the new settlement.

The two ships slowly worked their way west. When the winds allowed and the depths permitted, they dropped anchor close to shore and sent in the ship's boats to search for any sign either of the bay or of the Mississippi. The men always returned with the same disappointing news. By now, their dwindling water supply and provisions, barely adequate to begin with, were running dangerously low and had to be replenished. Although they could see an abundance of buffalo and goats, running along the shore, they were prevented from approaching by the strong, onshore winds, creating a heavy surf. The possibility of fresh game enticed them and overrode the dangers. Anchoring as close as possible, the boats were sent in to see if the ships could get any closer. They returned with the news that a shallow bank, with only four feet of water over it, prevented reaching a deep channel on the other side. For a while La Salle considered lightening the load of one of the ships to reduce her draft sufficiently to clear the bar, but before any decision could be made the wind changed, forcing him to weigh anchor. The next day they were prevented by an unfavorable wind from making another attempt, and reluctantly they resumed their journey.

Careful to keep within sight of the coast, they sailed west-southwest. At noon an observation of the sun placed their latitude at 28° 20' N latitude—a position quite near that which La Salle anticipated the mouth of the Mississippi to be. Since the latitude was changing quickly on the course they held, it was obvious that the coast was starting to trend toward the south. They were now at the western angle of the Gulf coast—La Salle's destination—yet there was no Mississippi. In its stead, on the morning of January 17, they discovered a "sort of river," whereupon they dropped anchor and sent one of the boats in to explore. Joutel, along with nine others, found that their "river" was really the tidal outflow from a bay, which lay behind a long, narrow spit of land. With the possibility that a river emptied into it, from which fresh water could be obtained, one of the men "went naked into the water to sound the bank." He found a channel deep enough for the ships. Then, with a great deal of difficulty, Joutel and his men managed to push their way against the current and into the bay. The "sort of river" they entered was Pass Cavallo, a narrow channel into Matagorda Bay on the Texas Gulf Coast.

Joutel created a smoke signal, to let La Salle know there was sufficient depth for the *Aimable* to enter, and then the men divided into two parties. The long boat, with three or four men, went in search of a river for fresh water, while the remainder of the party walked along the shore to hunt game. There were plenty of tracks of goats in the sand, and even herds of them were seen, but they could not get close enough to take a shot. In their stead, the men killed some ducks and other large game birds.

In the meantime, La Salle tried to bring the *Aimable* through the pass. But the current was too swift and erratic, and the channel too narrow to maneuver within. He was forced to return, drop anchor, and wait for the party of explorers. At sunset, they returned to the ship and gave La Salle an account of what they had seen. If they had found fresh water, La Salle would have been a happier man, but they did not. The next morning a favorable wind allowed them to once again be on their way. Now, rather than a northwest course, the compass showed their heading to be southwest. It wasn't very long, however, before the two ships were becalmed. As they wallowed in the long, glassy, lumpy seas, their sails hanging slack, La Salle considered whether it would be best to return to the "river" they saw the day before.

There was much in favor of the idea. For one thing, it was imperative that they replenish their fresh water supply. Another was their presumed position on the coast. The land now definitely trended in a north/south line, meaning that they had reached the western limit of the Gulf—hence the intended longitude of their destination. The latitude calculations showed they were already south of the mouth of the Mississippi. Accordingly, La Salle gave the orders to sail back. The two ships came to anchor in the same place as the previous day. La Salle kept his worries from Joutel and the rest of the men, but he could not deny them to himself. It was obvious that both the Bay of *Spiritu Santo,* as well as the mouth of the Mississippi had somehow been passed by. Given the conditions, it could easily enough have happened to the best and experienced mariners. At night, with no guiding lights, or during the day in fog, they could easily have slipped by the goal. Even with good visibility, the Gulf Coast is low and featureless, presenting no great headlands or other easily recognizable landmarks. The necessity of having to keep far offshore on account of the shallow water and numerous sandbanks made the matter that much more difficult.

Now there was an even greater urgency to find water, and the uncomfortable thought he had somehow misconceived the geography of the Gulf Coast prompted La Salle to a more thorough investigation of this place he had returned to. He resolved "to send a considerable number of men ashore, with sufficient ammunition, and to go with them himself, to discover and take cognizance of that country." All the men, including Joutel, embarked, but as they approached the shore they were once again enshrouded in fog. The small compass taken along, however, kept the boat headed toward land. Then, just as quickly as the fog descended, it began to lift, and the hazy outline of another ship was seen to approach. As she got closer, there was no doubt in anyone's mind that she was the *Joly.* All three vessels were finally reunited.

They quickly changed their pursuit for food and water and hurried out to greet her. They held a conference on what should be done next. Present were Captain Beaujeu, his lieutenant, Monsieur d'Aire, Sieur de Gabaret, second pilot of the *Joly,* several persons including clergymen, and of course, La Salle. Beaujeu and La Salle each accused the other of purposely separating from the rest of the fleet. After these recriminations, which resolved nothing, they settled down to determine exactly the place they were in and the course to be steered.

There were some who believed they had long since passed the Mississippi and that the currents had carried them farther west than they had imagined. Others were of the opinion they were near the Rio Magdalen, and they had to travel still farther west to reach their goal. La Salle tended to agree with the former notions and concluded that one of the shoals they saw almost two weeks ago might be the site of one of the two channels of the river, emptying into the sea. He had some doubts as whether to return there, but since the shoals were so near the latitude he had taken at the mouth of the Mississippi, he resolved to return.

La Salle proposed to divide the forces in the search; sending one part on foot over land until they found some river, while the three ships held the same course at sea to provide relief to the men ashore if needed. The idea held little appeal to Beaujeu who felt it put the men on shore at too great a risk. If they should lose contact with the ships, a good deal of time and effort would be spent trying to find them. Furthermore, it was a shallow, dangerous coast for the ships to sail close in. It would be safer, he said, if the soldiers disembarked, but remained where they were, and let the ships be the sole searchers of the possible other mouth of the river. By now the antagonism between the two leaders was so strong that no suggestion concerning authority, and course of action, had a chance of being accepted by the other person.

In the end, La Salle, believing that this place (Matagorda Bay), or somewhere very close by, contained one of the outlets of Mississippi, decided to establish a settlement here. Later, after the imperative needs of shelter, food, and water were taken care, he would lead a group to search for the other mouth which he thought was about a hundred miles to the northeast. There would be time afterward to look for the best possible harbor and mark its entrance to prevent mistakenly passing it, as had happened on this voyage. Even a regular port could be built.

The soldiers who traveled on the *Joly* were landed ashore, while some of the provisions aboard the *Aimable* were transferred over to Beaujeu for the return voyage to France. La Salle wrote a letter discharging Beaujeu from further service, as he had fulfilled the duty given him. Designating it as "from one of the mouths of the Colbert [Mississippi]," he said: This place being closer to where I must go by His Majesty's order, than are the other mouths of the river, I find myself obliged to ask you to hand over the soldiers which he has allotted me for this enterprise, and to ask you to disembark them from your vessel so that they can serve here while I make a reconnaissance of the Indians' villages and make an alliance with them for divers other schemes."

La Salle expressed his regret at "not having the honor" of being able to accompany Beaujeu as far as the eastern channel of the Mississippi, but felt it would be best to stay here with his men. This way, he said, it would prevent losing any more men and munitions which have already been reduced by the long voyage.

The land where His Majesty sent La Salle was believed to be near the Rio Grande; as such he was now well placed in a suitable location to fulfill his commitment to the king by attacking the Spanish and seizing the rich mines of Santa Barbara in New Biscay. In his journal, Abbé d'Esmanville claims that La Salle told him in the strictest confidence that these were his intentions. He would not search further for the river, said La Salle, "since he was already in the country where the King had sent him."

Almost a year and a half after leaving France on a voyage that took La Salle and close to three hundred persons a quarter of the way around the world, he had finally reached his destination. Here, La Salle would create a new settlement uniting all of New France in a string of forts reaching from the St. Lawrence River in the north to the Gulf of Mexico in the south. If he ever intended to play a part in Peñalosa's scheme or accede to the king's wish to invade Spanish territory, it certainly was not evidenced in any of his actions. All La Salle's efforts were directed toward finding the other mouth of the Mississippi, east of his present site (Matagorda Bay)—in the direction opposite that of New Spain and New Biscay.

MISERY AT MATAGORDA

As the *Joly, Aimable,* and *Belle* lay at anchor in the shallow water outside Matagorda Bay, a storm came up and lasted four days. The ships pitched and rolled mercilessly in the short, steep seas, and the men feared that at any moment the anchors might break loose. Pinned against a lee shore, they would be unable to claw their way free under sail and would quickly be dashed to pieces on the shore. As soon as practical, it was necessary to bring the ships into the bay behind Matagorda Peninsula, where they would be protected and lie more easily at anchor. La Salle named the bay St. Louis Bay and was convinced that somewhere one of the channels of the Mississippi discharged into it.

In 1844, Theodore Gudin, official painter to King Louis-Philippe (1830–1848), painted this scene of the *Belle*, *Le Joly*, and *Aimable* landing in Matagorda Bay, Texas. *Photo: courtesy of the Dallas Historical Society, Dallas, Texas.*

Sieur Barbier and the pilot of the *Belle* sounded the inlet to be sure there was sufficient depth for the ships to enter. They found ten to twelve feet of water over the bar, and within the bay there were five to six fathoms. Captain Beaujeu, unwilling to accept these findings, made his own soundings. According to him, there were only eight or nine feet of water over the bar, and although this was sufficient for the *Belle* and the *Aimable,* it was far too shallow for the *Joly.* La Salle, however, insisted there were twelve to thirteen feet of water, and even at low tide there were nine feet at the very least. He thought that if Beaujeu brought the *Joly* in at high tide, there would be no problem.

To settle the issue, the entrance was sounded once again by the pilots of all three ships, and stakes were set out to mark the channel. The *Belle,* which drew only seven and a half feet of water had no trouble entering the bay. But the *Aimable* required an extra foot of water, and at that, could make it only by reducing the cargo in her hold to increase her buoyancy. Accordingly, her cannon, the iron, and other weighty things were removed, bringing her draft to eight feet. Even though there was sufficient clearance of her keel over the bottom, the strong, erratic currents, and narrow, winding channel made it a difficult maneuver.

La Salle gave the orders to Captain Aigron to wait until half-tide and rising, which would be made known by a signal from the shore, to bring in the *Aimable.* The pilot from the *Belle* was also to have been aboard to assist in the entering, but Aigron refused outright, saying "he could carry in the ship without his help."

While waiting for the proper state of tide, La Salle noticed a large tree on the bank of the river which he judged would make a fine pirogue for exploring the bay and the rivers entering into it. He sent seven or eight workmen to cut it down and hew it into a serviceable craft. They had been gone only a short while, when two of the workmen returned, trembling in fright. They had been attacked by the natives, who carried off the other workers as captives.

The timing of this mishap could not have come at a worse time, for the *Aimable* was about to make the difficult entry into the bay, and La Salle wanted to be present to supervise. Nevertheless, he felt it was his duty to come at once to the aid of his men, and left in pursuit of the kidnappers. As he approached their camp, which stood on a small hill and consisted of fifty dwellings, he happened to turn around, and to his distress saw the *Aimable* under full sail approach the channel, but she was too close to the shoals. He could not run back to shout orders to Aigron, as he might have wished, for to do so might condemn his captured men. Resolutely, he continued toward the camp.

Then he heard the dreaded sound—the signal of disaster—of the firing of the cannon on the *Aimable*. She had run aground, with all sail set. La Salle had come too far now to be of any help to the foundering ship, and centered his efforts, instead, on establishing a friendly relation with the Indians. Wracked with anxiety over the stricken *Aimable,* La Salle kept the usual formalities of exchange of gifts and the sharing of food, as a sign of friendship and peace, to an absolute minimum. As with all the other tribes he encountered, La Salle gained their confidence and goodwill. As soon as he concluded negotiations for the release of his men, La Salle hastily returned to the scene of the disaster. His worst fears were confirmed, as he saw the *Aimable* on the shoals near the entrance and firmly aground.

All the orders he had given Aigron had been disobeyed. The *Aimable* was to have been towed through the channel by one of the longboats. Yet Aigron allowed one of his sailors to convince him they could do it under sail. Contrary to cries from the lookout atop the mainmast to steer toward the marked channel, Aigron maintained a course in the opposite direction. This placed them downwind of the channel and unable to come about to correct the error. As soon as the ship touched bottom, the pilot advised that they drop anchor to prevent being driven still harder aground. But the captain ignored this good advice, and instead, added still more sail. Perhaps he thought he could thus force his ship over the bar or tack back out to sea. But the sad result was that it put the ship all the more firmly on the bar.

La Salle, of course, believed that "the mischief had been done designedly and advisably" on the part of Captain Aigron. The engineer, Minet, was not so quick to judge Aigron, saying that he had acted on La Salle's orders, which were against the advice of himself, Beaujeu, and others. However, when Captain Aigron returned to France aboard the *Joly*, he was seized and put in prison for his "detestable actions."

There was no time now to engage in a lengthy discussion about what should have been done. The stranded *Aimable* contained in her hold almost all the ammunition, utensils, tools, and others goods necessary for the enterprise, and these had to be rescued as quickly as possible. With the long-boats from all three ships, plus a few pirogues borrowed from the Indians, La Salle's men began to ferry to shore as much they could. First, the gun-powder and flour were removed. By the time that was accomplished, night-time overtook them, and the remaining goods had to be left in the ship, to be taken ashore the following morning.

During the night, however, the situation worsened. The *Aimable*'s long-boat, tied to the stern of the ship, was either cut adrift or poorly tied to be-gin with and drifted off on her own. It ran aground, where, according to Joutel, it was "maliciously staved in." Also, during the night a strong on-shore wind sprung up, and the mountainous waves rolling in from the Gulf beat relentlessly against the hull of the *Aimable*. Unable to withstand these forces, the hull split open and tons of water rushed through, flushing her clean of the remaining cargo. As soon as there was daylight the men scram-bled to rescue the items that floated. They managed to save about fifty hogsheads of wine and brandy, some powder, and Indian corn. But the loss of other goods was extensive, and included nearly all the provisions, sixty barrels of wine, four cannon, 1,620 cannon-balls, 400 grenades, 4,000 pounds of iron, 5,000 pounds of lead, most of the tools, a forge, a mill, cordage, boxes of arms, nearly all the medicines, and most of the baggage of the soldiers and colonists.

At a hastily made camp by the side of the inlet, the saved boxes, bales, and casks, with piles of cordage, spars, and dismounted cannon, were strewn about in disarray. La Salle's nephew, Crevel de Moranget, was placed in charge of the camp, with orders to guard the few remaining possessions. Dejected men and homesick women wandered aimlessly around the tents and hovels made of bits of flotsam from the wreckage. What was to have been a glorious new settlement, bringing honor to the Sun King of France, uniting his kingdom of New France, was instead a rotting morass of a few salvaged goods and many disillusioned recruits. "They were all," says the en-gineer Minet, "sick with nausea and dysentery. Five or six died every day in consequence of brackish water and bad food." Like vultures flocking to the prospect of a feast from a dying animal, the Indians were drawn to the shore to witness the pathetic struggles of this small group of Frenchmen and anticipated the plunder within their grasp.

The hold of the *Joly* still contained cannons, cannon-balls, and a quantity of iron La Salle needed for his new settlement. Unfortunately, since they were the heaviest of all the supplies, before leaving France they had been placed in the deepest part of the hold to act as ballast. To remove everything else to get at them, while the ship leapt about in the heavy seas, was deemed by Beaujeu to be impossible. Even if he managed, he said, their weight might overturn the longboat before it reached shore. As an alternative, La Salle suggested that when Beaujeu reached the bay of *Spiritu Santo*, where he could anchor in sheltered water, that he unload the cannons there and bury them. By marking the location with stakes, La Salle could send the *Belle* at a later time to retrieve them.

This proposal had little appeal to Beaujeu, who did not want to risk being blamed for the loss of these valuable items if they could not be recovered or were discovered and taken by the Spanish. He told La Salle that he would much rather wait at *Spiritu Santo* until the *Belle* could come fetch them. Or, he would even return to St. Louis Bay in April, when the weather was more settled, to then make the transfer. Later, however, Beaujeu did manage to get some of the iron and six cannons out of the *Joly*; replacing them with four of his own to maintain the ship's trim. Though not the total amount of armament La Salle desired, Beaujeu thought that these, plus what was rescued from the *Aimable*, would be sufficient for La Salle's purpose.

Several times Beaujeu offered to sail to Martinique "to look for supplies and succor." La Salle rejected this idea, saying he did not wish to incur new expenses until he could show Seignelay "some solid achievement." A strong element of pride, as well as politics, doubtless entered into his decision.

Since Beaujeu had fulfilled his obligations to the minister, and to the king, by bringing La Salle and his men safely to the spot, assured to him to be one of the mouths of the Mississippi, there was little reason to remain. Departure of the *Joly* could be delayed no longer. As long as she remained on this exposed, perilous coast, she was in jeopardy. What the wind and seas would fail to accomplish in her destruction would be taken care of by the

Spanish if she were to be seen. On the 12th of March, Beaujeu bid a final farewell to La Salle and weighed anchor. From their letters, it appears they had settled their differences and parted amicably. Beaujeu wrote to La Salle:

I wish with all my heart that you would have more confidence in me. For my part, I will always make the first advances; and I will follow your counsel whenever I can do so without risking my ship. I will come back to this place, if you want to know the results of this voyage I am going to make. If you wish, I will go to Martinique for provisions and reinforcements. In fine, there is nothing I am not ready to do: you have only to speak.

DeBeaujeu

To which La Salle replied:

I received with singular pleasure the letter you took the trouble to write me; for I found in it extraordinary proofs of kindness in the interest you take in the success of an affair which I have the more at heart, as it involves the glory of the King and the honor of Monseigneur de Seignelay. I have done my part toward a perfect understanding between us, and have never been wanting in confidence; but even if I could be so, the offers you make are so obliging that they would inspire complete trust.

delasalle

When the *Joly* left for France, more than a few of La Salle's men, unable to face the certain hardships that lay before them, returned with it. Included was the engineer Minet, who could no longer get along with La Salle. From Matagorda Bay, Beaujeu steered the ship toward *Spiritu Santo,* but failing to find it, altered course toward Cape St. Anthony of Cuba. From there, he made his way to the Chesapeake Bay, where he was able to obtain provisions and at last reached Rochefort on July 5.

Minet was seized and imprisoned for deserting La Salle. Captain Beaujeu received less than the warm welcome he expected. He had sailed deep into the heart of the "Spanish Sea" and returned the *Joly* safely to France. He had escorted La Salle to that place which he claimed was one of the mouths of the Mississippi with the loss only a single vessel—*St. François.* Yet he was chastised by Seignelay who doubted Beaujeu's word that La Salle was where the king had sent him. In a letter to the Intendant of Rochelle, the minister wrote: "He seems to [place] this belief on such weak conjectures that no great attention need be given to his account, especially as this man has been prejudicial from the first against La Salle's enterprise."

AT LAST, LA SALLE HAD what his disposition demanded—the chance to act alone, and to make decisions without the interference of others. But tired, weakened, and full of self-doubt—perhaps already seeing the impending disaster ahead—he began to make choices uncharacteristic of him.

STRANGE IRRESOLUTION

The small spit of land on which the band of settlers found themselves, with their possessions heaped around, was clearly no place to build a fort. Totally exposed to winds from all directions, and visible to any passing Spanish vessel, it was necessary to find a better location. Already one ship had appeared but continued on its way without observing the Frenchmen. To move everything across the bay, however, required more than the one longboat they had left. La Salle sent several of his men over to the Indian camp to try and purchase some of the pirogues they had seen on their earlier visit.

They returned unsuccessful, but with the news that they saw there some of the goods from the wrecked *Aimable.* Bales of Normandy blankets, some of which had been cut and made into petticoats, as well as bits of iron from the ship had been pilfered. Normally, La Salle would have gone to the camp himself, and by virtue of the respect he always received through his speech and manners, would undoubtedly have returned, both with the pirogues and the stolen goods; all the while retaining the goodwill of the Indians. Such was the case in his dealings before, with the tribes of the Iroquois, Mi-

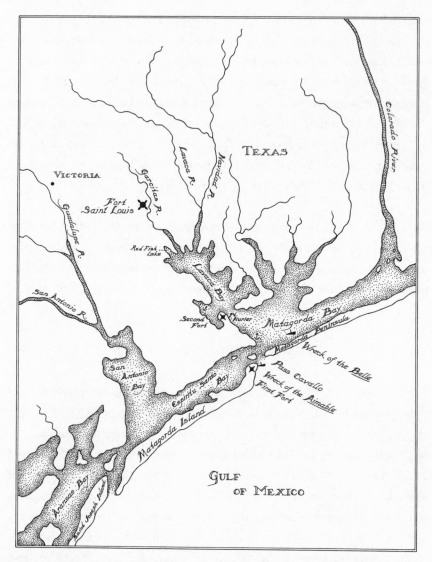

Location of the French forts established by La Salle on the Gulf coast of Texas, with shipwreck positions of the *Belle* and *Aimable*.

amis, and Illinois. This time, however, he sent his nephew Sieur Moranget and several others to do the task. It was La Salle's wish that they barter the stolen goods in exchange for the canoes, and that there be no violence. The choice of persons was most regrettable, for as Joutel says, "these gentlemen were more hot than wise."

They entered the camp with muskets in their hands, making it clear they would take what they wanted by force. Many of the Indians fled; those who remained could not understand that the Frenchmen wanted the blankets returned, and they too withdrew. Whereupon Moranget and his men entered the lodges and helped themselves, not only to the blankets, but some buffalo skins, and two canoes that they found.

Their return to camp was slow. Head-winds impeded their progress, and they were unfamiliar with managing the ungainly, long wooden canoes by poles, rather than with oars or paddles. As night came on, they stopped to rest, and as it was cold, built a fire to warm themselves. Foolishly they lay down to sleep. Worse yet, the sentinel they posted did the same.

When the natives returned to their lodges and realized all that had been taken, they took it as a declaration of war and resolved to be revenged. Drawn by the Frenchmen's campfire, the Indians soon found their foe and let fly a volley of arrows into the sleeping bodies. Two of the men were killed immediately, before return fire from their guns caused the Indians to flee. Sieur Moranget, with an arrow through one of his arms and another wound to the chest, made his way back to camp to inform La Salle. The dead were brought back to be given an honorable burial. It was a sad lesson they learned from failing to obey orders and having a sentinel disregard his duty.

The one quality La Salle always engendered among the Indian nations he dealt with and lived among—a mutual trust and peace—no longer existed. From now on they were at open war with that Nation. No trading was possible, and they always had to be on guard of attack. Sentinel guards were doubled to prevent any further surprises, and the penalty if found asleep on duty was severe.

Other lessons were quickly thrust upon the disconsolate group. There was more to fear in that hostile environment than the Spanish and the Natives. Nature could be equally cruel. The area was infested with venomous vipers, asps, and scorpions. More than one man died from the bite of the deadly rattlesnake. And two men perished when they went out onto the prairie where they were gored by buffalo. Others died when seized by alligators or succumbed to eating poisonous berries.

Some men deserted, preferring to live like savages among the savages than to suffer the wretched existence ahead of them in this strange and forbidding land. Others followed their example, but they were brought back by La Salle, who had one of the escapees hung and the rest condemned to serve him in the king's service for ten years.

Discontent was rife, and the frustrations felt by all led to plans to kill their own countrymen in order to get at the ammunition locked away. The bloody massacre was to begin with Joutel and then go on to Sieur le Gros, who lay in the warehouse still recuperating from wounds and thus unable to defend himself. Fortunately, one of the conspirators revealed the plot, and its execution was prevented.

Meanwhile the captain of the *Belle,* Sieur Hurier, ordered by La Salle to sound the bay and search for a more suitable location for the settlement, returned with his report. Opposite a point of land, which he named after himself, the *Belle* was brought to anchor, and a second fort created. From the start, it was planned to serve only as an intermediate station between the camp at the sea, and one to be selected later for a permanent habitation. The first fort was abandoned, and all its effects transferred to the new camp, with Joutel placed in command. He proceeded to create an enclosure using barrels and chests. Though totally inadequate as a defense against any attack, the new camp had the chief advantage that it was not visible to the prying eyes of the Spaniards.

The next few months were a busy time at the fledgling settlement on the banks of Matagorda Bay. The small rivers that entered the bay were brackish and unpalatable, and finding a source of fresh water continued to be a problem. Debilitated by an inadequate diet on the long voyage from France, the men found it difficult to obtain food from the bounteous supply that surrounded them. The buffalo, goats, and numerous game birds of all sorts were not easily felled. Most of the men were not trained as hunters or soldiers, and they had very poor marksmanship. What little ammunition not lost in the shipwreck had to serve the dual purpose of protecting them from hostile Indians, as well as used to procure food.

Joutel commented on the abundance of freshwater and saltwater fishes, oysters, eels, and tortoises. Here too, inexperience and lack of proper equipment thwarted the harvesting of these foods. However, eggs, both of land and sea turtles were easily taken. More cautious now of the numerous rattlesnakes the men learned to kill the deadly snake before they became its victim and found that "their flesh was not amiss." If not altogether their favorite food, at least it was preferable to eating alligator.

Attempts to start a garden failed. Various seeds and grain they put into the ground were either lost through drought, or eaten by birds or beasts. Many seeds, damaged by the saltwater, failed to sprout.

Daily, more of the settlers were laid to rest in the graveyard. Of the 180 people who landed to start the new colony, fifty-seven were already dead. Some died from the tropical diseases acquired during their stay at Santo Domingo, others from general malnutrition. Those men and women who did not fall victim to the Indians' arrows died from eating poisonous berries or were stung or bitten by poisonous animals. And there were those who seemed to languish and expire out of sheer despair over their situation.

By now it was clearly evident to La Salle that they were not at the mouth of the Mississippi. It was unlikely, even, that it entered any of the numerous lagoons of St. Louis (Matagorda) Bay. Since this place was destined to be a base from which all future explorations to find the river would be made, it was imperative to start a permanent settlement; one that was better sited and constructed than either of the two earlier forts.

The place La Salle finally selected for the new fort, named by him Fort St. Louis, was five miles up the Garcitas River. On the west bank of that river, one of several rivers that empty into Lavaca Bay, construction began on the new fort. Its location on the highest point of land on the river's bank gave an uninterrupted view of the surrounding countryside. Herds of buffalo dotted the great level prairies that stretched endlessly to the north, west, and south. Below the fort, the Garcitas River wound its way through a green valley. Timbers and planks rescued from the stricken *Aimable* and posts laboriously cut from nearby trees were used to create housing and a stockade. Lodging, divided into apartments, was made from assorted scraps of wood and covered with buffalo hides to provide shelter. All the structures were surrounded by palisades made from some stakes. Within the space of two months, all the work was completed. The sole protection of the fort consisted of eight cannons, a hundred muskets, and an equal number of cutlasses. Everything yet remaining in the earlier forts—some bars of iron, twenty packs of iron to make nails, and tools—was transferred to Fort St. Louis.

The enterprise thus far bore no resemblance to the glorious dreams promoted by La Salle and endorsed by King Louis XIV. The harsh reality of the settlers existence was far different than the glittering promises made to them back in France.

Those persons selected to found La Salle's new colony were ill-suited for that purpose. How much he was directly responsible for the selection, or whether it was the result of appointments by his agents who thrust them upon La Salle, is uncertain. But there is no uncertainty in Father Le Clerckq's assessment that the colonists "were vagabonds, and beggars, quite devoid of the industry and skill so necessary to settlers in a wilderness country." As for the 150 soldiers, they were "more wretched beggars, soliciting alms, many too deformed and unable to fire a musket." And the mechanics engaged at La Rochelle were found, once they arrived at Matagorda Bay, to know nothing at all.

Undaunted by the endless stream of failures, La Salle urged his men even harder to complete their tasks. Failure to meet his expectations brought on a swift, and at times often unjust, punishment. Under the pressure to make his dreams become a reality, La Salle was becoming a stern and harsh man. In the past, men remained loyal to the man and embraced his goals. They followed him willingly. Now, their allegiance to La Salle was one borne of necessity, and loyalty was an order, not a choice. There was little chance of survival on their own, should they attempt to desert.

CONTINUAL MISFORTUNES

Even if the colony at Fort St. Louis managed to flourish and become a success, without a connection to the Mississippi River, it would be a useless endeavor. Its very existence was based on being the final fort in a long line of forts, where goods from the interior of New France could be transported to the ocean and on to France. The Mississippi River was the vital element that united all of New France. Without it "all was futile and meaningless; a folly and a ruin." Once major construction on Fort St. Lewis was completed, La Salle shifted his energies to again searching for the Mississippi. In his absence, Joutel was left in command of the fort. Under his charge were the lives of thirty-four men, women, and children. Of that number, three were Récollet Friars, and Sieur Hurier, who would take command if anything should happen to Joutel. La Salle left specific instructions with Joutel that he was not to let anyone back into the fort unless they brought with them a written order from himself. As for the natives, contrary to La Salle's usual manner of establishing and maintaining peaceful relationship, he instructed Joutel to have no communication with them. Should they approach, he was to fire upon them.

On the last day of October (1685) La Salle set out to search for the Mississippi, or the "fatal river," as Joutel called it. He took with him fifty men, including his brother Abbé Jean Cavelier, to thoroughly explore St. Louis Bay in the hope he may thus find one of the river's channels. La Salle and his companions kept along the shoreline, while the *Belle* followed by sea. Those on the boat were to take soundings of the bay and make note of suitable places along the coast for anchoring. Each absorbed in their own duties, the two groups became separated. The pilot of the *Belle* did as was ordered, but grew overconfident and careless. One night, rather than remaining aboard the boat, the pilot and crew went ashore. They built a fire, perhaps to cook some meat or for the heat and companionship of a flame. Afterward, they lay down to sleep. Foolishly neglecting to have a guard maintain vigil, they were surprised by an Indian attack. All six of the men were slaughtered and their canoe smashed. When the *Belle* failed to return, as previously arranged, La Salle himself went in search of the missing boat and crew. He found the sad remains of the poor wretches, their scattered carcasses torn and shredded, half devoured by wolves. The *Belle,* which was to transport the colonists to the Mississippi, and their only means of returning to France, was moved to a safer place farther up the bay. La Salle placed a number of men aboard to protect the boat, with strict instructions "not to stir from that place until they had heard from him, and not to go ashore, unless with a good guard and necessary precautions."

The loss of the pilot and crew was yet another of the constant setbacks.

They were not the only ones, however, to afflict La Salle. One of his men, Sieur Duhaut (the elder of two Duhaut brothers), who accompanied him on the shore search, paused a bit to repair his shoes. When he tried to catch up with the rest of the group he mistakenly followed a path beat in the grass by buffalo, thinking it to be the trail of his companions, and became completely lost. For nearly a month he struggled to find his way back to Fort St. Louis, surviving on wild game for food. It was the middle of January, and ten weeks since the expedition first started, before Duhaut finally found the fort. At first Joutel was apprehensive about admitting him, for to do so was contrary to the orders given him by La Salle. In the end, overcome by the desire to learn any news about the fate of his leader, Joutel relented.

No one could have suspected at the time how grievous an error it was to allow Duhaut to rejoin the group. He endured his wanderings, traveling only at night to avoid constant danger from the natives, without a single companion to ease his misery and give him hope. During this time of personal trial Duhaut had excessive time to reflect on his woes and the circumstances that were rapidly propelling him to his death. One man, he thought, was responsible for all his travails—La Salle. The seed of his hatred toward La Salle was planted, and quietly, the malignant sprout grew within him until it finally burst forth fourteen months later, in a deed of foul treachery.

By the end of March, La Salle and his band of Frenchmen stumbled back to Fort St. Louis. Only eight of the original twenty were left. They were fatigued in the extreme, and their clothes hung in tatters. For the four and a half months of suffering, La Salle had accomplished little. They had encountered various Indian nations, but managed to avoid any warfare. One tribe, not so hostile as the others, informed La Salle that the Spaniards were universally hated by all tribes of the region. Had he wished, it would have been an easy matter to enlist their aid in launching an attack on Spanish settlements and New Biscay. But it was the farthest thing from his mind. At this time, he could scarcely keep his own small group alive, let alone launch an attack on others. Once again he failed to find the fatal river.

During La Salle's absence, Joutel tried his best to cheer the spirits of the disconsolate colonists. He was a staunch supporter of La Salle's endeavors and a devoted friend, but he also recognized the changes that were occurring in his leader's behavior. "When M. de la Salle was among us," says Joutel, "pleasure was often banished. Now there is no use in being melancholy on such occasions. It is true that M. de la Salle had no great cause for merry-making, after all his losses and disappointments; but his troubles made others suffer also."

Joutel encouraged entertainment in the evenings with singing and dancing. And he kept their minds and bodies busy with work to keep them from dwelling upon their misfortunes. On account of the shipwreck, the anvil they brought lay somewhere under water, but in its stead a cannon-ball was used to fashion needed items out of iron. Everyone was kept busy with various tasks—hunting, fishing, dressing hides, and building. Trees were cut down and hewn into timbers, and grass was mowed so that it would grow fresh again for their cattle. Providing for their spiritual needs was to Joutel one of the most important parts of his program. The chapel he had them build was the most spacious structure in the fort, and a full church routine was rigidly adhered to.

All these efforts, however, could not stay the pervading aura of doom. Complaints and worries smoldered within the colonists. One of the dissidents was Father Maximus Le Clercq, who kept memoirs concerning La Salle's conduct and condemned him on several occasions. Joutel managed to get hold of these memoirs and immediately burned them to prevent the further spread of discord. The main fomenter of these discontents was the elder Duhaut, who took the opportunity to promote a revolt. He told the people in Fort St. Louis that La Salle would never return, and the only hope of remaining alive was to follow him as their leader. But before his plans of mutiny were acted upon, Joutel caught wind of the affair. He severely reprimanded Duhaut, threatening him with imprisonment if he persisted in this activity. The lenity he showed was an act that Joutel later deeply regretted.

SHORTLY BEFORE RETURNING to Fort St. Louis, La Salle dispatched several men to look into the well-being of the *Belle*. With the pilot gone and the vessel manned only by a few inexperienced sailors, he was exceedingly anxious over its safety. A few days later the searchers returned to the fort, bearing calamitous news. The *Belle* was not at the place they had left her, and no messages were left to indicate why she departed, or where.

La Salle, the victim of acts of treachery before, came to but one conclusion. The crew had deserted the colony and sailed the *Belle* to the West Indies or back to France. The loss of the ship was a tragedy, since it was the only means of transporting the colonists to the Mississippi and their last hope of ever returning to France. All the more fatal to the enterprise was the loss of the contents of her hold. Believing that the ship was a safer place than the fort in which to store his personal belongings and items important for sustaining the colony, La Salle had placed everything aboard the *Belle*. With the loss of the ship went all his clothing and personal effects, plus a quantity of stores, ammunition, tools, and many articles to be used for trade with the Indians.

So stunning was the blow of this latest disaster to La Salle, that his last remaining bit of physical strength gave way, and he became dangerously ill. Concern for his recovery was uppermost in everyone's mind. As Jean Cavelier wrote, "we had no resource but in the firm guidance of my brother [La Salle] whose death each of us would have regarded as his own." Almost a full month elapsed before La Salle sufficiently regained his health and was ready to start another expedition. The situation was desperate and called for daring measures. Through disease, accidental death, and Indian assaults, the 180 souls of the colony had dwindled to forty-five. This time La Salle would continue his search by land until he came to the Mississippi. Then, he would ascend the river to Fort St. Louis on the Illinois, and from there proceed to Montreal where he could send a report to France and implore aid for his colony on the Gulf coast. Accompanying him on this journey were twenty others, including his brother Jean Cavelier, his nephew, Moranget, and the Récollet priest Anastase Douay. Toward the end of April (1686) the pitiful looking group, their clothing scavenged off the wrecked *Aimable* or taken from the dead bodies of their comrades, parted company with Joutel and the remaining colonists. Only those too ill to travel were left behind.

They were gone only a few days when Sieur Chefdeville, the Marquis de la Sablonnière, and four others showed up at the fort. These were the sole survivors from the lost *Belle,* and from them, Joutel learned the woeful fate of La Salle's vessel. While the *Belle* was still safely at anchor, Sieur Planterose and six others went ashore in a canoe to search for fresh water. They took with them four or five casks to fill. By evening they had not yet returned, and the captain of the ship set an anchor light as a beacon to guide them safely back. But the light went out, and neglectfully, was never re-lit. The men in the canoe were never seen again. Either they drowned when their overloaded boat was swamped in rough water, or while ashore, were attacked and killed by the Indians. Those who remained on the *Belle* waited until there was no more water left, and all the food was consumed. During this time, several more died. To wait any longer condemned them all to certain death. They weighed anchor and resolved to sail the *Belle* back to Fort St. Louis. Two things conspired against them in their efforts. There were only a few men left now, and these were weak from hunger and thirst and inexperienced in sailing. Also, they were caught by a sudden storm, and the *Belle* broke free from her anchor. Totally uncontrolled, she was sent scudding across the bay. The crew hastily tried to reset the anchor, but before it could take hold, the violent northerly wind drove the boat to the other side of the bay where it ran hard aground on a sandbar.

Without the ship's boat, lost a few days earlier, the men had no way to reach shore. As best they could, they constructed a raft from barrels and planks to get to the narrow spit of land (Matagorda Peninsula) close by. But it was so poorly made, that the first to use it were all drowned. A second raft, built better than the first, successfully brought the remaining passengers to shore. Several trips were made back to the *Belle* to salvage what they could. Some sails, rigging, and personal items—linen, clothes, and papers—belonging to La Salle were saved. The distance back to the mainland was too great to swim across, and the peninsula was devoid of trees with which to build a suitable boat. For three months they languished on that barren beach, until providentially they found a canoe, and the survivors were able to return to Fort St. Louis and bring the sad tale with them.

TOWARD THE FATAL RIVER

La Salle planned to let the heat of summer days pass before making a final, determined effort to reach Canada and bring succor to Fort St. Louis on the bay. But illness prevented him from making a start until the beginning of January 1687. Reduced to clothing made from stitched-together scraps of canvas sails taken from the remains of the *Belle* and wearing strips of dried buffalo hide in place of shoes, La Salle took leave of the fort. What few possessions deemed useful were packed on five horses traded for from the Indians.

This time, seventeen men accompanied him, including: Henri Joutel, his brother Abbé Cavelier, his two nephews Moranget and Cavelier, the rebellious Duhaut, Liotot the surgeon, and an ex-buccaneer named Hiens. Only twenty souls remained in the colony. Of these, half were women and priests. Sieur Gabriel Barbier was placed in command of the settlement until La Salle returned. Their limited protection against Indian attack consisted of muskets, cutlasses, and eight cannons—but without cannon-balls. In place of the cannon-balls, they could be filled with nails and scraps of iron. Abbé Cavelier remarked that what appeared at first to be a pleasant land, now "seemed an abode of weariness and a perpetual prison."

It was a quiet occasion, unmarked by any ceremony, when the two groups separated. Though no one expressed the thought aloud, the tears, tenderness, and sorrow at leave-taking betrayed the inner thoughts of all; they would never see each other again.

As before, it was a toilsome march across prairies, through marshes and woods. Streams and rivers, swollen by frequent rains, had to be crossed, either by wading waist deep through the water or on crudely constructed rafts. The need to constantly be on guard against Indian attacks added to their difficulties. By necessity they treated the various tribes they encountered with the greatest caution until it could be determined whether or not they were hostile. At times, the wanderers were taken into the Indian villages and treated with the greatest courtesy. There would be feasting, an exchange of presents, and the ritual smoking of the peace-pipe. In other villages, however, feigned hospitality by day changed to malevolence at night.

The Murther of Mons.ʳ de la Salle

M. Vander goukt Scal:

Engraving of the Murder of Sieur de La Salle.

For two and a half months the small band of Frenchmen slowly made their way north northeast, crossing the Brazos and Trinity Rivers. During this time, resentments, barely kept under control, erupted into quarrels, which in turn developed into a conspiracy of murder. The genesis of the plot began simply enough when they neared a place La Salle had been to before on one of his earlier journeys. At that time, he hid a cache of Indian wheat and beans. Since provisions were now running low, and they were close by, La Salle dispatched Sieurs Duhaut, Liotot, Hiens and two others to retrieve the much needed food. They had no trouble finding the spot, but everything was rotten and quite spoiled. As luck would have it, as they were returning empty handed, two buffalo appeared, which they killed. One of the men was sent for a horse to bring back the meat back to the camp.

La Salle sent Moranget, along with his servant, de Male, for the first load. When he got there, Moranget found to his dismay that they already smoked the meat, though it was not dry enough. The four men had set aside the marrow-bones and other choice pieces of beef to roast for themselves. Enraged at their greedy behavior, Moranget snatched everything away, telling them he would make sure that none of them would have anything of it to eat.

If this incident was but an isolated squabble, it might perhaps have resulted in nothing further than bitter recriminations. But Duhaut had never forgiven, or forgot, his travail during the solitary month of his trek to Fort St. Louis and the chastisement he received from Joutel once he got there. Moranget's harsh behavior echoed that of his uncle, La Salle, and ignited Duhaut's wrath. The surgeon Liotot also had cause for wrath. His brother (or nephew) had been killed by the Indians on one of La Salle's previous journeys, and he had secretly sworn vengeance. The conspirators, all in agreement, withdrew and together resolved a bloody revenge. The first to be murdered was Moranget, followed by two of La Salle's most faithful supporters—his servant Saget, and Nika, the Shawanoe hunter who had long accompanied him. They waited until night, when everyone was asleep, then crept upon their unsuspecting victims. Liotot was the executioner. With an axe, he hacked away at Moranget's head. Then he did the same with the servant and the Indian. The other villains—Duhaut, Hiens, Teissier, and l'Archevêque—stood by and watched, ready with their guns to fire if there was any resistance.

Then, in order to save themselves and finish the massacre, the assassins planned to kill La Salle. They consulted among themselves as to the fastest method to effect it, and concluded they would do the same as they had done to Moranget—knock his brains out. But since they were distant from

La Salle's camp by some miles and separated by a river swollen by recent rains, the plot had to be postponed for several days.

Meanwhile, La Salle became anxious over the absent men and the failure of Moranget to return, bringing with him the buffalo meat. He decided to see for himself the cause of the delay. Some sort of foreboding, or the presage of misfortune, overtook La Salle, for before departing he inquired whether anyone heard Duhaut, Hiens, or Liotot express any discontent. Hearing nothing to cause concern, he set out to find them. As he approached the camp of the murderers, he spotted l'Archevêque and asked for his nephew, Moranget. L'Archevêque replied that he was wandering about somewhere. At that same time, Duhaut, who had hid among high weeds, raised himself, and fired his pistol. Two shots rang out at the same time, those of Duhaut and l'Archevêque. Duhaut's was true to the mark and pierced La Salle's brain so that "he dropped down dead on the spot, without speaking one word."

The Récollet Father, Anastase Douay, who stood by La Salle's side, witnessed the entire event. He was paralyzed with fright, certain that he was to be the next victim. But Duhaut assured Douay that he had no cause for fear. All he wanted, he said, was revenge against Moranget "because he had designed to ruin him," and La Salle, for "the ill usage" he received from him.

The sound of the shot brought forth all the other traitors. They tore off La Salle's shirt, and vented all their malice, scorn, and derision, "in vile and opprobrious language." When their rage cooled, they dragged his naked body into the bushes and left him there, without burial, to be devoured by buzzards and wolves. "Such was the unfortunate end of Monsieur de la Salle's life," wrote Joutel, "at a time when he might entertain the greatest hopes, as the reward of his labours."

UNENDING VIOLENCE

Without any opposition, Duhaut arrogantly assumed leadership of the rest of the expedition. Rather than killing off everyone else, eliminating all witnesses, as he had originally planned, Duhaut remained with the others as they proceeded toward the Mississippi. Joutel and Abbé Cavelier resented being under the authority of the murderer of their leader, but yielded, fearful that if they resisted, they too would fall victims. Their devotion to La Salle did not extend to martyrdom on his behalf.

They continued the journey, passing through various Indian villages, where they were well treated. By chance, at one of these villages, Joutel came upon some deserters from one of La Salle's earlier expeditions. They had taken to living like savages, among the natives, and were barely recognizable to their own countrymen. These deserters confirmed what Joutel had heard earlier from the Indians. The great river they sought lay only forty leagues away, toward the northeast.

As they got closer to the French settlements, Hiens began to be apprehensive about what might happen to him once the truth was known about La Salle's assassination. He preferred to return to Fort St. Louis by the bay than continue any further with Duhaut. Hiens enlisted the aid of the two French deserters, Ruter and Grollet, plus twenty-two natives, in his plan of revolt. He sought out Duhaut and spoke to him, saying: "You have decided to go on to the French settlements. It is a danger which we dare not encounter. I therefore demand that you divide with us all the arms, ammunition, and goods we have. You then may pursue your own course and we will pursue ours."

Without waiting for a reply from Duhaut, Hiens immediately shot him through the heart. Briefly, he staggered about, then dropped dead. The accomplice, Ruter, shot Liotot. But he was not so quick to die and lived for several hours afterward. It took two more pistol shots before his convulsed body lay still. Father Douhy, present at the execution wrote: "His [Liotot] hair, and then his shirt and clothes took fire, and wrapped him in flames, and in this torment he expired." The two bodies were then buried. L'Archevêque, Duhaut's servant, was also to have been killed, but he managed to escape.

Thus, said Joutel, "those murderers met with what they had deserved, dying the same death they had put others to."

The next day Hiens held a conference with Joutel. They agreed to divide their remaining possessions, and the two parted amicably, each going their separate way. Of the original twenty persons who left Fort St. Louis for Canada, the number was now seven: Joutel, Father Douay, Abbé Cavelier, and his nephew, young Cavelier, and three others. Through May and into June, they continued their journey toward the northeast, and by September, reached the fort and settlement of Fort St. Louis on the Illinois.

It would be difficult to say who felt the greater joy on that afternoon in September 1688 when Joutel and his companions entered the fort; those who endured the long and difficult travel over eight hundred miles of wilderness, or the Frenchmen and Indians in the fort who welcomed news about their lost leader, La Salle. When pressed for news about his health and the well-being of the new colony, Joutel and Abbé Cavelier practiced a strange deception. They said "he was in good health when he left us." In itself, this statement was true, for though they knew about his death, they were not witness to it. Father Douay, and Teissier, who did see him killed, neither contradicted them by telling the truth nor supported the lies by affirming of the story. Instead, they maintained a silence.

Joutel and Abbé Cavelier led everyone to believe that La Salle was with the colony and that they were appointed to return to France in order to procure more supplies. At length, they arrived at Québec, where they embarked on a ship and safely reached Rochelle, France, on October 9, 1688. Until then, they had kept the news of La Salle's death a secret. Joutel's motives for concealing the truth are unclear. Those of Abbé Cavelier, however, appear to have been his desire to get possession of family property before it was seized by La Salle's creditors. Francis Parkman, in his work about La Salle's voyages, wrote: "The prudent Abbé died rich and very old . . . having inherited a large estate after his return from America."

The revealed news about La Salle's death and the desperate condition of the Texas colony on Matagorda Bay little interested King Louis XIV. His only response to Joutel's pleas for aid was to send an order to Canada to have the murderers arrested, if they should appear there.

TRAGIC ENDING

The capture of one of La Salle's four vessels, the *Saint-François,* on the coast of Santo Domingo, had alerted Spanish authorities to French intruders into the region they considered their own. In the next five years, ten expeditions were sent out from New Spain to search the Gulf Coast, from Vera Cruz to Florida, for them. The viceroy of Mexico, Conde de la Monclova, made every effort to find, and expel, the French intruders. He and other Spanish authorities were certain that the sole purpose of a French settlement in this region was to have a base for their ships to attack and conquer New Spain.

In 1686, the viceroy set out two vessels, *Nuestra Señora del Rosario* and *Nuestra Señora de la Esperanza,* respectively commanded by Captain Martin de Rivas with Juan Enriquez Barrato as chief pilot, and Captain Antonio de Iriarte with Antonio Romero as chief pilot. These two ships, of a type called piraguas, were specially constructed for the expedition. Essentially, they were oversized long boats, propelled by oars as well as sail, and carried six cannons each. Their shoal draft and easy maneuverability facilitated the search along the low-lying coast, with its shallow waters.

The captains were charged with carefully examining all the rivers and inlets along the Gulf coast, from Tampico, Mexico, to the latitude of 30° N, where they expected to find the Bay of Espiritu Santo. On December 28, 1686, the two vessels left Tampico, where they had taken on two natives to act as pilots and interpreters. On March 30, 1687, they found the remains of a vessel, judged to be French, on the Rio de las Flores, near the mouth of the present-day San Antonio River. Five days later, in a bay thirteen leagues to the east, they found the wreckage of the *Belle.* To this bay they gave the name San Bernardo, the same as La Salle's St. Louis Bay, and now called Matagorda Bay. The French coat of arms, still visible, and fleur-de-lis were unmistakable evidence of her origin. It was assumed that this must be one of La Salle's vessels, but they could not corroborate it as the interpreters were unable to understand the language of the natives.

Since there was no evidence in sight of any settlement, they continued the search. As instructed, they sailed east to the bay of *Espiritu Santo* (Mobile Bay) without finding any further signs of a settlement. To them, the

low, swampy coast along the way seemed totally inappropriate for a settlement of any kind, and the Mississippi River was ignored as "unworthy of
any examination." Rivas and Iriarte reasoned that there was no need to go
beyond Mobile Bay, for any French settlement there would soon be made
known, through the Indians, to the Spanish nearby. Six months after departure, the two vessels returned to Vera Cruz.

At a meeting in Mexico City, the diary and maps from the expedition
were reviewed and compared with a letter received from the Spanish ambassador in London. This letter included an official account (available after
Beaujeu's return to France) of La Salle's voyage, his failure to find the
mouth of the Mississippi, and of the wreck of the vessels. The two documents agreed with each other, and they were certain the ships they found
were those of La Salle's expedition. There was no knowledge, though, of
any settlement on the Garcitas River. Concluding that La Salle, and all his
men, died from drowning, starvation, or Indian attack, the viceroy wrote to
King Carlos (Charles) II of Spain. Dated July 25, 1687, it reads:

> The whole gulf of Mexico has been examined with the most exact diligence
> possible . . . without there having been found in it or on its entire coast any port,
> river or bay in the possession of enemies or of Europeans, or any signs of settle-
> ment or fortification anywhere. . . . Wherefore the whole monarchy of Your
> Majesty is to be congratulated; for, although this kingdom would never be en-
> dangered by a settlement of enemies along this coast, since they could be dis-
> lodged, it is much better that no such settlement should exist, and that the many
> plausible falsehoods that have been told both here and in Spain concerning this
> matter should be so felicitously disproved.

The next year, evidence arose to the contrary. A Frenchman, living
among the Indians north of the Rio Grande, was captured by the governor
of Coahuila in New Biscay. Most likely, he was one of the early deserters
from La Salle's colony, and he told his captors about Fort St. Louis. His story
was confused and contained many contradictions. But undeniably he was
French and found living deep within Spanish territory. Rumors reaching the
governor tended to confirm his account. Indians who ranged the lands of

Texas visited Spanish missions in New Biscay. They told about "white men dressed in armor . . . who returned at intervals to their wooden boats on the sea. One of these boats was said to have been wrecked."

In the spring of 1689, the governor dispatched an expedition by foot, commanded by Captain Alonso de León, with the captive Frenchman as guide. On April 22, 136 leagues distant from Coahuila, the long-sought-for settlement was reached. The scene was one of total desolation and carnage. Decaying bodies, pierced with arrows and their heads crushed by war-clubs, were strewn about. Broken guns and cutlasses, chests and barrels, books with pages torn out, and shattered ecclesiastical ornaments lay rotting in the mud.

The surrounding Karankawa Indians, resentful of the white man's en-croachment in their territory, watched La Salle's last expedition leave, re-ducing the number by half to guard the fort. Daily, they saw the remaining settlers within the fort succumb to starvation or die from the epidemic of smallpox. No resistance was left against the Indian massacre. No one was spared. Even the priests, Father Zénobe Membré, Maxime Le Clercq, and Abbé Chefdeville, who had come to devote themselves to missionary work among the Indians, met a violent death at their hands. In addition to the bodies found in the fort, three other skeletons were found out on the prairie. Captain León assumed that the bodies of the rest of the colonists had been thrown into the river, to be eaten by alligators.

From some of the Indians, de León ascertained that several captives—a few children—had been taken, and that four Frenchmen were living among one of the distant Indian tribes. These were sent for with assur-ances that they would be well treated. Two of them, distrustful of the Spaniards, refused to come on their bidding, saying they preferred to live among the Indians. The two others turned out to be l'Archevêque, the accomplice of Duhaut to La Salle's murder, and his companion, Jacque Grollet, one of the French deserters. They were taken to Mexico City where they gave further information about La Salle's colony, and from there, sent to Spain. Disregarding the promises made to them, they were thrown into prison. Later, they were sent back to New Biscay to work in the mines.

From all evidence, it appears that those who accompanied Hiens after his parting with Joutel were killed by the Indians. And Hiens was killed in a quarrel by Rutter, another of the deserters who turned to living a life among the Indians. Thus, "in ignominy and darkness died the last embers of the doomed colony of La Salle."

On March 20 of 1687, at the age of forty-three, the life of Rène-Robert Cavelier de la Salle came to an abrupt finish. Before he sailed from France on that last fateful voyage, La Salle wrote a farewell letter to his mother in which he expressed "good hope of a happy success" to the enterprise. La Salle would not have embarked if only he had known when he penned these words that this voyage, rather than bring honor and glory to the family name, would submerge it in a barrage of doubt, misunderstanding, and criticism lasting for centuries; rather than a happy success culminating in the greatest achievement of his career, it would result in his death by means most foul and treacherous; and rather than extend France's domain in North America from the Appalachian to the Rocky Mountains, and from Hudson Bay to the Gulf of Mexico, this venture would mark the start of dismemberment of France's power in the New World.

But La Salle did not know, and fate denied him the destiny he desired.

CONCLUSION

For eighteen years, La Salle safely journeyed over thousands of miles of rivers and lakes. He endured physical hardship from a climate harsher than he had ever known. Deprivation of sleep and sustenance were near constant companions in his travels; while deceit and abandonment by those he depended upon thwarted and slowed progress toward his goals. Yet La Salle attained what he had set out to accomplish. Traveling through totally un-explored lands, peopled with tribes who were at best helpful and at worst capable of the cruelest savagery of torture and cannibalism the mind can conceive, La Salle paddled his canoe down the length of the Mississippi River, finally reaching the mouth of that great river where it enters into the Gulf of Mexico.

He ably demonstrated his ability to organize men, and constructed a string of French and Indian fortified settlements that ranged from Fort Frontenac on the St. Lawrence river, along critical junctions of the Great Lakes and into the very heartland of North America.

These new communities reinforced and strengthened France's territorial claims in the New World and enabled her to economically compete with the English and Dutch already established along the eastern seaboard. It also gave France the hope of perhaps wresting wealth from the Spanish in the south and west.

By international accord, occupying the mouth of the Mississippi gave France the right to claim all the territory through which this river flowed, including the land drained by its tributaries. In honor of his sovereign, King Louis XIV, La Salle named the land "Louisiana." On that momentous occasion on April 9, 1682, France gained a land equal in size to half of all of Europe. Added to her ownership of the St. Lawrence River and its tributaries, France now owned a significant portion of the entire North American continent. Her domain extended from Hudson Bay to the Gulf of Mexico and from the Appalachian Mountains to the Rocky Mountains.

Yet, for all this, history has not been kind to Réne-Robert Cavelier de la Salle. No great rivers or lakes have been named after him to perpetuate the memory of his deeds. "The saddest circumstances of all in regard to the memory of this celebrated man is that he was regretted by but few, and that the failure of his enterprises made him seem a mere adventurer to those who judge only by appearances"—thus, concluded Charlevois.

True, La Salle discovered no new continents nor found that elusive passage connecting two oceans. He cannot even be said to have *discovered* the Mississippi River. Others—Soto, Moscoso, Jolliet, Marquette, and Hennepin—had led the way before him. But La Salle was the first to conceive the idea of an inland waterway extending from Montréal, in Canada, all the way to the Gulf of Mexico. Accomplishing this grand concept, he united an entire continent with a means to effectively transport goods and people, and paved the way for subsequent settlement and French colonization in the valley of the Mississippi. Errors he made in the course of his ventures were pursued honestly and courageously, though the results were not always as he may have wished.

La Salle was not a person content to drift along on the currents and eddies of chance, but expended every effort possible to achieve what he had undertaken, until the last breath of his life was treacherously taken from him. He deserves better than the fate history has accorded him.

PART VIII

Renascence of the Belle

For over three-hundred years, the *Belle* lay buried beneath the waters of Matagorda Bay, in mute testament to the shattered dreams of La Salle. In time, not only was the fate of the *Belle* forgotten, but the noble accomplishments of that French explorer faded from the minds of people.

La Salle's settlement on the Gulf coast of Texas, and the shipwreck of two of his vessels there, are of importance nationally and internationally in the history of the French colonial period in the New World. To the state of Texas, they are of particular interest, as they are an intimate part of its history and cultural patrimony.

In 1978, the Texas Historical Commission (the state agency for historic preservation) began looking for the shipwreck of the *Belle*. Her general location in Matagorda Bay was known from historic records, and Spanish maps made during the expedition of Rivas and Iriarte in 1688. The total area to be searched in Matagorda Bay is not large, nor is the water deep. However, its murky water prevents any possibility of visually finding the wreckage. To facilitate the search, the Texas Historical Commission used a photon magnetometer. Dragged behind the stern of a boat, this sensitive metal detector is able to recognize underwater magnetic anomalies. Throughout the first seasons, many anomalies were located in the bay and tested. None, however, showed promise of being the *Belle*.

By building a wall around the vessel, and pumping out the water, the *Belle* was able to be excavated from dry land. *Photo: courtesy of the* Victoria Advocate, *Victoria, Texas.*

In 1995, with fresh funding, the search was renewed in the area the *Belle* was suspected to lie. On the very first day a promising magnetic reading was recorded, and a scuba diver sent down to investigate. Feeling with his hands through the silt, he came upon a lead shot and a bronze buckle. Then, his hands ranged over the surface of a long, cylindrical object. It was a heavily ornamented bronze cannon. They knew now what they found had to be the *Belle.* No other shipwrecks, of this antiquity, were known to be lost in this part of Matagorda Bay. Absolute confirmation, however, would have to wait until later. Divers also recovered a number of other artifacts: pewter plates, jars, glass beads, and bronze falconry bells (used as trade items), and large quantities of lead shot. A large part of the wooden hull remained intact.

The problem was how to best excavate the ship without destroying valuable archaeological information in the process. They resolved it by building a coffer dam around the historic remains. A double wall, made from interlocking steel plates, was driven into the floor of the bay. Though the depth of the water was only twelve feet, the plates had to extend an additional

The hull of the *Belle* as it appeared at the excavation site in Matagorda Bay in 1997. *Photo: courtesy of the Texas Historical commission.*

Cannon retrieved from the *Belle*. *Photo: courtesy of the* Victoria Advocate, *Victoria, Texas.*

forty-one feet beneath the sea floor to prevent seepage. Then, the water was pumped out, leaving a dry "hole in the water," in the center of which lay the exposed *Belle.*

As layers of sand and mud were carefully removed, the full extent of the ship and its contents was revealed. A third of the timbers and planks of the *Belle*'s hull remained intact. On the starboard side, the direction she listed to when sinking, everything from the waterline to the bottom of the keel was present.

The archaeologists were amazed at the remarkable state of preservation. The grain of the wood was clear enough to determine what kind of tree it came from—mostly oak, with some elm, birch, and maple. In the bow of the ship they found a seven-hundred-foot-long coil of anchor rope, of which a hundred foot length was removed in a single piece. Other pieces of rope were still clinging to pieces of sailcloth. There were birch-bark containers, probably brought back from Canada by La Salle, in which the stitching was visible. Others items included wooden bowls, shovels, hair, fabric, and leather shoes.

Normally, one never finds such a perfect state of preservation of organic material that has been under water this long a time, especially in the Gulf of Mexico, or any of its associated bays. The warm water there supports a wealth of bacteria and marine organisms, such as toredo worms, which quickly eat up organic material. Also, in shallow water, as in Matagorda Bay, wave and surge action reach down to the very bottom and quickly breaks up everything. The scientific team surmised that the unique preservation was attributed to the ship being completely covered with clay and sand almost as soon as it sank. Totally sealing the ship and its contents, it created an anaerobic environment, in which the bacteria and worms could not live. All the lead, in the form of shot and musket balls, most likely helped to produce a toxic environment against these organisms. Then too, when the ship went down, she was only two years old and still in excellent condition.

Once the eight-hundred-pound cannon was brought up and cleaned of the accretions covering it, there no longer was any doubt that the shipwreck was the *Belle*. On the gun's breach, a large letter "L" capped with a crown—the royal crest of the Sun King—showed that the cannon was cast during the reign of King Louis XIV. Toward the muzzle, the emboss of two crossed anchors, surmounted by a scroll bearing the name Le Compte de Vermandois, more specifically dated it to some time between 1669 and 1683, when the Count of Vermandois was the Admiral of France. As befitting this royal gift to La Salle, the cannon is covered with ornate decorations of acanthus and palm leaves, fan shells, and fleur-de-lis. The lifting rings, normally a simple, functional element, here, are in the form of leaping dolphins. Altogether, four of the ship's five cannons were retrieved. The remaining, missing cannon, may have been snagged by a fisherman's net and displaced.

From the hold of the ship, a stack of pewter plates gave further confirmation of its identity. Stamped on the bottom of the plates were the initials of one of La Salle's officers, Sieur de le Gros. Several documents with La Salle's signature were also found, mainly related to preparations for the expedition and procuring of supplies.

After all the artifacts have been properly cleaned and have undergone conservation procedures to prevent deterioration, they will be permanently housed at a museum, yet to be determined. Important articles will become part of traveling exhibits and local museum exhibits. Plans are now under way for the Texas Historical Commission, working in conjunction with the French Museum, Musée de la Tatihou, to build a full-scale replica of the *Belle*. But it will take another four years before the reborn *Belle* is afloat.

Like re-creations of other historic vessels—Henry Hudson's *Halve Maen* (*Half Moon*), and John Cabot's *Matthew*—the *Belle* will be a floating museum. In its travels, people will have the opportunity for direct contact with the ship, and renew their interest in this important part of our nation's history.

Engraving of La Salle as an old man.

ENDNOTES

IN CONTEST FOR THE NEW WORLD [PART I]

p. 3   Thatcher, J.B., Christopher Columbus, p. 181

CANADA, OR THE NOUVELLE FRANCE [PART II]

p. 15   Publications of the Champlain Society, Royal Fort
              Frontenac, p. 17

p. 17   Charlevoix, *History and General Description of New France*,
              Vol. II, p. 162

p. 17   Publications of the Champlain Society, Royal Fort
              Frontenac, p. 86

p. 23   Charlevoix, op. cit., Vol II, pp. 55, 56

p. 27   Ibid, Vol. III, p. 223

p. 33   Parkman, F. *France and England in North America*, Vol. I,
              p. 1320

p. 33   Ibid, p. 1322

p. 33   Ibid, p. 794

p. 33   Charlevoix, op. cit., Vol. III, p. 194

p. 54   Publications of the Champlain Society, op. cit., p. 17

p. 56   Tonti, C., *An Account of Monsieur de La Salle's Last
              Expeditions and Discoveries in North America*, p. 3

p. 60   Publications of the Champlain Society, op. cit., p. 116

p. 66   Margry, P., *Relation of the Discoveries and Voyages of Cavelier
              de La Salle from 1679–1681: The Official Narrative.* Vol. I,
              pp. 337, 338

BEYOND THE GREAT LAKES TO THE MISSISSIPPI
[PART III]

p. 72   Galinée, Recit . . ., p. 32

p. 73   Hennepin, L., *A New Discovery of a Vast Country in America.* pp. 54, 55

p. 74   Ibid., p. 82

DESCENT TO THE GREAT RIVER'S MOUTH
[PART IV]

p. 111, 112   Abbott, J., *The Adventures of the Chevalier De La Salle and His Companions,* pp. 246, 247

p. 117   Fortier, A., *History of Louisiana,* Vol. I, p. 25

p. 119, 120   Parkman, F., op. cit., p. 941

GEOGRAPHIC KNOWLEDGE EXPANDED [PART V]

p. 125   Navarette, M, Collection of the Voyages and Discoveries

p. 129   Margry, op. cit., Vol. II, pp. 382, 383

A CARTOGRAPHIC DILEMMA [PART VI]

p. 152   Habig, M, *The Franciscan Pere Marquette, and, A Critical Biography of Father Zenobe Membré.* p. 253

p. 153   Hennepin, L., *A New Discovery of a Vast Country in America,* p. 199

p. 158   Winsor, J., *Narrative and Critical History of America,* Vol. IV, p. 209

A BOLD AND GLORIOUS VENTURE [PART VII]

p. 171   Margry, P., op. cit., Vol. II, p. 399

p. 171   Ibid, Vol. II, p. 384

p. 173   Parkman, F., op. cit., p. 963

p. 174   Margry, P., op cit., Vol. II, p. 408

p. 175   Parkman, F., op cit., p. 967

p. 182   Shea, J.G., *Early Voyages Up and Down the Mississippi by Cavelier, St. Cosme, Le Seur, Gravier, and Guignas*, p. 17

p. 185   Herrera, Historia Generale, dec. i, lib. IX, cap. 10

p. 219   Dunn, W.E., *The Spanish Search for La Salle's Colony on the Bay of Espiritu Santo, 1685–1689*, p. 351

RENASCENCE OF THE *BELLE* [PART VIII]

p. 222   Charlevoix, op. cit., Vol. IV, pp. 95, 96

Appendix I

Rivers and Lakes
with Their Various Names

St. Lawrence River

Grande Rivière de Canada (early name)

River of Hochelaga (named by Jacques Cartier)

Iroquois River

Catarakoui River

Sault St. Louis

Caughnawaga

On the St. Lawrence River at town of Hochleaga (present-day Montréal). Farthest point reached by Jacque Cartier.

Mississippi River

Mississipy (in use among the Ontaonas [Algonquin?] Indians)

Colbert River (named by Marquette for M. Colbert, Minister to King Louis XIV)

Rivière de Baude (named by Jolliet for Baude, the family name of Count Frontenac)

Grand Rivière

Cucagua (as called by De Soto's historian, Garcilaso de la Vega)

Portions of the River (Indian names attributed to)

Gustacha, Chucagua, Malabouchia, Namese-Sipon, Tapata, and Ri Falls of St. Anthony of Padua (section of river at present-day St. Paul and Minneapolis)

Lake Pepin (a widening of the river in Minnesota; named after one of the Frenchmen accompanying Du Lhut when he rescued Hennepin).

Minnesota River

St. Peter River

St. Joseph River

Miamis River

Missouri River

Pekitanoui (named by Marquette)

Rivière des Osages

Rivière des Emissourittes, or Missourits (called by La Salle)

Ohio River

Ouabache [Wabash] (noted on some earliest maps)

Ohio (meaning "Beautiful River," called by the Iroquois)

Olighin-cipou (called by the Ottawas)

Rivière Baudrane (named by La Salle)

Ouabouskiaou (called by Marquette)

Illinois River

Rivière Seignelay (named for Marquis de Seignelay, Marine and Colonial Minister to King Louis XIV). In La Salle's time the name Seignelay was applied to the Illinois R. through all its course, including the Kankakee R.

Rivière des Macopins

Rivière e la Divine (named by Jolliet)

Checagou (called by the Indians)

Portions of the River

Lake Peoria (a widening of the river)

Fat Pimiteoui (meaning "Fat Lake," called by the Indians)

Vermilion River (Red River) A branch of the Illinois

Rivière Aramoni (Indian name for "red")

Kankakee River (a branch of the Illinois R.)

Theakiki, or Haukiki (later corrupted to Kiakiki)

Red River (near Texas–Mexico border).

Rivière Seignelay

Arkansas River

Rivière Bazire (named by Jolliet, in honor of a merchant in Canada who in 1673 helped support Frontenac's plan to build Fort Catarakoui)

Niagara River

Onguiaahra, or Ongiara (on some early maps—1641 and 1657)

Des Plaines River

Rivière La Divine

Oswego River

Chouagueu

Wisconsin River

Ouisconsin, Misconsin, or Miskonsing (named by Marquette)

Rio Grande

Rio Bravo

Rivière de la Magdelaine

Rio de las Palmas (River of Palms)

Lake Michigan

Lake of the Illinois, later, Lake Illinois (called Lac des Illinois, or Missihi-ganin, by Jolliet)

Lac Dauphin

Lac Mitchiganong

Green Bay

Bay de Puants

Lake Superior

The Upper Lake

Lake Condé, or Lac de Condé

Lake Supérior (named by Jolliet)

Lac Tracy (named by Marquette in honor of the governor-general of Canada)

Lake Huron

Kitchigami (called by the Indians)

Grand Lac (named by Champlain in 1632)

Karengnondi (named by Hennepin)

Lac d'Orleans

Mer douce des Hurons

Lake St. Clair

Salt Water Lake (named by Champlain)

Tsiketo

Lac de la Chaudière

Lac des EaDes Sallées

Lac Ste. Claire (named by Hennepin, who passed through this lake on Aug. 12, 1679 on the fête-day of Ste. Claire)

Lake Erie

Lac Teiocha-routiong

Lac Conte (named after Prince Conti)

Lake Ontario ("Beautiful Water")

Lac St. Louis (named by Champlain, 1615)

Lac Frontenac

Lac Ontario (named by Jolliet)

Lac des Iroquois (labeled by Dutch cartographer, Hondius)

l'Ontario de St. Loys (labeled by cartographer N. Sanson, 1659)

Spirit Lake

Lake of the Issati (perhaps Lake of the Woods in Minnesota)

Valley of the Mississippi River

Manitoumie

Frontenacie (named by Jolliet)

Colbertie (named by Marquette)

La Louisiane (named by La Salle)

Gulf of California

Bay of Vermillion ("Red Bay")

Mobile Bay

Bay de Espiritu Santo (Bay of the Holy Spirit, named by the Spanish)

Baia de Culata ("Muddy Bay")

Mar Pequeña ("Small Bay")

Bay of Rio del Espiritu Santo

Appendix II

Indian Tribes

Five Nations (Iroquois)—Called by themselves "The Long House" or "The Five Cabins." Called by the English "Five Nations."

    Seneca (Tsonnontouans) Were the westernmost, strongest, and most numerous of the Iroquois tribes.

    Cayuga (Oiogouins, Goyogouins)

    Onondaga (Onnotaés, Hounontages) Called themselves "People of the Hills." The central, and most influential of the Iroquois tribes.

    Oneida (Onneiouts, Honnehiouts)

    Mohawk (called Aguiers, or Aniés, by the French) Occupied the lower half of the Mohawk River Valley. They were the fiercest, most implacable, and most treacherous of the five nations.

    Tuscarora (Later joined the Iroquois, which afterward were called the Six Nations)

Eries (Nation of the Cat) (Erigas, Erichronon, Riguchronon) Occupied the territory along the south shore of Lake Erie

Neutral Nation (Attiwandarous) Inhabited a region on the north shore of Lake Erie, eastward across the Niagara to Detroit. Called "Neutral" on account of their neutrality in the war between the Hurons and Iroquois. Nonetheless, they were "abundantly ferocious" and at war with the Algonquins.

Delaware

Mohegan (*Loups* in French) "Wolf People." Early residence in upstate New York, then moved to Conneticut

Shawanoe

Cenis

Algonquin Tribes (Outagamis) Called Rénards [fox] by the French, and Foxes by the English.

> **Illinois Nation**
>
> > **Peoria** Inhabited region along the Illinois River.
> >
> > **Tamaroa** Below mouth of Missouri River, on eastern (Illinois) side of the Mississippi
> >
> > **Kahokia**
> >
> > **Moigwena**
> >
> > **Michigamea**
> >
> > **Kaskasia** Along the Illinois River
>
> **Miamis** Closely related to the Illinois Tribes
>
> **Mascoutein** In Wisconsin. Called First Nation by the Algonquin.
>
> **Oniatanon** Settled mainly along the Wabash River. Were called Weas by the English.
>
> **Kickapoo** In southern Wisconsin. Closely allied to the Mascoutens, whom they finally absorbed.

Ottowa

Huron (Wyandot) "People of the Peninsula." Geographic location northeast of Lake Huron

Sioux (Nadouessious)

> **Iowa Tribe** (Aiouas) Called Nadoessi Mascouteins, or "Sioux of the Prairies" by André, 1676. Were first established in southern Minnesota, but early in the nineteenth century they dwelt on Iowa and Des Moines Rivers in present-day Iowa.
>
> **Ottoes**
>
> **Issanti** A tribe of the Dakota confederacy, whose early home was on Spirit Lake, Minnesota
>
> **Oüadebaton**
>
> **Chougasketon**

Osage

Missouris (Messorites) A Sioux tribe allied to the Iowas and Ottoes

Tintonha

Tribes Resident in Wisconsin

Menomonie (Called Folle Avoine by the French) Resided on the Menomonie River

Pottawattamie Near the borders of Green Bay

Winnebagoe Also near the borders of Green Bay

Sacs On the Fox River.

Outagamie (Fox) On north flowing tributary of the Arkansas River

Arkansas On west bank of the Mississippi R., near the mouth of the Arkansas River

Kappas, or **Quapaws**

Topingas, or **Tongengas**

Torimans

Osotonoy, or **Sauthois**

Chickasaw, or **Chicachas**

Natchez

Taensa A small tribe closely allied in language and customs to Natchez

Choctaw

Quinipissa

Appendix III

French Forts

Fort Frontenac

At the eastern end of Lake Ontario. First called Fort Catarokouy. Rebuilt and renamed as Fort Frontenac by La Salle in 1675.

Fort Conti

On Niagara River, below the cataract. Built in 1678 by La Salle. Controlled the passage from Lake Ontario to Lake Erie. Key to control of all the Great Lakes to the west, as well as control of the Ohio Valley.

Fort Miamis

Near the St. Joseph River (Miamis R.) at the southern end of Lake Michigan. Built in 1679 by La Salle.

Fort Crêvecoeur ("Fort Heartbreak")

On Illinois River below Lake Peoria. Built in 1680 by La Salle.

Fort Beaubarnais

On Lake Pepin of Mississippi River.

Fort Prudhomme

On east bank of Mississippi R., at Third Chickasaw Bluff. Below mouth of the Ohio R., near Memphis, Tennessee. Built in 1682 by La Salle.

Fort St Louis

On the Illinois River. At *Le Rocher* ("Starved Rock"). Built in 1682 by Henri de Tonti and La Salle.

Fort Duquesne

Where the Monongahala and Alleghany Rivers join to form the Ohio River.

Fort Detroit

Center of French power in the West. Controlled the passage from Lake Erie to Lake Huron.

Fort Michillimackinac

Controlled passage from Lake Huron to Lake Michigan.

Fort Ste. Marie

At outlet of Lake Superior.

Fort St. Louis

On Garcitas River, Texas. Built in 1685 by La Salle.

BIBLIOGRAPHY

Abbott, John S. C. *The Adventures of the Chevalier De La Salle and his Companions.* New York: Dodd and Mead Publishers, 1875.

Anderson, Melville B., trans. *Relation of the Discoveries and Voyages of Cavelier de La Salle from 1679 to 168: The Official Narrative—The Caxton Club.* Chicago, 1901.

Balesi, Charles J. *The Time of the French in the Heart of North America—1673–1818.* Chicago: Alliance Française, 1996.

Bolton, Herbert E. "The Location of La Salle's Colony on the Gulf of Mexico." *Southwestern Historical Quarterly* 27: 177–189.

Charlevoix, Pierre-François-Xavier de. *History and General Description of New France.* Translated with notes by John Gilmary Shea. New York: John Gilmary Shea, 1872.

Cormier, Louis-Philippe. *Lettres de Margry a Parkman—1872–1892: Cahiers du Centre de Recherche en Civilization Canadienne-Française.* Editions d'Universite de'Ottawa,1977.

Delanglez, Jean. *Some La Salle Journeys.* Chicago: Institute of Jesuit History, 1938.

Dunn, William Edward. *The Spanish Search for La Salle's Colony on the Bay of Espiritu Santo,1685–1689.* Austin, Tex.: Texas State Historical Association. Reprint from *Southwestern Historical Quarterly* 19, no 4. (April 1916).

Fortier, Alcee. *A History of Louisiana.* (5 vols.) Vol. I. *Early Explorers and the Domination of the French.* Baton Rouge, La.: Claitor's Book Store, 1966.

French, B. F. *Historical Collections of Louisiana: Part I. Historical Documents from 1678–1691.* New York: Wiley and Putnam, 1846.

French, B. F. *Historical Collections of Louisiana, Part III.* New York: D. Appleton & Company, 1851.

Galloway, Patricia K., ed. *La Salle and His Legacy: Frenchmen and Indians in the Lower Mississippi Valley.* Jackson: University Press of Mississippi, 1982.

Gravier, Gabriel. *Etude sur une carte inconnue, la premiaere dressoee par Louis Joliet en 1674 apres son exploration du Mississippi avec le P. Jacques Marquette en 1673.* Paris: Maisonneuve et cie, 1880.

Habig, Marion A. *The Franciscan Pere Marquette, and, A Critical Biography of Father Zenobe Membré.* New York: Joseph F. Wagner, Inc., 1934. Published in *Franciscan Studies,* 13.

Hamilton, Peter Joseph. *Colonial Mobile.* Mobile, Ala.: University of Alabama Press, Southern Historical Publications, No. 20, 1976.

Hamilton, Raphael N. *Marquette's Explorations: The Narratives Re-examined.* Madison: University of Wisconsin Press, 1970.

Hennepin, Father Louis. *A New Discovery of a Vast Country in America.* Reprinted from the Second London Issue of 1698. Intro. notes and index by Reuben Gold Thwaites. Vols. I and II. Toronto: Coles Publishing Company, 1903.

Holmes, Vera Brown. *A History of the Americas: From Discovery to Nationhood.* New York: Ronald Press Company, 1950.

Joutel, Henri. *Joutel's Journal of La Salle's Last Voyage: Performed by Monsr. de la Sale, to the Gulph of Mexico to find out the Mouth of the Missisipi River.* London: J. Baker, 1714. Reprint Burt Franklin, New York, 1896.

Kellogg, Louise Phelps, ed. *Early Narratives of the Northwest: 1634–1699.* New York: Scribners Sons, 1917.

Lamontagne, Leopold, ed. *The Publications of the Champlain Society: Royal Fort Frontenac.* Texts selected and translated from the French by Richard A. Preston. Toronto: Champlain Society, 1958.

Le Clercq, Father Chrestien. First Establishment of the Faith in New France. Vols. I, II. John Gilmary Shea, trans. Paris: Amable Auroy, 1691. J. G. Shea (Pub.), New York, 1881.

Legislature de la Province de Quebec. *Nouvelle-France: Documents Historiques. Correspondance echangee entre les Autorites Francaises et les Gouverneurs et Intendants.* Vol. I. Publies par ordre de la legislature de la Province de Quebec. Quebec: L. J. Demers & Frere, 1893.

Margry, Pierre. *Daecouvertes et âetablissements des Français dans l'ouest et dans le sud de l'Amâerique septentrionale, 1614–1698; mâemoires et documents inaedits recueillis et publiaes par Pierre Margry.* New York: AMS Press, 1974. Reprint of 1879–88 ed. published by Maisonneuve, Paris.

Margry, Pierre. *Relation of the Discoveries and Voyages of Cavelier de La Salle from 1679–1681: The Official Narrative.* Melville B. Anderson, trans. From the printed Collection of P. Margry, for the Caxton Club. Chicago: Lakeside Press, 1901.

Marques, A. H. de Oliveira. *History of Portugal.* Vol. I: *From Lusitania to Empire.* New York: Columbia University Press, 1972.

Marshall, Orsamus H. *The First Visit of De La Salle to the Senecas, Made in 1669.* Translation of Galinée mss: Recit d'un ami de l'abbé de Galinée by Abbé Eusebe Renaudot. Read before the Buffalo Historical Society, 1874. Privately printed.

Ogg, Frederic Austin. *The Opening of the Mississippi: A Struggle for Supremacy in the American Interior.* New York: Haskell House Publishers, 1969.

Osler, E. B. *La Salle.* Ontario: Longmans Canada Limited, Don Mills, 1967.

Parkman, Francis. *France and England in North America:* Vol. I. *Pioneers of France in the New World. The Jesuits in North America. La Salle and the Discovery of the Great West. The Old Régime in Canada.* New York: Library Classics of the United States, 1983.

Pelletier, Monique. *Les Globes de Louis XIV—les sources Françaises de l'oeuvre de Coronelli.* Kent, Eng.: Imago Mundi Ltd. c/o Lympne Castle, 1982. Published in *Journal of the International Society for the History of Cartography* 34.

Scaife, Walter B. *America: Its Geographical History, 1492–1892.* With a Supplement titled: *Was the Rio Espiritu Santo of the Spanish Geographers the Mississippi?* Baltimore: Johns Hopkins University Press, 1892.

Schlarman, J. H. *From Quebec to New Orleans: The Story of the French in America.* Belleville, Ill.: Beuchler Publishing Company, 1929.

Shea, John Gilmary. *Early Voyages Up and Down the Mississippi by Cavelier, St. Cosme, Le Seur, Gravier, and Guignas.* Albany, N.Y.: Joel Munsell, 1861.

Taylor, E. L. *La Salle's Route Down the Ohio.* Ohio Archaeological and Historical Publications. Vol. 19. Published for the Society by F. J. Heer, Columbus, Ohio, 1910.

Tonti, Chevalier. *An Account of Monsieur de La Salle's Last Expeditions and Discoveries in North America*. London: J. Tonson, Publisher, 1698.

Winsor, Justin. *Narrative and Critical History of America*. Vol. II. *Spanish Exploration and Settlements in America from the Fifteenth to the Seventeenth Centuries*. Vol. IV. *French Exploration and Settlements in North America, and those of the Portuguese, Dutch and Swedes, 1500–1700*. Vol. V. *The English and French in North America, 1689–1763*. Boston: Houghton, Mifflin and Company, 1886, 1887.

Weiss, Arthur James. *The Discoveries of America to the Year 1525*. New York: G. P. Putnam's Sons, 1884.

INDEX

Mascouten Indians, 92, 240

Matagorda Bay, 194–201; *Belle* (ship) found in 1995, 225–29; Indians at, 196, 197, 198–99, 201–3, 207, 220; La Salle's murder at, 213–15; La Salle leaves, 207; loss of *Belle* (ship) at, 209, 211; settling at, 201–6; Spanish find evidence of French at, 218

Membré, Zénobe: on beauty of Mississippi River, 117; and colonization of Gulf of Mexico area, 132; death of, 220; on La Salle's persistence, 104; on latitude of mouth of Mississippi, 152, 163, 163–64; preaching to Indians, 109; role of, 70, 77–78

Mémoire sur les Affairs de l'Amerique (La Salle), 126

Menomonie Indians, 241

Mer douce des Hurons. *See* Huron, Lake

Mexico: exploration of, 135–38; France's desire to find route to, 67–68; map of, *144*

Miami Indians: buffalo hunting by, 84; conflict with Iroquois, 96, 101–2; rumors spread by, 87; tribal relations, 240; uniting with Illinois Indians, 103

Miamis, Fort, 95, 243

Miamis River. *See* St. Joseph River

Michigamea Indians, 240

Michigan, Lake, 237

Michillimackinac, Fort, 244

Milot, Jean, *14*, 197, 198, 200

Minnesota River, 236

Misconsin (river), 237

Miskonsing (river), 237

Missihiganin (river). *See* Michigan, Lake

missionaries. *See* Franciscan missionaries; Jesuits; Récollet missionaries; Sulpician missionaries

Mississippi River: beauty of, 117; belief that discharged into Bay of Holy Spirit, 160–61, 162; church's reaction to expedition/discoveries, 118; discovery of, 147, 222; exploration of, French, 49–54, 156–58; exploration of, motives for, 105–6; exploration of, Spanish, 146–48; fear of, 86–87; idea of passage to Pacific from, 158; importance to New France, 206–7; Indians along, 109–10, 116;

information about learned from Indians, 86–87, 90; latitude where enters Gulf of Mexico, 151–56; mouth of, arriving at, 111–14; mouth of, exploration of, 143, 146; mouth of, oversight of, 140–41; naming of, 164; other names for, 235; preparations and plans for exploring, 106; voyage to, 107–8. *See also* Gulf of Mexico

Mississippi River, mapping of, *115*, 164: adjustments made after La Salle's expeditions, 161–62; discharging into Gulf of Mexico, 162; by Franquelin, 160, *161*, 163; by Hennepin, 160, 163; by Jolliet and Marquette, 156–60

Mississippi River Valley, 66–104; Indians in, 71; map of, *165*; navigating Great Lakes on way to, 71–72; navigating Niagara River on way to, 71–72; other names for, 238

Missouri Indians, 241

Missouri River, 108, 158, 236

Mobile Bay: belief that Mississippi River discharged into, 160–61; mapping of, 160–61, 162–63; maps of, 142–43; mistake in navigating to, 188–90; other names for, 238

Mohawk Indians, 15, 30, 37, 239

Mohegan Indians, 240

Moigwena Indians, 240

Montezuma, 136, 137

Montréal, Canada: Indians in area of, 29–30; La Salle's settlement in, 30–31; La Salle in, 29–36

Montreal Canoe, 39

Monts, Pierre du Gaust de, 12, 31

Moranget, Crevel de, 198, 202, 203, 214

Moscoso Alvarado, Luis de, 147–48

Muddy Bay. *See* Mobile Bay

murder of La Salle, 213–15

Musée de la Tatihou, 229

Nadoessi Mascoutein Indians, 240

Nadouessious Indians, 240

Narváez, Pánfilo de, 143, *144*, 146, 148–49

Natchez Indians, 241

Nation of the Cat, 239

Navarrete, Martin Fernández de, 141–42

navigation, early methods of, 1

Neutral Nation (Indians), 239

About the Author

Donald S. Johnson is a commercial artist, cartographer, boatbuilder, and freelance writer, who has written numerous articles on maritime history, sailing, and navigation. He is the author of *Charting the Sea of Darkness: The Four Voyages of Henry Hudson* and *Phantom Islands of the Atlantic*. Both volumes have won critical acclaim. Johnson's *Cruising Guide to the Coast of Maine* is the sailors' bible in the waters of the region. When not sailing or lecturing, he makes his home in Perry, Maine.

OTHER COOPER SQUARE PRESS
TITLES OF INTEREST

AFRICA EXPLORED
Europeans on the Dark Continent, 1769–1889
Christopher Hibbert
344 pp., 54 b/w illustrations, 16 maps
0-8154-1193-6
$18.95

African Game Trails
An Account of the African Wanderings of
an American
Hunter-Naturalist
Theodore Roosevelt
New introduction by H. W. Brands
600 pp., 210 b/w illustrations
0-8154-1132-4
$22.95

ANTARCTICA
Firsthand Accounts of Exploration
and Endurance
Edited by Charles Neider
468 pp.
0-8154-1023-9
$18.95

ARCTIC EXPERIENCES
Aboard the Doomed *Polaris* Expedition
and Six Months Adrift on an Ice-Floe
Captain George E. Tyson
New introduction by Edward E. Leslie
504 pp., 78 b/w illustrations
0-8154-1189-8
$24.95 cloth

BEYOND CAPE HORN
Travels in the Antarctic
Charles Neider
414 pp., 14 maps
0-8154-1235-5
$17.95

CARRYING THE FIRE
An Astronaut's Journeys
Michael Collins
Foreword by Charles Lindbergh
512 pp., 32 pp. of b/w photos
0-8154-1028-6
$19.95

THE DESERT AND THE SOWN
The Syrian Adventures of the Female
Lawrence of Arabia
Gertrude Bell
New introduction by Rosemary O'Brien
368 pp., 162 b/w photos
0-8154-1135-9
$19.95

EARLY AMERICAN NATURALISTS
Exploring the American West, 1804–1900
John Moring
320 pp., 10 b/w photos
0-8154-1236-3
$26.95 cloth

EDGE OF THE JUNGLE
William Beebe
New introduction by Robert Finch
320 pp., 1 b/w photo
0-8154-1160-X
$17.95

EDGE OF THE WORLD:
Ross Island, Antarctica
A Personal and Historical Narrative of Ex-
ploration, Adventure, Tragedy, and Survival
Charles Neider
with a new introduction
536 pp., 45 b/w photos, 15 maps
0-8154-1154-5
$19.95

THE FABULOUS INSECTS
Essays by the Foremost Nature Writers
Edited by Charles Neider
288 pp.
0-8154-1100-6
$17.95

GREAT SHIPWRECKS AND
CASTAWAYS
Firsthand Accounts of Disasters at Sea
Edited by Charles Neider
256 pp.
0-8154-1094-8
$16.95

THE GREAT WHITE SOUTH
Traveling with Robert F. Scott's Doomed
South Pole Expedition
Herbert G. Ponting
New introduction by Roland Huntford
440 pp., 175 b/w illustrations, 3 b/w maps
& diagrams
0-8154-1161-8
$18.95

IN SEARCH OF ROBINSON CRUSOE
Daisuke Takahashi
256 pp., 23 b/w photos
0-8154-1200-2
$25.95 cloth

THE *KARLUK*'S LAST VOYAGE
An Epic of Death and Survival
in the Arctic, 1913–1916
Captain Robert A. Bartlett
New introduction by Edward E. Leslie
378 pp., 23 b/w photos, 3 maps
0-8154-1124-3
$18.95

KILLER 'CANE
The Deadly Hurricane of 1928
Robert Mykle
264 pp., 15 b/w photos
0-8154-1207-X
$26.95 cloth

THE LIFE AND AFRICAN
EXPLORATIONS OF DAVID
LIVINGSTONE
Dr. David Livingstone
656 pp., 52 b/w line drawings and maps
0-8154-1208-8
$22.95

MAN AGAINST NATURE
Firsthand Accounts of Adventure and
Exploration
Edited by Charles Neider
512 pp.
0-8154-1040-9
$18.95

MY ARCTIC JOURNAL
A Year among Ice-Fields and Eskimos
Josephine Peary
Foreword by Robert E. Peary
New introduction by Robert M. Bryce
280 pp., 67 b/w illustrations, maps, & diagrams
0-8154-1198-7
$18.95

MY ATTAINMENT OF THE POLE
Frederick A. Cook
New introduction by Robert M. Bryce
680 pp., 45 b/w illustrations
0-8154-1137-5
$22.95

A NEGRO EXPLORER
AT THE NORTH POLE
Matthew A. Henson
Preface by Booker T. Washington
Foreword by Robert E. Peary
New introduction by Robert A. Bryce
232 pp., 6 b/w photos
0-8154-1125-1
$15.95

THE NORTH POLE
Robert Peary
Foreword by Theodore Roosevelt
New introduction by Robert M. Bryce
480 pp., 109 b/w illustrations, 1 map
0-8154-1138-3
$22.95

THE SOUTH POLE
An Account of the Norwegian Antarctic Ex-
pedition in the *Fram*, 1910–1912
Captain Roald Amundsen
Foreword by Fridtjof Nansen
New introduction by Roland Huntford
960 pp., 155 b/w illustrations
0-8154-1127-8
$29.95

STANLEY
The Making of an African Explorer
Frank McLynn
424 pp., 19 b/w illustrations
0-8154-1167-7
$18.95

THROUGH THE BRAZILIAN
WILDERNESS
Theodore Roosevelt
New introduction by H. W. Brands
448 pp., 9 b/w photos, 3 maps
0-8154-1095-6
$19.95

TUTANKHAMUN
The Untold Story
Thomas Hoving
408 pp., 43 b/w photos
0-8154-1186-3
$18.95

THE VOYAGE OF THE *DISCOVERY*
Scott's First Antarctic Expedition, 1901–1904
Captain Robert F. Scott
Preface by Fridtjof Nansen
New introduction by Ross MacPhee
Volumes I & II

Volume I
712 pp., 147 b/w illustrations
0-8154-1079-4
$35.00 cloth

Volume II
656 pp., 123 b/w illustrations
0-8154-1151-0
$35.00 cloth

Available at bookstores; or call 1-800-462-6420

COOPER SQUARE PRESS
200 Park Avenue South
Suite 1109
New York, NY 10003